Digital Detectives

Chandos

Information Professional Series

Series Editor: Ruth Rikowski
(email: Rikowskigr@aol.com)

Chandos' new series of books is aimed at the busy information professional. They have been specially commissioned to provide the reader with an authoritative view of current thinking. They are designed to provide easy-to-read and (most importantly) practical coverage of topics that are of interest to librarians and other information professionals. If you would like a full listing of current and forthcoming titles, please visit www.chandospublishing.com.

New authors: We are always pleased to receive ideas for new titles; if you would like to write a book for Chandos, please contact Dr Glyn Jones on g.jones.2@ elsevier.com or telephone +44 (0) 1865 843000.

Digital Detectives

Solving Information Dilemmas in an Online World

Crystal Fulton
Claire McGuinness

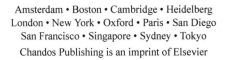

Amsterdam • Boston • Cambridge • Heidelberg
London • New York • Oxford • Paris • San Diego
San Francisco • Singapore • Sydney • Tokyo
Chandos Publishing is an imprint of Elsevier

Chandos Publishing is an imprint of Elsevier
50 Hampshire Street, 5th Floor, Cambridge, MA 02139, USA
The Boulevard, Langford Lane, Kidlington, OX5 1GB, UK

Notices
Knowledge and best practice in this field are constantly changing. As new research and
experience broaden our understanding, changes in research methods, professional practices,
or medical treatment may become necessary.

Practitioners and researchers must always rely on their own experience and knowledge in
evaluating and using any information, methods, compounds, or experiments described
herein. In using such information or methods they should be mindful of their own safety
and the safety of others, including parties for whom they have a professional responsibility.

To the fullest extent of the law, neither the Publisher nor the authors, contributors, or
editors, assume any liability for any injury and/or damage to persons or property as a
matter of products liability, negligence or otherwise, or from any use or operation of
any methods, products, instructions, or ideas contained in the material herein.

British Library Cataloguing-in-Publication Data
A catalogue record for this book is available from the British Library

Library of Congress Cataloging-in-Publication Data
A catalog record for this book is available from the Library of Congress

ISBN: 978-0-08-100124-0 (print)
ISBN: 978-0-08-100131-8 (online)

For information on all Chandos Publishing publications
visit our website at https://www.elsevier.com/

Working together
to grow libraries in
developing countries

www.elsevier.com • www.bookaid.org

Publisher: Glyn Jones
Acquisition Editor: Glyn Jones
Editorial Project Manager: Harriet Clayton
Production Project Manager: Debasish Ghosh
Designer: Maria Ines Cruz

Typeset by TNQ Books and Journals

*We dedicate this book to the digital detectives in our classrooms,
whose needs and insights have inspired this book.*

CONTENTS

LIST OF FIGURES

LIST OF TABLES

ABOUT THE AUTHORS

Dr Crystal Fulton is a senior lecturer in the School of Information and Communication Studies, University College Dublin, Ireland, where she has taught in the areas of information literacy, information and public services, information and communication behaviour, and social media for over 17 years. Her teaching takes a collaborative, problem-solving approach aimed at promoting self-constructed learning practices to help students become more independently analytic. She is a dedicated innovator in educational practice, continuously introducing new and interesting classroom techniques and assessment to encourage student engagement in learning, ranging from the adoption of new technologies that support learning, such as synchronous virtual seminars, to new courses to address educational gaps, such as her unique course to help doctoral students become effective instructors. She has long used blended and online teaching and learning, pioneering her school's first course to be offered completely online. She has won the University College Dublin's President's Teaching Award (2010–2012) for excellence in contributions to teaching. She has delivered papers at international conferences on teaching and learning, and she has published in this area. Her book, *Information Pathways: A Problem-Solving Approach to Information Literacy*, was published in 2010.

Dr Claire McGuinness is a part-time lecturer in the School of Information and Communication Studies, University College Dublin, Ireland. She has been teaching and researching information and digital literacy for more than a decade, and she was awarded a PhD in Library & Information Studies in 2005. Claire is module designer and coordinator of two information and digital literacy modules at the undergraduate and postgraduate levels in the School of Information & Communication Studies, in which she endeavors to combine theory with practice and to use active and e-learning methods to engage her students and encourage them to learn. As the director of undergraduate studies, Claire has extensive experience in supporting students as they move through their programmes. She is particularly interested in pedagogy and instructional training for information professionals, and since 2004 her advanced instructional module has aimed to prepare trainee information professionals in the masters and diploma programmes for the teaching work that they often are expected to undertake in the workplace. Claire has published a number of articles and book chapters on information literacy and academic-librarian collaboration, and her book, *Becoming Confident Teachers: A Guide for Academic Librarians*, was published in 2011.

FOREWORD

What is a **Digital Detective**, and how can you become one? While your first thought upon reading the title of this book might have been CSI, Criminal Minds, or even Sherlock Holmes, the textbook you are about to read is not really about catching villains, solving crimes, or analyzing crime scenes (although the skills and competences we discuss might certainly help!). Rather, our motivation is driven by a concern for catching *errors*, solving *information dilemmas*, and analyzing *information resources*. As students in the twenty-first century, your experience of higher education is very different from the experience of those born in the predigital era, and our aim with this book is to help you to deal effectively and efficiently with the challenges you may encounter on your path through the digital world.

Since the inception of the Word Wide Web in the early 1990s, the ways in which information is created, presented, accessed, modified, analyzed, shared, and communicated have undergone unprecedented change. We now live in a *social media world*, where speed, connectivity, and mobility are the name of the game. Study after study reveals a culture of constant connectivity—an "always on" lifestyle—where information is readily available at the touch of a button or the swipe of a screen. Learning is no longer bound by the walls of a classroom, but can take place wherever and whenever you choose, as long as you possess the tools, connectivity, and know-how to achieve your goals. Being digitally literate in the twenty-first century is a multifaceted state and may be defined in many different ways; from simply knowing which button to press to a deeper, context-based situational awareness, the spectrum is complex and wide. As "digital natives," perhaps you feel the burden of expectation. Born into the digital era, and growing up with the Web, maybe you have a sense that you should *know* more, and *be* more skilled, when it comes to digital tools and resources. That you should somehow be a digital expert by virtue of the decade of your birth. This is a lot to live up to. As we know, however, there is *no* body of innate digital skills, attributes, and competences that sets one generation apart from the other; all of us must learn how to operate comfortably in this environment, and the greatest lessons of all come from figuring out how to solve the problems and dilemmas we encounter on a day-to-day basis. This is where we come in.

The dilemmas that we address in this book are drawn in no small measure from our experience as instructors in an educational institution that has become increasingly technology-enabled since we first began to teach. Throughout the years, we have observed our students as they grapple with the different gadgets and applications that have emerged, from laptops, smartphones, and tablets to the databases, e-books, and digital library collections that have transformed scholarly communication. Where our classrooms were once furnished with overhead projectors, now they are enabled with Wi-Fi and equipped with smartboards, audience response systems, and software for recording audio and capturing lectures. Much of our teaching has shifted to the virtual arena, with the roll out of learning management systems and digital learning objects such as e-tutorials. The world of education has changed forever—mostly for the better—and with it our learning behaviors. However, with change comes challenge, and the explosion of technology-enabled learning generates as many questions as it does solutions to problems. Here we strive to answer the questions that you might have about the best way to engage with digital resources in your learning and to instill a sense of confidence as you make your way through a world where *digital* is now the norm.

Using this book, you will develop and hone your detection skills by considering a series of meaningful dilemmas that you may encounter in your education and in life in general. Through our research and our interaction with many groups of students over two decades, we have identified the digital stumbling blocks that trip students up again and again: for instance, whether you can safely use Web sources for college work, how to avoid plagiarizing the work of others or using material illegally, and whether Google is an acceptable place to search for information. We avoid answering these questions with a simple yes or no; rather, we ask you to reflect deeply on your *own* instincts and behavior and to consider the reasons *why* certain courses of action are preferable to others when it comes to digital information. At this point, the skills, attributes, and competences required to be digitally literate have been well-documented in many different sources, but less so the different scenarios and contexts in which these skills should be applied. In becoming full-fledged digital detectives, it is our wish that you are never again caught out by a digital dilemma, in whatever circumstances you find yourselves. We hope that this textbook can take you at least part of the way there. The rest is up to you!

C. Fulton and C. McGuinness
September 2015

ACKNOWLEDGEMENTS

Our many thanks go to our colleagues, families, and friends who have generously given us their support during the writing of this textbook. We also are indebted to Chandos Publishing/Elsevier, especially Dr Glyn Jones and Harriet Clayton, for the opportunity to undertake this book project.

CHAPTER 1

The Digital Landscape, Scholarship, and You

Welcome to higher education! As a student about to embark on a programme of university learning, or as a student in the early stages of a university programme, this book is for *you*. Here, you will be presented with new ideas, new learning opportunities, and new ways of experiencing learning. Digital learning environments, resources, and tools will form a significant part of your learning and will also pose significant challenges of their own. Because many aspects of the digital world are new and changing quickly, you may sometimes feel unsure of how to utilize aspects of the digital world to achieve your learning goals and how to do so effectively and ethically. If you do feel this way, you are not alone. Digital dilemmas present themselves continuously throughout our interaction with the digital world, and learning how to resolve them is all part of this exciting journey. For instance, have you ever done one of the following?

- copied a line of text or a picture from a webpage and pasted it straight into a project or paper you were working on?
- found *all* of the information for a project on one single website?
- asked for help with a problem on a social media website?
- typed a full sentence into the Google search box?
- found a definition of a word on Wikipedia?

This book will help you to decide whether the actions you take in managing your learning and preparing coursework are the *right* ones and will help you to develop the skills and strategies to make good decisions always.

This opening chapter sets the scene by introducing you to the educational landscape that frames the learning experiences of undergraduate students in an increasingly digital environment. A variety of digital tools and resources have transformed information seeking and learning over the past two decades. The virtual learning environment has also changed how we access learning. It is essential to consider the impact of these changes on how learning is acquired. As we explore the expanding role of digital learning in university education, we also consider some of the essential themes around effective digital learning, framed as digital dilemmas, which

Digital Detectives
ISBN 978-0-08-100124-0

1

are covered in this text to assist you as you develop from digital native to digital citizen.

In this chapter you will:

- contextualize learning, in particular digital means of learning, in the university environment.
- gain an overview of this text.
- consider your learning goals in conjunction with using this text.

1.1 THE CHANGING WORLD OF EDUCATION

Education is changing. As a university student today, you will find yourself in a different educational environment from that of past graduates. You may be aware of the rapidly changing environment around you, as more and more digital entities pop up, encouraging you to sign up, log in, share, like, collaborate, upload, download… the list goes on. Significantly, digital resources abound, creating an abundance of information that can be easily accessed. By and large, this is a wonderful advantage and has transformed knowledge development, research, and learning over the past decades. However, identifying digital content that is appropriate for *academic* purposes can also be very challenging, and this is where we come in.

The development of intelligent analytical skills that enable you to discern reliable digital content is now essential for success not only in education but also in the workplace and other everyday life contexts. The transition from secondary education to university marks a leap to an advanced level of learning, and this includes an increased emphasis on independent critical thinking and analytical skills. As a result, it is crucial to develop effective and efficient means of utilizing digital information as early as possible for success in academic work.

As students like you enter university, they are often assumed to be able to locate, access and download information with ease. However, in reality, they may not recognize issues surrounding the quality of the information found and the ethical issues relating to its use. The boundless growth of digital information and the constant emergence of new formats make decisions about the quality of information more and more difficult.

1.2 DIGITAL TECHNOLOGIES AND RESOURCES
IN UNIVERSITY LEARNING

Digital tools and devices now play a significant role in university education. More and more students are bringing mobile computing devices, including laptops, tablets, and mobile phones, with them to the classroom. What do *you* bring? In addition, the university environment provides instant access to a variety of digital tools and resources, including software, scholarly databases, Internet resources, and Wi-Fi communication, that facilitate communication and information retrieval.

When harnessed in a positive, meaningful and student-centred way, digital resources and technologies offer a powerful and engaging means of attaining learning outcomes and enhancing the overall learning experience. Although born into the digital era, however, today's students often do not see the learning possibilities in the multimedia resources and tools, such as apps, that they use primarily for leisure. They can find themselves confused and stressed by the *digital dilemmas* that they encounter in their places of education, especially when making the challenging transition from secondary to higher education.

Students may experience this as a conflict between the range, variety, and ease of access to web-based online resources and the traditional image of higher education as primarily oriented around formal textbooks, monographs, and research papers. Students may make poor information choices as a result of their lack of knowledge of how online sources are created, disseminated, organized, and presented. This book aims to resolve this conflict by empowering undergraduate students to make the most of all types of digital resources, while adhering to academic standards and behaving ethically with regard to the information they collect and produce in the online environment.

1.3 WHAT CAN I LEARN FROM THIS TEXT?

This book challenges you to become an independent and confident *Digital Detective* who critically scrutinizes web-based digital information to ascertain its authenticity, veracity, and authority, and who uses this information in a discerning way to complete academic tasks successfully. By learning to select and use digital information appropriately, you will be empowered to function at a higher level of digital information fluency, acting as a discerning consumer of, and effective contributor to, web-based information.

This book contains a series of key *digital dilemmas* that you might face when engaged in academic tasks. By exploring the solutions to these real-life digital dilemmas, you will develop a range of essential skills and strategies for interacting with digital information in the context of your studies. Using this book, you will learn the following critical skills for learning in the digital environment:

- discover how resources on the Web are created, organized, filtered, located, and accessed.
- select and use relevant information appropriately from overwhelming multi-format search returns.

- learn to think critically about the process of finding, using, and creating information on the Web and via other digital sources.
- successfully harness Web resources to complete academic tasks.
- avoid the perils of plagiarism and behave ethically with regard to all digital information formats.
- learn how to discern misinformation on the Internet and engage in safe online practices.
- become a savvy Internet user who understands how to present yourself online and who is aware of and can control the digital footprints that you create.

This text aims to address the issues surrounding digital research from your perspective as a student, addressing real-life critical stumbling blocks that can prevent you from engaging fully and productively with learning situations as you move into the world of higher education. Multiple opportunities for reflection and practical exercises that facilitate practice and implementation of the skills gained from the text in an authentic online environment accompany discussion and examples of common digital dilemmas.

1.4 LEARNING BY CHAPTER

This book offers a situated, problem-solving approach to deepen your analytical and research skills. Each chapter focuses on a practical, real-life dilemma, as reported by instructors and students themselves, that undergraduate students typically experience in the course of their academic studies. The dilemma addressed in each chapter is used to reveal the broader contextual issues that frame the problem you are exploring, leading to a deeper understanding of the digital environment. Practical and accessible strategies and skills for dealing with information anxiety in the digital environment are proposed.

To gain the most from this text, exploring the entire text is recommended. However, you may also find dipping into particular chapters helpful as your university education progresses and you encounter different questions around digital information. To assist you, a summary of chapters and dilemmas covered in this text is provided below.

1.4.1 Chapter 2: Your Learning in a Digital World

In Chapter 2, you are challenged to step back and consider your *own* information seeking and learning strategies, to question the assumptions that lie at the bottom of your approaches to academic tasks, and to explore whether there might be more effective ways of performing in the academic environment. Importantly, you will assess your own digital literacy level to provide a baseline on which you can build as you progress through this textbook and develop your digital skills. Remember that learning is a process. This chapter helps you to examine this process as your personal learning journey, in which you will set learning goals for your overall learning, appropriately incorporating digital tools and resources to support your learning needs.

1.4.2 Chapter 3: Aladdin's Cave
1.4.2.1 The Dilemma: "I Can Just Google This, Can't I?"
This chapter explores the power of Internet search engines for academic work and focuses specifically on Google, since this is often people's first port of call when confronted with a problem, query, or academic task. This chapter shows you how to adopt a clever, strategic approach to your searching, so that you can ensure the items you retrieve on Google are suitable for the task at hand. It also goes *behind the scenes* of Google to explain how search results are ranked and how searches are becoming increasingly personalized for individual users.

1.4.3 Chapter 4: Wiki or Won't I?
1.4.3.1 The Dilemma: "I Can Use Wikipedia for College Assignments, Can't I?"
This chapter acknowledges the ubiquity of Wikipedia as *the go-to* information source of our time and its popularity among students when researching for scholarly assignments. However, students may receive conflicting messages about the suitability of Wikipedia as an academic source and may feel uncertain about using it. Here, we explore the general issues surrounding the use of freely available, collaboratively authored sources, such as wikis for academic work, and we advise students on how to ensure that the sources they select are appropriate for the task at hand.

1.4.4 Chapter 5: Judgement Day
1.4.4.1 The Dilemma: "When I Find Information on the Web, How Can I Tell Whether It's Okay to Use It for College Assignments?"
This important chapter invites you to consider the meaning of *quality* when applied to information resources found on the Web. You will be challenged to explore your own perceptions of *good* and *bad* information sources and to think about your decision making around the selection of

resources in any given context. We also examine some evaluation models for digital information, focussing on the criteria for assessing the quality of the different kinds of information that you find on the Web, from webpages to videos and infographics.

1.4.5 Chapter 6: Finders Keepers

1.4.5.1 The Dilemma: "No Password? No Problem! If I Can Download It, I Can Use It and Share It, Right?"

The tricky question of copyright and intellectual property in the online world is addressed in this chapter. Digital information is easy—almost too easy—to download, copy, and add to our work. Using digital information without acknowledging the origin of the material is considered a form of plagiarism, and the penalties for making this mistake can be severe. To avoid this danger, you will be guided in the ethical use of material that appears online, in particular to recognize the need to give credit to creators of information you decide to use for your assessment and to provide appropriate attribution for a variety of digital sources of information.

1.4.6 Chapter 7: In Too Deep

1.4.6.1 The Dilemma: "I Can't Find the Full Texts of Anything from My Class Reading List on the Internet. Why Not?"

This chapter introduces you to the Deep Web and reveals to you how the full texts of scholarly and formally published information resources may not show up in general Internet searches, because they are locked behind subscription paywalls or are otherwise inaccessible to general Internet users. In addition, in this chapter, we demonstrate how the use of scholarly search engines, such as Google Scholar and Microsoft Academic Search, can be used effectively to locate academic information, follow citation trails, and identify key authors. We conclude by exploring the concept of open access, which is a movement to ensure that research data are disseminated cost-free on the Web.

1.4.7 Chapter 8: It's Only Words…

1.4.7.1 The Dilemma: "Searching is Searching, Whether You're on the Web or Using One of the Library Databases, Right?"

This chapter takes a close look at scholarly databases and similar resources, such as Web-Scale Discovery Services, and considers the important ways in which they differ from the vast resource *databases* that constitute web-based search services, such as Google and Bing. We compare databases with the

Web in terms of the suitability of the information for college work, the essential differences in how these resources are constructed, and the implications of database structure for searching. The importance of creating effective search strategies is also discussed, including Boolean logic, advanced searching, and other useful tricks of the trade.

1.4.8 Chapter 9: All Play and No Work

1.4.8.1 The Dilemma: "Social Networking Sites Are Just for Fun and Friends. I Can't Use Those Sites for College Work, Can I?

Social media tools have a constant presence in our daily lives. Regardless of the task at hand, the expression "there's an app for that!" often seems to be true. Choosing social media tools to support our learning, particularly with ongoing tasks and learning management, can be a daunting task. How can social media tools best serve your learning? What impact does our digital imprint created through social media participation have on our digital reputation? This chapter introduces you to the plethora of social media tools, resources, and apps, and explores the ways in which they can be used to support your learning and research.

1.4.9 Chapter 10: Truth or Dare

1.4.9.1 The Dilemma: "Misinformation and Hoaxes on the Internet Are Easy to Spot. I Won't be Caught Out, Will I?"

As true digital detectives, in this chapter, you are guided in how to spot when information on the Web and in other digital environments may be false, deliberately misleading, and designed specifically to defraud you. You will also become familiar with a range of strategies to protect yourself from the consequences of fraudulent or hostile online activity, such as identity theft, phishing, malware, and payment fraud. You will reflect on how fast-moving social networking sites, such as Twitter, have accelerated the speed at which false information can *go viral* and how critical skills are now more crucial than ever to help you discern the good from the bad.

1.4.10 Chapter 11: A Hidden Agenda

1.4.10.1 The Dilemma: "People See Only What I Want Them to See on the Web. I Control My Online Reputation, Don't I?"

In this chapter, the focus is on your *digital footprint*, or the trail of *digital crumbs* that you leave behind in the online environment through your multiple interactions in digital spaces, including email, e-commerce, social media, and content creation. You will consider the importance of online reputation management in today's world and discover the means of figuring out how you appear to others online. You will also learn how to manage your online image through controlling your privacy and ensuring that positive content appears when others search for you online.

1.4.11 Chapter 12: Fact or Fiction? Negotiating New Learning Spaces

1.4.11.1 The Dilemma: "Real Learning Has to Take Place in a Classroom, Right?"

This final dilemma addresses potential concerns about online learning as you transition from an environment that uses technology only marginally to a learning experience that may be highly technology-mediated. We explore learning management systems, e-tutorials, collaborative authoring tools, podcasts, and many more e-resources, as well as ways to organize our digital learning, such as personal information management. Importantly, we consider how approaches to learning online may differ from the traditional classroom environment and how we can utilize this environment in our university learning.

1.5 CHAPTER CHALLENGES

At the end of every chapter is a list of *Challenges*. These are practical exercises and problem-solving designed to embed your learning in each chapter. We recommend that you work through each challenge, referring to the content in a given chapter for support. You will find that some challenges, such as learning diaries and time management calendars, require your attention continuously throughout your work with this textbook, whereas other exercises and critical analyses are self-contained in a chapter. We hope that you find the challenges helpful and that you try all of the challenges presented.

1.6 LET'S BEGIN OUR WORK TOGETHER...

Now, it's time to get started. The digital world is yours to explore and to use effectively to support your learning at university. The tips and strategies in this textbook have been compiled to help you make the most of the digital environment. Remember that increasing your digital literacy will enable you to participate effectively as a digital citizen—a goal well worth attaining in the increasingly digital world around us.

We hope you enjoy your learning journey through this textbook!

CHAPTER 2

Your Learning in a Digital World

One of the first essential tasks for a digital detective is to understand the meaning of *digital literacy*. What is digital literacy? How does it fit with your learning needs for university? What are your learning needs for university? This chapter challenges you to step back and consider your *own* information seeking and learning strategies in the current digital environment, to question the assumptions that lie at the bottom of approaches to academic tasks, and to explore whether there might be more effective ways of performing in the academic environment.

In this chapter, you will:
- consider the meaning of digital literacy.
- reflect on your own learning strategies.
- explore ways of learning in a digital context.
- consider effective means of managing learning in the digital environment.

By the end of the chapter, you should have a better understanding of your own level of digital literacy, as well as some ideas on how you might leverage digital tools and resources for learning at university.

2.1 WHAT IS DIGITAL LITERACY?

The term *digital literacy* is attributable to Paul Gilster (1997), who referred to digital literacy as a logical extension to literacy, defining the term as "the ability to understand and use information in multiple formats from a wide range of sources when it is presented via computers." While digital literacy has been associated with positive social engagement, for example, as an attribute of engaged citizens and employees, defining this term has proven to be complex, because the digital environment is constantly changing (e.g., Pangrazio, 2014). In definitions, there is often an emphasis on mastery of skills and tools. The United Nations Educational Scientific and Cultural Organization (2013) echoes Gilster's definition:

> [Digital literacy is] the ability to use digital technology, communication tools or networks to locate, evaluate, use and create information. It also refers to the ability to understand and use information in multiple formats from a wide range of sources

Digital Detectives
ISBN 978-0-08-100124-0

9

when presented via computers, or to a person's ability to perform tasks effectively in a digital environment.

UNESCO (2013)

Digital technologies, as well as the digital information involved, are equally important to digital literacy. Digital devices, such as computing and communication instruments, and tools, such as databases, enable access, management, and creation of digital information. These means of interacting with digital information are viewed as networking devices, rather than simply computing devices. The digital information itself offers the digital material to be acted upon. Our capabilities, demonstrated through our interaction with this digital environment, determine our level of digital literacy.

According to the American Libraries Association's Digital Literacy Task Force (2011), a digitally literate person is someone who:

- *possesses the variety of skills – technical and cognitive – required to find, understand, evaluate, create, and communicate digital information in a wide variety of formats;*
- *is able to use diverse technologies appropriately and effectively to retrieve information, interpret results, and judge the quality of that information;*
- *understands the relationship between technology, life-long learning, personal privacy, and stewardship of information;*
- *uses these skills and the appropriate technology to communicate and collaborate with peers, colleagues, family, and on occasion, the general public; and*
- *uses these skills to actively participate in civic society and contribute to a vibrant, informed, and engaged community.*

ALA Digital Literacy Task Force (2011)

The European Union refers to digital literacy as *digital competence* and includes this in its standard of eight key competencies for lifelong learning:

Digital Competence can be broadly defined as the confident, critical and creative use of ICT [Information and Communications Technologies] to achieve goals related to work, employability, learning, leisure, inclusion and/or participation in society. Digital competence is a transversal key competence which, as such, enables us to acquire other key competences (e.g., language, mathematics, learning to learn, cultural awareness). It is related to many of the 21st Century skills which should be acquired by all citizens, to ensure their active participation in society and the economy.

Ferrari (2013)

This EU report offers a self-assessment tool for evaluating digital literacy or competencies in five areas (information retrieval, evaluation, and management; communication; content creation; safety in the digital environment; and problem solving) with three proficiency levels: A, foundation level; B, intermediate level; C, advanced level (Ferrari, 2013).

This self-assessment rubric (Figure 2.1) can help you to identify your own digital competencies by inviting you to consider your strengths and weaknesses in the digital environment. This self-evaluation will help you consider areas for improvement, so that you can start planning how to fill any gaps in your digital skills.

2.2 LEARNING AT UNIVERSITY: WHERE DO I START?

University education, particularly in the first year, can be daunting. University education provides significant freedom, enabling students to design their education to satisfy their learning goals within the framework of a degree programme. To make the most of learning in this unique environment, it is essential to plan ahead. This requires you to consider carefully your learning goals and how you can achieve them.

Start by visualizing learning. What do you think *learning* means? Where does learning take place? For example, in the university environment, where and when would you feel that you were learning? There are no right or wrong answers to these questions; learning can be perceived differently by individuals, and different approaches to learning may be more effective for different people. University education provides a range of formal learning opportunities, including lectures, tutorials, seminars, computer-assisted labs, and so on. A range of digital opportunities may be present in these learning contexts. It is important to consider how learning may be associated with the presence of digital technologies and information. Consider how you learn and the essential supports for your learning.

Students often think about their learning in terms of what they must do to demonstrate learning, that is, assigned tasks for course credit. Remember that the process of learning is important here as well. Continuously improving how you learn will help you succeed with the learning you must achieve in a given situation. Breaking down the process can help you visualize the different aspects of learning; for example, learning in the context of an assigned task may be considered in terms of analyzing the task to be completed and the information required to complete the task, gathering evidence to complete the task, completing the task, and reviewing feedback about the finished product.

While working through an understanding of the process of how we learn, it can be useful to record your thoughts as you explore your learning. A common piece of advice—one meant to encourage you to reflect on your learning as it happens—is to keep a learning journal. Start now with ideas about the meaning of learning to you and the contexts in which it happens, as well

	A—Foundation	B—Intermediate	C—Advanced
Information	I can do some online searches through search engines. I know how to save or store files and content (e.g., texts, pictures, music, videos, and web pages). I know how to go back to the content I saved. I know that not all online information is reliable.	I can browse the internet for information and I can search for information online. I can select the appropriate information I find; I can compare different information sources. I know how to save, store or tag files, content and information and I have my own storing strategy. I can retrieve and manage the information and content I saved or stored.	I can use a wide range of strategies when searching for information and browsing on the Internet. I am critical about the information I find and I can cross check and assess its validity and credibility. I can filter and monitor the information I receive. I can apply different methods and tools to organize files, content and information. I can deploy a set of strategies for retrieving and managing the content I or others have organized and stored. I know whom to follow in online information sharing places (e.g., micro blogging).
Communication	I can interact with others using basic features of communication tools. (e.g., mobile phone, VoIP, chat or email). I know basic behaviour norms that apply when communicating with others using digital tools. I can share files and content with others through simple technological means. I know that technology can be used to interact with services and I passively use some. I can collaborate with others using traditional technologies. I am aware of the benefits and risks related to digital identity.	I can use several digital tools to interact with others using more advanced features of communication tools (e.g., mobile phone, VoIP, chat, email). I know the principles of online etiquette and I am able to apply them in my own context. I can participate in social networking sites and online communities, where I pass on or share knowledge, content and information. I can actively use some basic features of online services. I can create and discuss outputs in collaboration with others using simple digital tools. I can shape my online digital identity and keep track of my digital footprint.	I am engaged in the use of a wide range of tools for online communication (emails, chats, SMS, instant messaging, blogs, micro blogs, SNS). I can apply the various aspects of online etiquette to different digital communication spaces and contexts. I have developed strategies to discover inappropriate behaviour. I can adopt digital modes and ways of communication that best fit the purpose. I can tailor the format and ways of communication to my audience. I can manage the different types of communication I receive. I can actively share information, content, and resources with others through online communities, networks, and collaboration platforms. I am actively participate in online spaces. I know how to get actively engaged in online participation and I can use several different online services. I frequently and confidently use several digital collaboration tools and means to collaborate with others in the production and sharing of resources, knowledge, and content. I can manage several digital identities according to the context and purpose. I can monitor the information and data I produce through my online interaction, I know how to protect my digital reputation.
Content creation	I can produce simple digital content (e.g., text, or tables, or images or audio, etc.). I can make basic changes to the content that others have produced. I can modify some simple function of software and applications (apply basic settings). I know that some of the content I find may be covered by copyright.	I can produce digital content in different formats (e.g., text, tables, images, audio, etc.). I can edit, refine, and modify the content I or others have produced. I have basic knowledge of the differences between copyright, copyleft and creative commons and I can apply some licences to the content I create. I can apply several modifications to software and applications (advanced settings, basic programme modifications).	I can produce digital content in different formats, platforms and environments. I can use a variety of digital tools for creating original multimedia outputs. I can mash up existing items of content to create new ones. I know how different types of licences apply to the information and resources I use and create. I can interfere with (open) programmes and modify, change or write source code, I can code and programme in several languages and I understand the systems and functions that are behind programmes.
Safety	I can take basic steps to protect my devices (e.g., using anti-viruses and passwords). I know that I can share only certain types of information about myself or others in online environments. I know how to avoid cyber bullying. I know that technology can affect my health, if misused. I take basic measures to save energy.	I know how to protect my digital devices, I update my security strategies. I can protect my and others, online privacy. I have a general understanding of privacy issues and I have basic knowledge of how my data are collected and used. I know how to protect myself and others from cyber bullying. I understand the health risks associated with the use of technologies (from ergonomic aspects to addiction to technologies). I understand the positive and negative aspects of the use of technology on the environment.	I frequently update my security strategies. I can take action when the device is under threat. I often change the default privacy settings of online services to enhance my privacy protection. I have an informed and wide understanding of privacy issues and I know how my data are collected and used. I am aware of the correct use of technologies to avoid health problems. I know how to find a good balance between online and off line worlds. I have an informed stance on the impact of technologies on everyday life, online consumption, and the environment.
Problem solving	I can ask for targeted support and assistance when technologies do not work or when using a new device, programme or application. I can use some technologies to solve routine tasks. I can make decisions when choosing a digital tool for a routine practice. I know that technologies and digital tools can be used for creative purposes and I can make some creative use of technologies. I have some basic knowledge, but I am aware of my limits when using technologies.	I can solve easy problems that arise when technologies do not work. I understand what technology can do for me and what it cannot. I can solve a non routine task by exploring technological possibilities. I can select an appropriate tool according to the purpose and I can evaluate the effectiveness of the tool. I can use technologies for creative outputs and I can use technologies to solve problems. I can collaborate with others in the creation of innovative and creative outputs, but I don't take the initiative. I know how to learn to do something new with technologies.	I can solve a wide-range of problems that arise from the use of technology. I can make informed decisions when choosing a tool, device, application, software, or service for the task I am not familiar with. I am aware of new technological developments. I understand how new tools work and operate. I can critically evaluate which tool serves my purposes best. I can solve conceptual problems taking advantage of technologies and digital tools. I can contribute to knowledge creation through technological means. I can take part in innovative actions through the use of technologies. I proactively collaborate with others to produce creative and innovative outputs. I frequently update my digital competence needs.

Figure 2.1 DIGCOMP's digital competence self-assessment framework.

as the learning outcomes you wish to achieve. Track your progress throughout your studies, so that you can identify your learning successes and points where you might try alternative learning approaches to achieve further.

Keeping a record of learning will enable you to document learning as a process and, critically, to understand how you learn. The journal will also help prepare you for continuing the learning process beyond university. Learning to learn and monitoring your progress are crucial early steps in becoming an effective, lifelong learner. As a lifelong learner, you will be better positioned to maintain essential digital competencies.

2.3 HOW PEOPLE LEARN IN DIGITAL AND BLENDED SPACES

Just as individuals have learning preferences in the offline world, they may also have learning preferences in the digital world. However, digital learning is about more than tools and resources alone. Connectivity is essential; for example, if you identify a technology that you feel supports your learning, consider also how the technology increases your connectivity. How does the technology connect you to other people, devices, and networks?

Learners in a digital world can benefit from the flexibility that the digital space offers. However, while students may feel that they are digital natives who are very comfortable with technology, they may not understand the extent to which learning can be connected to the digital. Digital learning may occur in offline, online, and blended spaces. For example, some instructors use Twitter to poll students about a given topic in the traditional offline lecture setting. Students may complete assessments, such as tests, through a university's learning management system (e.g., Blackboard).

A recent popular trend has been MOOCs—formally known as a *massive open online courses*—in which learning materials, ranging from traditional items, such as readings, to digital learning supports, such as videos, can be openly accessed via the Internet for a range of topics. In addition to self-study, a MOOC offers a community space where students can discuss topics with instructors or other students. Various mobile device apps, such as Coursera, offer easy access to MOOCs. MOOCs have been found to cost significant amounts of money to run and update periodically (e.g., Parr, 2015; Stein, 2013). In addition, MOOC completion rates have been observed to be a fraction of initial enrolment (e.g., Sandeen, 2013; Stein, 2013), suggesting a possible disconnect at some point between learner and the completely digital learning environment of the MOOC.

2.4 HOW CAN A DIGITAL CONTEXT ENHANCE MY LEARNING?

Importantly, the digital learning environment can provide personalized learning. Instructors and students can use the digital environment to enhance learning, and this raises two important considerations for learning. First, reflect on why an instructor might incorporate one or more digital elements into your learning; digital tools and resources are added to your learning environment for a specific pedagogical reason. Second, think about how you can finesse your learning with digital tools and resources that are already familiar to you. Is there an app that you may have used previously that you might repurpose for greater learning now?

Think carefully about your learning goals and how digital tools and resources might support you. Using technology in your learning environment not only accustoms you to new digital opportunities and possibly advances your use of existing technologies, but also helps you to develop digital skills that you can take with you after you complete your university education.

2.5 BEING A REFLECTIVE DETECTIVE: MANAGING YOUR OWN LEARNING

Managing your own learning is a significant task that must be started as soon as possible to enable you to take charge and maintain control of your learning. University life offers an abundance of academic and extracurricular activities. While social life at university can provide entertainment as well as social learning, take care to organize your overall university experience so that you have sufficient time for both forms of activities. As you work through this textbook, you will learn about opportunities to use digital tools and resources effectively to help you organize your time and your approach to a variety of academic tasks, such as reading, note-taking, studying, and preparing for assessment.

2.6 CHALLENGES

Before you delve into the digital dilemmas presented in the next chapters, consider your own learning needs and approaches by completing the following exercises.

1. Evaluate your own digital literacy using the self-assessment template offered by the European Union (Figure 2.1). Identify areas where you might improve your digital literacy. Because digital literacy is part of lifelong learning, make a plan now for continuous improvement. Identify specific chapters in this textbook that may be particularly helpful to you in achieving this goal.

2. Start and keep a learning journal, as described in this chapter.
   a. Set your personal learning goals to build digital competencies for your first year of university.
   b. Add tasks and deadlines for these tasks, which will help you to achieve your learning goals.
   c. Update your learning journal regularly throughout the academic year. Choose a time each week when you can pause and reflect on your progress, review learning goals, and revise and add to your learning goals as necessary.
3. How might digital devices, such as mobile phones, facilitate your university learning? Complete the following list of your digital device use.
   Remember to return to this exercise periodically and add devices and/ or uses for learning.

List the top five digital devices you use now.	Describe briefly how you currently use each device to help you learn.	Consider some additional, new ways you might utilize each device to achieve your personal learning goals.
1.		
2.		
3.		
4.		
5.		

4. How might digital tools, such as mobile phone apps, facilitate your university learning? Complete the following list of your digital tool use for learning.
   Remember to return to this exercise periodically and add digital tools and/or uses for learning.

List the top five digital tools you use now.	Describe briefly how you currently use each tool to help you learn.	Consider some additional, new ways you might utilize each tool to achieve your personal learning goals.
1.		
2.		
3.		
4.		
5.		

5. How might digital information facilitate your university learning? Complete the following list of your digital information use for learning. Remember to return to this exercise periodically and add digital information used for learning.

List five examples of digital information you have used academically.	Explain how you made effective and appropriate use of this information in each case to achieve your learning goals.
1.	
2.	
3.	
4.	
5.	

REFERENCES

ALA Digital Literacy Task Force. (2011). *What is digital literacy?* ALA. Office for Information Technology Policy. Retrieved from http://connect.ala.org/node/181197#sthash. LtRAktge.dpuf.

Ferrari, A. (2013). *DIGCOMP: A framework for developing and understanding digital competence in Europe.* Joint Research Centre (JRC): Scientific and Policy reports. Report EUR 26035 Seville, Spain: JRC, European Union. Retrieved from https://ec.europa.eu/jrc/sites/default/files/lb-na-26035-enn.pdf.

Gilster, P. (1997). *Digital literacy.* New York: Wiley Computer Publications.

Pangrazio, L. (2014). Reconceptualising critical digital literacy. *Discourse: Studies in the Cultural Politics of Education,* 1–12. http://dx.doi.org/10.1080/01596306.2014.942836.

Parr, C. (2015, April 23). MOOCs: Fluctuating rates in online investment. *Times Higher Education.* Retrieved from https://www.timeshighereducation.com/news/moocs-fluctuating-rates-in-online-investment/2019816.article.

Sandeen, C. (2013). Assessment's place in the new MOOC world. *Research & Practice in Assessment* 8: 5–12.

Stein, K. (2013, December 5). PENN GSE study shows MOOCs have relatively few active users, with only a few persisting to course end. *PENN GSE Graduate School of Education Press Room.* Retrieved from https://www.gse.upenn.edu/pressroom/press-releases/2013/12/penn-gse-study-shows-moocs-have-relatively-few-active-users-only-few-persisti.

United Nations Educational Scientific and Cultural Organization (UNESCO). (2013). *Global media and information literacy assessment framework: Country readiness and competencies.* Paris, France: UNESCO.

CHAPTER 3

Aladdin's Cave

3.1 THE DILEMMA: "I CAN JUST GOOGLE THIS, CAN'T I?"

It's a familiar scenario. You have been given a college assignment, which asks you to write a paper on a topic you know little about, for example, the *greenhouse effect*, since your professor is interested in environmental issues. Although you have heard of it, you are not sure where to start, but you will need a lot of information to write a complete paper. Where should you look first? Chances are that you will resort to the resource that you always turn to first: Google, of course. However, when you enter the phrase *greenhouse effect* in the search box, you quickly discover that there are 7,680,000 search results for this query! The first one is Wikipedia, which you have been told by your professor that you cannot use. The others might be okay, but there are just so many links. How do you select the sources to use for your paper? *Is Google really helping you at all, or just making you more confused?*

When it comes to academic assignments, it cannot be denied: Google is the research tool of choice for students like you, and it begins before you even walk through the college gates. A survey by the Pew Internet Research and American Life Project asked teachers which sources their students were *very likely* to use for a typical research assignment; 94% of them said Google or other online search engines (Purcell *et al.,* 2012). Another study by the Project Information Literacy team found that, although college freshmen students did use other sources as well, such as academic journals, many of them often did a Google search for an unfamiliar topic first, then took the keywords they found through the Google search and used them in the library databases to make their searches more accurate (Head, 2013). However, some of the students who were surveyed said that they preferred to stick to searching Google because it was what they were familiar with from high school. What do *you* do? There are many reasons why you might turn to Google first when you have an information problem: it's simple, straightforward, very fast, and, after all, you almost always find *something* you can use. When it comes to college work, however, there are some things you should know about Google and how it works so that you can make good decisions

Digital Detectives
ISBN 978-0-08-100124-0

about when you should and shouldn't use it for your assignments. You should read this chapter together with Chapter 7 to expand your understanding of how to use the Internet effectively for academic work.

In this chapter, you will:

- reflect on your *attitude* toward Google (and all Internet search engines) as a tool for college work.
- consider how you *select* the online sources to use from the list of search results you retrieve when using Google.
- learn how search engines *locate*, *index*, and *retrieve* sources in response to search queries.
- discover how Google *ranks* the list of search results that you receive in response to your query and how to use this information to help you *judge* which sources to select.
- become aware of *search personalization* and how it can affect your search results.
- learn how to *refine* and *optimize* your searches using Google's search features and operators. In other words, become Google-wise!

3.2 CAN I JUST GOOGLE IT?

The web is not the Internet. Although many people, (including some who should know better), often confuse the two. Neither is Google the Internet, nor Facebook the Internet.

Naughton (2014)

The answer to this dilemma is both no and yes! Google *can* be used for college work, but it is unwise to think that you can *just* Google anything. The quotation above should be taken seriously. While Google is a tremendous tool, it does not—indeed *cannot*—provide the perfect single solution to any information problem, especially the information problems that you will encounter in higher education. This chapter shows you how to be smart and savvy about using Google to find exactly what you need or at least to set you in the right direction. The basic Google search page is deceptively simple, although this user friendliness is one of the reasons it is so popular. Behind the clean, uncluttered interface, with the occasionally intriguing Google Doodle, lies a highly sophisticated mechanism that continuously, even endlessly, contrives to impose some degree of order on the unruly mass of free-floating information on the World Wide Web. Understanding, even at a most basic level, how this mechanism works is an important step to becoming a skilled digital detective in the *Googleverse*.

3.3 BUT FIRST: INDEXES!

To understand how an Internet search engine works, it is useful to first make sure that you know what an *index* is. Most people's experience of an index might be the alphabetical list of words or authors' names that you find at the back of a book, which shows you exactly where you can find particular topics or names in the main text of the book. You use an index to avoid having to flick through every page in the entire book in the hope of finding the passage you are interested in or trying to remember which page contains the passage you are looking for. The process of indexing a book involves selecting important words, phrases, or names on every single page and listing them separately in alphabetical order, along with the page numbers where they appear. A single term could be indexed to just one or to several pages in a book, depending on its importance in the context of the book's subject matter. In a way, you can think of an index as a *map* to the content of a book, with directions on how to find the location of words and phrases to make precise searching easier. The function of an Internet search engine is to do just that; however, instead of a single book, Internet search engines attempt to provide a map or index to the *entire content* of the Web and to make that index easily searchable by users. This mapping means you can avoid having to "flick through" the entire Web to find what you need. The workings of search engines are explained below.

3.4 HOW SEARCH ENGINES FIND INFORMATION FOR YOU

An important thing to be aware of is that the process of Web searching is *automated*. This means that there is no direct human involvement in picking out and serving up your search results (although it is, of course, humans who create and fine-tune the mechanisms of the search engine). The basic function of an Internet search engine is to match a user's query to the index that has been created of the content of webpages. To do this, search engines perform more or less three key tasks:

1. They continually search the Web, scanning for updates to existing websites and for new websites that have been created.
2. They send this information back to a central depository or database, creating an index of all of the words they find and pointing to the location of these words on the Web. The index is updated constantly because everything changes frequently on the Web.

3. They enable you, the searcher, to enter queries, which then are matched against the index, and they provide you with a list of the uniform resource locators (URLs), or links, that best match your query in your list of search results.

To carry out these functions, search engines, including Google, consist of four basic components:

1. Web crawlers or *spiders*: There is constant activity behind the scenes of the search page that you see before, during, and after you enter your query. To use the jargon of the Web, "spiders" are simply automated programs, or robots, that *crawl* from webpage to webpage by following the links on each page. As they crawl through the Web, the spiders collect information from each page—for example, updated or new content—and send it back to the index. Spiders usually start their journey through the Web at particularly popular webpages or servers, following every link that they find there and spreading out quickly. However, it *is* possible to avoid the spiders. In some cases, when website owners do not wish their pages or parts of their pages to be crawled and indexed, the robot exclusion standard is applied; this is a protocol that instructs spiders *not* to index the words on a particular page nor to follow the links. The pages in question do not, therefore, show up in the search results for that particular search engine. You should be aware that, because of this, many pages might not be found by performing a basic Web search. Using a search engine to trawl through the Web is far from an exhaustive strategy. We discuss this particularly in Chapter 7, when we explore the "Deep Web."

2. Index: The index of a search engine is enormous. Webpages often are indexed under *every single word* that appears on the page, in the titles and subtitles, as well as the URL of the page itself, the URLs of other pages that appear on the page, and any metatags, image files, and so on—although different search engines do have different approaches to *spidering*. For example, some search engines do not index small words like *a* and *the*, whereas others index only the 100 most frequently used words on a page. In the early days of the Internet, a search engine would index maybe a couple of hundred thousand webpages; nowadays, as the Internet continues to grow, search engines such as Google must index hundreds of *billions* of pages. In a typical index, such as at the back of a book, words are listed with just the page number(s) on which they occur. If a search engine index were to follow this approach, it would mean that each word on a webpage would be indexed with just the URL where it could be found. In reality, however, this is not a useful way to store information about a webpage because it takes no account of the context, or the importance of that word on a particular page. As a result, there would be no way for a search engine to *rank* its search results in a helpful way for searchers. Search engines must include more information about the words in their indexes; for instance, they might include the number of times a word appears on a page, or they might give a heavier *weighting* to certain words to indicate their importance. We look at search result ranking more closely in Sections 3.5 and 3.6 below.

3. **Search engine program:** The third component is the program that searches through the index and attempts to retrieve webpages that correspond most closely to the query that a searcher has input into the system. You should understand that when you type a query into a search engine, you are not, in fact, searching *the Web*. Instead, you are searching the *index* that has been compiled through the crawling activities of the spider, which in turn points you toward the pages themselves. Search engines use complex *algorithms* to search the index when a query is entered. An algorithm is "a process or set of rules to be followed in calculations or other problem-solving operations, especially by a computer" (Oxford Dictionaries, 2015). Algorithms differ from search engine to search engine. The results from a Google search might differ from those retrieved from Bing or Yahoo!, depending on the information scanned by the algorithms and how *relevance* is determined. The algorithms used by the various search engines are closely guarded secrets; the commercial potential of the Web, and the marketability of the data that are collected about users, have led to ferocious competition between search engine developers to attract the most users. If a search engine provider were to reveal its *secret formula*, this could potentially leave it open to manipulation by website owners who wish to push their sites up the rankings or allow it to be copied by competitors. Equally, however, concerns that the secrecy of search engine algorithms means that no one really knows exactly how search results are ranked have also recently been expressed; for example, could they be deliberately skewed toward particular sites, or are they designed to exclude others (Vasager & Fontanella-Khan, 2014)? Awareness of these potential concerns enables us to make informed decisions about the quality of the information that we find on the Web.

4. **User interface:** The user interface is the part of the search engine that you see and interact with. It is the page where you enter and refine your query, and where your results appear when the search is complete. At its

most basic, the user interface consists of a simple search box, into which you type your terms and press "enter." Think of the Google homepage, which is laid out with the simplest of designs. However, search interfaces also usually provide access to an *advanced* search page, where you can adjust your search query and apply various parameters and limiters to allow you to carry out the most precise search possible. (How to create an effective search strategy is the subject of Chapter 8.) The page where your results appear is called the *search engine results page* (SERP). Most search engines do not just display links to websites on this page, but they do group results from their image or video databases. Google, for example, also serves up a list of *related searches* for situations where searchers may not be sure what they are looking for. Studies of searcher "first click behavior" have shown that the *order* or ranking of results on the SERP is extremely important in terms of the links searchers choose. For example, one study showed that search results that appear in the part of a SERP that has to be *scrolled down* to are very rarely clicked on; that is, links that do not appear on the visible part of the SERP are less likely to be viewed by the searcher (Hochstotter & Lewandowski, 2009). Other studies have also shown that very few users move on to the second SERP after carrying out a search on a search engine (Barry & Lardner, 2010). For commercial entities that rely on user clicks to increase their business, this is a serious matter. Search engine marketing is the name given to the strategies that are applied by business owners to drive users to their websites. The issue of search result ranking is discussed in the following section.

3.5 HOW DOES GOOGLE DECIDE THE ORDER OF THE SEARCH RESULTS LIST?

When you carry out a search using Google, what assumptions do you make about the order of the search results that you receive? Take a moment to consider your search behavior. Do you, for example, assume that the search results that appear first are the most useful or relevant to your query? Or do you diligently scroll through every single result served up by Google to determine which links are the most important? *How do you decide which result to click on first?* Understanding how search engines such as Google *rank* their search results is essential because it empowers you to make better decisions about the sources that you use. In the case of search engines, first might not always mean first rate.

You have probably noticed that when you carry out a search, two types of results appear: *sponsored links* and normal, or organic, links. The sponsored links usually stand out by being labeled as *ads* or being otherwise marked as separate from the organic links—by being displayed in a sidebar, for example. Sponsored links occur when commercial entities or other parties *purchase* the right to be displayed on the SERP once a particular keyword or combination of terms is entered, which may give them some competitive advantage in the marketplace, especially when search results are location-based. The organic links, by contrast, are the results that the search engine has deemed to be the most suitable matches for the query that was entered by the searcher. How the order of Google search results is determined is explained below.

3.6 PAGERANK: GOOGLE'S RANKING SYSTEM

As mentioned before, search engines generally work by matching the words in a searcher's query to the words in its index of webpages. However, without some means of determining which results are potentially the most useful, the most relevant, and of the highest quality, the links that appear would be random and unlikely to satisfy your information need. If ranking was based, for example, on the number of times your search terms appeared on the webpages retrieved, it would then be possible for website creators to manipulate the search engine results by including certain keywords multiple times on the page. This type of manipulation is known as *keyword stuffing*, and search engine developers have sought ways to prevent it. Google's search results are ordered by a trademarked metric known as *PageRank*™, the exact details of which have never been made known publicly. However, we can still glean some basic insight into how it works.

PageRank assigns a numerical score to each webpage, which determines how far up the SERP the webpage appears for a given query. A higher score means a higher ranking and a higher probability that a webpage link will be clicked on by the searcher (remember first-click behavior!). To understand how this score is calculated, it is helpful to think of the process almost as a popularity contest for websites, where ranking is based on the number of *votes* that a website receives! However, unlike the X Factor or other reality shows, the votes are not cast by humans; rather, the popularity of an individual website is determined partly by the number of *incoming links* to that website and the quality of the sites that provide these links. In simple terms, the more links there are *to* your site from other high-quality website, the higher your site will be ranked on the SERP by the Google search engine. The logic behind this system is that other websites are more likely to link to sites with perceived high-quality content than average or low-quality sites. However, even within this process, *votes* from different sites are not all considered equal. Links from sites that are themselves considered high quality (i.e., those with a high PageRank score) are more valuable than incoming links from lower-quality sites. Moreover, *votes* from sites that seem to be less discriminating and link to hundreds of other pages count for much less than those from sites that link only to a selected few. This system encourages website creators to consistently produce high-quality and up-to-date content, which in turn encourages more pages to link to these webpages.

Although there are an estimated 200 other factors counted in the PageRank algorithm, including keyword position, density, multimedia, and broken links, incoming links from other sites are believed to be the most important criterion. However, search results are increasingly being influenced by factors that relate directly to *your* online behavior. The next section explains how.

3.7 WHAT IS A *FILTER BUBBLE*? THE PERSONALIZATION OF SEARCH RESULTS

Have you ever noticed that when you carry out a search, sometimes the results seem to be almost spookily tailored to your interests or to your location? Have you seen ads popping up on various websites that you visit that seem to suggest just the kind of products or services that you are currently interested in? It can occasionally seem like the search engine can read your mind, and, in a way, it can. For example, you may have spent 20 minutes searching for a new pair of winter boots, and the next day, when you are browsing through Facebook, an ad for the precise kind of leather boot you are searching for pops up in your newsfeed. How is this possible, when everybody who searches Google is effectively searching the same *database* of Web content? When searching Google and, increasingly, other search engines, one of the most important things to be aware of is how a number of factors specific to you, including your geographic location, *previous search history*, browsing behavior, and a myriad of other online *click signals*, influence the results that you receive when performing a new search. In 2005 Google introduced *personalized search* to the normal Google search for Google account holders (later applied to all users of Google search); this feature forever changed the way information is delivered to individuals when using Web search engines. Personalization of content is also a feature you may have noticed on the social media sites that you use; for example, your Facebook newsfeed might seem to include only items that you are interested in and exclude posts from *friends* whom you do not interact with much and probably wouldn't read anyway. This increasing customization of Web content is called a *filter bubble*, described as follows:

> The new generation of Internet filters looks at things you seem to like – the actual things you've done, or the things people like you like – and tries to extrapolate. They are predictive engines, constantly creating and refining a theory of who you are and what you'll do and want next. Together these engines create a unique universe of information for each of us – what I've come to call a filter bubble – which fundamentally alters the way we encounter ideas and information.
>
> **Pariser (2011, p. 9)**

Personalized search works by building a profile of your search habits over time through the placement of *cookies*, which are "small files that websites put on your computer hard disk drive when you first visit" (Microsoft Safety & Security Center, 2014). The longer you interact with a search engine, more data about your search behavior are stored. These data then are used to try to predict the type of content that you are more likely to engage with and that may be more relevant to your needs. For example, if you are a lover of independent music and often visit www.pitchfork.com, the search engine will learn over time that you like this site, and it will boost the site in search result ranking when you perform music-related searches. You might have a friend, on the other hand, who prefers classical music and frequently browses the BBC's www.classical-music.com, which then receives a ranking boost for her searches. If you both searched for "top albums of 2015," your search results might look rather different, despite both of you using the same search engine. Personalized search is, therefore, the reason why two people performing the same search on different browsers might not get the same results.

3.8 WEB AND APP ACTIVITY

Search personalization on Google works in two main ways. First, if you are logged into your personal Google account and have *Web and App Activity* (search history) turned *on*, information about the searches you carry out and details of your browser and app activities are recorded and stored, including the following:

- *Searches you have done on Google products, like Search and Maps*
- *Whether you searched from a browser or an app*
- *Your interactions with search results, including which results you click*

- *Ads you respond to by clicking the ad itself or completing a transaction on the advertiser's site*
- *Your IP address*
- *Your browser type and language*
- *Results that are returned, including results from information on your device (like recent apps or contact names you searched for) and private results from Google products like Google+, Gmail, and Google Calendar.*

Google (2015)

If you do not wish for Google to record your search behavior, you can turn Web and App Activity *off* by first logging into your *Account History* page at www.google.com/history, where you will be prompted to enter the login details for your Google account, if you are not already logged in. If you are logging in from the basic Google homepage, click on *Settings* in the bottom right-hand corner, then on *History* to bring you to the Web & App Activity page. You will arrive at a default screen that shows you a record of your Web and App activity on Google, including your past searches and content that you have browsed on this browser and other apps. Figure 3.1 displays the Web & App Activity screen in Google Chrome.

You can expand this page to show your other activities by clicking on the menu at the top right-hand corner (three vertical dots on Google Chrome), then on *Settings.* On this page, you have the option to *Show More Controls.* Clicking on this option brings up all of your activity, including:

- your searches and browsing activity.
- places you go.
- information from your devices.

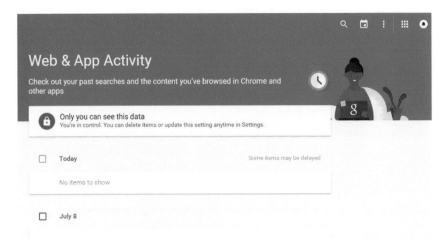

Figure 3.1 Google Web and App activity.

- your voice searches and commands.
- videos you search for on YouTube.
- videos you watch on YouTube.

On this page you have the option to *remove* selected search items or to *delete* the entire history of your searches. For each item, you will see a slider button to the right. If the button is blue and has been moved to the right, your activities are being recorded by Google. To *pause* the recording, simply slide the button to the left for each item, and the button will turn gray, which indicates that the activity on each item is no longer being recorded. Clicking on *Manage Activity* for each of these items provides you with a detailed history of your activities for time periods that you can specify by selecting from a dropdown menu. You can also delete specific activities, as you wish. Figure 3.2 shows the control screen.

If you choose, you can also download a full copy of your data from Google from this page. Simply click again on the menu at the top right-hand corner (three vertical dots on Google Chrome), then select *Download Searches*. This option enables you to create an archive of all of your past searches. Google then emails you when the archive is ready to download. You will receive a zip file containing your data, which you can download to your device or view in Google Drive.

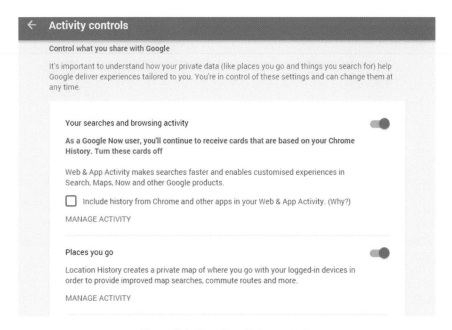

Figure 3.2 Google activity controls.

3.9 INTERNET PROTOCOL ADDRESS

The other way that Google records searches is through the *Internet protocol (IP) address* of your computer. The IP address is "the numerical Internet address assigned to each computer on a network so that it can be distinguished from other computers. [It is] expressed as four groups of numbers separated by dots" (IAB Ireland, 2015). While Google is not able to link your search behavior with your *personal* Google account, it records the searches of anyone who uses that specific *device* to search the Web. Furthermore, if you do not delete your browsing history, anyone who uses that device after you will be able to see your searches. If you want to find the IP address of your device, there are various websites that will detect it for you, including http://whatismyipaddress.com and www.howtofindmyipaddress.com. Alternatively, if you simply enter "IP address" into the Google search box, it will display the IP address of the device you are using as the first search result!

It is up to you whether you allow your searches to become personalized. You may like the idea of searches being tailored to your interests, particularly when it comes to things like searching for vacations, events, music, and leisure activities. The downside of personal search, which has been flagged by authors like Pariser (2011), is that you could sometimes miss important information that is excluded from your search results because it does not fit with your search history. Being aware of this issue can help you to make an informed choice about how you wish to set up your search strategy.

3.10 HOW DO I BECOME GOOGLE-WISE?

The key to being Google-wise is to become familiar with and know how to use the different settings, functions, and operators that are available to optimize your search experience. Being Google-wise not only allows you to perform more precise and useful searches but also empowers you to increase or decrease the level of personalization of your search experience—or at least to be aware of the potential effects of personalization on your search results. In this section we look at three specific aspects of Google searching that will help you to hone your digital detective skills:

- Priming your search (e.g., search settings, history, location)
- Google advanced search
- Google search operators

Google and other search engines allow you to perform exceptionally precise searches by adding and combining a series of operators that allow you to dictate, for example, the *type* of source or the location, including position, on a page or URL the search engine should look for using your search terms. Being Google-wise means that you are adept at creating search strategies that filter out much of the irrelevant information and serve up results that you will potentially find useful.

3.10.1 Google Search Settings: Priming Your Search

Before you even *begin* to search, however, you should take a few minutes to set up Google exactly as you want. To do this, click on *Settings* at the bottom of the main Google search page and then on *Search Settings*, where you are presented with a number of options that you can set up according to your preferences:

- **Safe search filters:** You can use this setting to filter sexually explicit content from your search results; you also have the option to "*lock*" this setting if you want to prevent others from changing it.
- **Google instant predictions:** You may have noticed that as you begin to type a query into the Google search box, a list of suggested search terms appears underneath the box and changes as you add more letters to your search terms. This is Google's attempt to predict what you might be searching for and is based on the popularity of previous searches. The *Instant Predictions* setting is where you tell Google whether you want it to show you these suggested terms as you type in your queries. You can tell it to *always* do this, to do this only when your computer is *fast enough*, or *never* to do this, depending on your preference.
- **Number of results per page:** If you are using Google Instant Predictions, 10 results per search results page will automatically be displayed. However, if you opt out of instant predictions, you can specify the number of results that you would like to appear on each search page, from 10 to 100.
- **Where results open:** Here, you can tell Google to open results in a new window in your browser, if you prefer. You might do this to avoid having to repeatedly use the back button to browse through your search results.
- **Search history:** As mentioned before, you can choose to enable or disable search history or to remove selected results from your search history.

- **Spoken answers:** Where voice search is enabled, such as in the Google app on your mobile device, you can specify whether answers should also be spoken or delivered in text only.

3.10.2 Google Advanced Search

Advanced Search is also accessed by clicking on *Settings* in the bottom right-hand corner of the screen on the main Google page. As with all databases, advanced search enables you to be extremely precise about how you search, through cleverly combining search terms to narrow or broaden a search and through applying various filters that give precise instructions to the search engine with regard to the documents, images, or other source types that you wish to retrieve.

Within advanced search, you can tell Google to find webpages with various properties:

- **Contain *all* of the words that you enter:** This means that only results that contain all of the words will be displayed. Results that only contain one or the other word will be excluded. This corresponds with the Boolean *AND* operator, which is explained in Chapter 8.
- **Contain an *exact* word or phrase:** You can use this if you want to make sure that certain words appear beside each other in the webpages that you retrieve. This is the same as *phrase searching*, which is discussed in Chapter 8.
- **Contain *any* of the words you enter:** This means that the results you get will contain one, some, or all of the words you enter. This is useful when you are not sure what the *best* search term to use is. You can use more than one term to make sure you do not miss anything. This is the Boolean *OR* operator.
- **Contain *none* of certain words that you specify:** If you want to make sure that particular words are excluded from your search, you can use this function. This is the Boolean *NOT* operator.
- **Fall within a specific range of numbers:** This might include units of measurement, monetary values, and so on.

Advanced Search also enables you to apply certain filters to your search, in addition to the functions described above, to refine it even more. For example, you can further narrow your results by language, region of publication, or last webpage update to ensure currency. Some of the other parameters here can be extremely useful in filtering out unwanted webpages or telling Google that you want only results of a certain type. For example, you can tell Google to indicate the *reading level* of the documents you retrieve, or to retrieve results at only a basic, intermediate, or advanced reading level. The "*filetype*" parameter can be especially helpful when you are trying to find more official or academic-type information because it enables you to specify the format of the results found. For example, you can tell Google to retrieve *only* PDF or Word documents, which could be useful since a lot of journal articles and official reports are in PDF format. If you are looking for slide presentations that people have uploaded after conferences, you can tell Google to retrieve only results in PowerPoint format, using the .ppt extension. Other formats include Excel and Shockwave Flash. Last, Google Advanced Search enables you to specify the *usage rights* of the documents and images you find. This is a very important search feature, especially if you are searching for images that you can cut and paste into a document or webpage of your own and you wish to avoid copyright infringements, which can lead to legal action. The following different usage rights included in this search filter:

• Not filtered by license
• Free to use or share
• Free to use or share, even commercially
• Free to use or share or modify
• Free to use or share or modify, even commercially

These usage rights are discussed in greater detail in Chapter 6, which deals with copyright and intellectual property rights on the Internet.

3.10.3 Google Search Operators

As if the search functions described above were not enough, Google also allows you to use a range of specialized search operators, which enable you to give very precise instructions to Google about, for example, where on a webpage you wish the engine to search for specific words or the type of source to retrieve. This is a useful function that enables you to build searches very quickly using the basic Google search box. By including an operator along with a colon in front of a search term, you can tell the search engine to do different things. Some of the most useful operators are laid out in Table 3.1

For example, imagine you wish to find out whether there are any documents or reports from University College Dublin (UCD) about *information literacy*. How can you accurately approach this search? You might consider entering a search string like this in the Google search box:

information literacy site : ucd.ie filetype:pdf

Table 3.1 Google Specialized Search Operators

filetype:	This is the same as the filetype function in Google Advanced Search. Combining this operator with an extension, such as pdf, doc, or ppt, instructs the search engine to retrieve only items in that particular format. For example, searching for "digital literacy" **filetype:doc** retrieves only Word documents that are about digital literacy.
site:	This allows you to search within a particular site or domain. For example, a search string **site:thetimes.co.uk** instructs the search engine to search only the website of the UK newspaper *The Times*.
inurl:	The inurl operator ensures that the search terms are found within a particular URL; for example, a search for **inurl:digital** means that Google will retrieve results where the word *digital* appears in the URL of the site.
allinurl	Where you are entering more than one search term, this operator ensures that they all appear in the URL of the sites retrieved.
intitle	The **intitle** operator allows you to specify that your search term should appear in the title of the webpage.
allintitle:	This is the same as above, but is applied when you are entering more than one search term.
inanchor:	The anchor text is the clickable text that you see on a webpage, which indicates a hyperlink. With this search operator, you can ensure that your search term appears in the anchor text.
allinanchor:	As above, but with more than one search term.
related:	This is a very useful operator when you come across a website that you really like. It allows you to find similar websites. For instance, **related:bbc.co.uk** searches for websites that are close to the BBC site and retrieves sites such as CNN.com, Reuters.com, and the *Guardian* website.
link:	The **link:** operator allows us, in a way, to apply a PageRank of our own! **link:** finds all the pages that link to a particular website. This allows us to make judgments about the quality of a website; for example, if many high-quality sites provide incoming links to a website we are interested in, we can draw a reasonable conclusion that the website itself must be of good quality.
define:	This operator asks Google for definitions of terms, which are gathered from pages on the Web, including Wikipedia.
info:	The **info:** operator gives you information about a specific URL, including the cached version of the page, similar pages, and pages that link to the site.

Table 3.1 Continued

cache:	As we described previously, Google gathers information from webpages by "crawling" (following link to link), where it takes a "snapshot" of each page at a particular point in time before indexing the page content. This snapshot that Google takes is also known as the **cache**, and this operator allows you to retrieve a particular website as it appeared the last time the Googlebot crawled it. You should remember that a page may have changed since it was last crawled. Searching for cached pages can be useful if some information seems to have disappeared from a page since you last viewed it and Google has also not crawled it since then.

In record time, you are presented with almost 100 results, including journal articles written by UCD staff and held in the online research repository, module descriptors, newsletters, course brochures, and book reviews. The search worked extremely well.

3.11 EXTRA TIP: REFINE YOUR SEARCH ON THE RESULTS PAGE

While you can create very specific search strings before hitting *Enter*, Google also allows you to apply further limiters to your search on the search results page itself (see Figure 3.3). You can instruct Google to refine the search results by country, time (of publication or creation), reading level, and specific location. You can also choose the specific Google database that you wish to search, for example, images, videos, news, books, and more.

3.12 GOOGLE WITH CARE

Googling is always a possibility, but to be a really effective search engine user, you need to go beyond your comfort zone and really learn how to make the most of the different tools and functions in the system to get the results that you need. Take your searching seriously. While clicking on the first result might be the quickest and most convenient option, you should understand that ranking might not necessarily correspond with the best or most relevant information for your query. Take time to think about the type, format, and quality of information you need, and use Google search operators to narrow down your search before you click the *Go* button. Be aware of the potential effects of personalized search and make a decision about the level

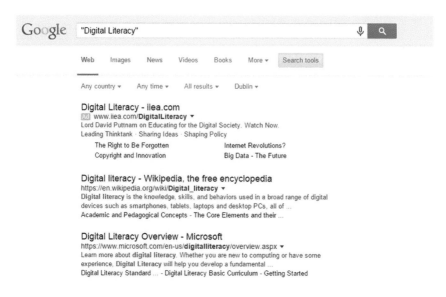

Figure 3.3 Google search results page: search limiters.

of privacy that you wish to maintain. Above all, understand that Google is just one of a wide and varied range of search tools that you can use to complete your college work and that it should never be considered a *one-stop shop* for your information needs.

3.13 OTHER SEARCH ENGINES

There is no doubting Google's ubiquity and popularity as a search engine. According to StatCounter (2015), in the 12 months before July 2015, Google accounted for *89.96%* of worldwide desktop, mobile, tablet, and console Internet searches. Although Google is indeed the *go-to* search engine of our time, you should not forget that there are many alternative search engines that you can also choose, each with unique features and search interfaces that are worth exploring. Some of the other major Internet search engines include the following:

* **Bing** (Microsoft)**:** www.bing.com
* **Yahoo!:** https://ie.yahoo.com
* **Ask.com:** www.ask.com
* **Aol.com:** www.aol.com
* **Wolframalpha:** www.wolframalpha.com
* **Exalead:** www.exalead.com/search

Whichever you choose, always take the time to explore the basic and advanced search settings of each search engine, as well as the additional options and features that may be included. You should also read the *About* section to understand the mission and coverage of each search engine, and their privacy policies, and to keep informed about the data that are collected about your search activity. Protecting your privacy online is discussed further in Chapter 11.

3.14 CHALLENGES

If you want to be smart Google searchers, you must practice. Here are some challenges to complete on your way to becoming Google-wise:

1. Find a PDF document about *information literacy* produced by the American Library Association (Hint: This organization's name is usually abbreviated to ALA).

2. How many websites link to the CNN websites? What are the first five websites listed?

3. Find a PowerPoint presentation about *digital literacy in Australia*. Who created the first presentation that comes up in the SERP?

4. Find a definition of *hypochondriac* on the Web. Which of the first three definitions that you find do you feel is the most trustworthy?

5. Find five websites that are similar to www.webmd.com.

6. Find an image of a dolphin that you are free to modify and use for noncommercial purposes. Who created the image that you have chosen?

REFERENCES

Barry, C., & Lardner, M. (2010). A study of first click behavior and user interaction on the Google SERP. In *In 19th international conference on information systems development (ISD 2010). Prague, Czech Republic, August 25–27, 2010*. Retrieved from http://hdl.handle.net/10379/1492.

Google. (2015). *Google accounts help. Google web & app activity*. Retrieved from https://support.google.com/accounts/answer/54068?hl=en.

Head, A. J. (2013). *Learning the ropes: How freshmen conduct course research once they enter college, project information literacy research report*. Retrieved from http://projectinfolit.org/images/pdfs/pil_2013_freshmenstudy_fullreport.pdf.

Hochstotter, N., & Lewandowski, D. (2009). What users see – structures in search engine results pages. *Information Sciences, 179*(12), 1796–1812.

IAB Ireland. (2015). *Digital glossary – IP address*. Retrieved from http://iabireland.ie/research-case-studies/glossary/digital-glossary.

Microsoft Safety & Security Center. (2014). *What is a cookie?* Retrieved from http://www.microsoft.com/security/resources/cookie-whatis.aspx.

Naughton, J. (March 9, 2014). *25 things you might not know about the web on its 25th birthday.* The Guardian. Retrieved from http://www.theguardian.com/technology/2014/mar/09/25-years-web-tim-berners-lee.

Oxford Dictionaries. (2015). Retrieved from: http://www.oxforddictionaries.com.

Pariser, E. (2011). *The filter bubble: What the internet is hiding from you.* London: Penguin Viking.

Purcell, K., Rainie, L., Heaps, A., Buchanan, J., Friedrich, L., Jacklin, A., et al. (2012). *How teens do research in the digital world.* Pew Internet & American Life Project. Retrieved from http://www.pewinternet.org/2012/11/01/how-teens-do-research-in-the-digital-world/.

StatCounter GlobalStats. (2015). *Search engine (desktop, mobile, tablet, console).* Retrieved from http://gs.statcounter.com/#all-search_engine-ww-monthly-201408-201507-bar.

Vasager, J., & Fontanella-Khan, J. (September 15, 2014). *Berlin pushes Google to reveal search engine formula.* Financial Times. Retrieved from http://www.ft.com/cms/s/0/9615661c-3ce111e4973300144feabdc0.html#axzz3K4nl0o7P.

CHAPTER 4

Wiki or Won't I?

4.1 THE DILEMMA: 'I CAN USE WIKIPEDIA FOR COLLEGE ASSIGNMENTS, CAN'T I?'

You have just been given the assignment of writing a big essay for one of your classes. Included in the instructions is a line that makes your heart sink: "You may not use Wikipedia as a source." Wikipedia may have seemed a handy source to use to find information about many topics, and everyone you know uses Wikipedia, so why is it taboo to use in university?

Wikipedia is a controversial source of information. It is common for students to receive conflicting messages about the suitability of Wikipedia as an academic source. Many instructors forbid the use of Wikipedia, not only to avoid potentially inaccurate information, but also to encourage students to adopt formal, recognized sources of information prepared by known subject experts.

While some researchers have shown that the accuracy of Wikipedia articles is comparable to that of more traditionally known and used encyclopedias, such as *Encyclopaedia Britannica*, Wikipedia has not lost its notoriety as a potentially error-ridden source. Why?

No source is perfect. The key here is to understand the usefulness of a source and then to apply it appropriately to your learning. To do this, we must understand how Wikipedia articles are created and managed. This requires an exploration of collaborative authoring and its potential advantages and disadvantages for academic purposes.

In this chapter, you will:

• learn to define and identify collaborative authoring.
• identify the types of information contained in Wikipedia entries.
• explore how Wikipedia works, including how content is created and maintained, and who is responsible for content.
• consider how Wikipedia meets criteria for credibility.
• analyze how and when you might best utilize Wikipedia articles for your academic work.
• learn how to start making your own contributions to Wikipedia content.

Digital Detectives
ISBN 978-0-08-100124-0
39

4.2 WHAT IS COLLABORATIVE AUTHORING?

Collaborative authoring is participative creation of content. In other words, this is content that we all help to develop and manage. Specific activities are associated with collaborative authoring, including the following major authoring tasks:

- creating new textual or multimedia content
- monitoring content
- editing content
- correcting and/or removing errors or misinformation
- updating content
- organizing content

These tasks reflect the process involved in collaborative authoring, as illustrated in Figure 4.1.

The process is fluid and iterative. Contributors may begin at different points in the process. For example, a collaborator might begin by editing or verifying the content created by others—a good strategy to learn the social rules or conventions followed in a particular collaborative space, including, tone, level, and forms of content. Alternatively, a collaborator might jump right in as a content

Figure 4.1 Major authoring tasks in collaborative authoring.

creator. As a contributor gains experience in a given collaborative context, more advanced opportunities, such as monitoring content, will follow.

4.3 THE ANATOMY OF A WIKIPEDIA PAGE

Most of us have used Wikipedia at some point; however, we may or may not have explored some of the features that make Wikipedia most useful for our academic work. Let's take a moment now and review a typical Wikipedia article as we would usually see it displayed on the Internet. Figure 4.2 shows an article about Wikipedia in the encyclopedia, Wikipedia.

Figure 4.2 Wikipedia article about Wikipedia.

While the length and appearance of articles do vary, there are several common features of Wikipedia entries. These components provide not only an easily recognizable template for scanning and reading a Wikipedia article, but also particular areas of content of potential use for research purposes. Common elements of a Wikipedia article, as shown in Table 4.1, include a *title*, *contents*, a *general facts table*, the *article* itself, and *links to other articles*.

Table 4.1 Common Elements of Wikipedia Articles

Title	As is the case in any encyclopedia, the title of a given entry is always found at the beginning of a Wikipedia article. The title usually suggests the focus of the article. Articles may be proposed by anyone; however, proposed titles are vetted and approved by official editors in the Wikipedia community before becoming part of Wikipedia.
Contents	*Contents*, located in a box at the top left of an article, offers a table of contents outlining sections and subsections of the article. This list provides a route map to the text of the article. This is similar to a table of contents you find at the beginning of a book. Contents provides an opportunity for you to consider the areas covered in an article and assess whether you wish to read the whole article or pinpoint specific sections to read in depth.
General facts table	This is a table found at the top right of an article, and it provides a quick reference summary of factual information about the topic. In our example above of the Wikipedia article about itself, the logo of Wikipedia is provided in this box, as well as the Web address, slogan, numbers of users, and so on.
Article	The article itself may have a variety of subheadings, depending on the topic and the development of the article. Some articles appear as stubs, that is, articles in the very early stages of development, whereas others may contain a great deal of content.
Links to other articles	Throughout an article, you will find links to other Wikipedia articles. Simply click on line of blue text to go to a particular article. This form of linking adds embeddedness to Wikipedia content, which is useful for connecting the reader to additional information that may help contextualize information provided in a given article.

Another common element found in a Wikipedia article is an area that provides details of materials used to create the article or of relevance to the article, which may be of use for your own research. As explained in Table 4.2, there are different sources found in a Wikipedia article.

Table 4.2 Source Elements on a Wikipedia Page

Sources	Near the bottom of an article in Wikipedia, there are sources or references to the literature used in the article and recommended as additional reading. Look for the following headings:
1. See also	The subheading *See also* does exactly as it suggests. This section provides a list of links to other related topics. If you select a See also link, you will be taken to articles gathered under the topic heading provided. That could be a single Wikipedia page or a list of links to articles related to your original topic.
2. References	The *References* section provides a list of citations to the sources used in constructing an article. Citations are provided in order of appearance of material used within the article. Depending on how an article has been prepared, the list may be numbered, with numbers connecting to specific positions within the text of the article. Alternatively, the reference list may be a list of items used to construct the article in general, and the Notes section may, instead, be used to provide a numbered list of citations. Take care to examine these sections and understand the nature of the content provided.
3. Notes	The *Notes* section may provide any additional notes regarding the article. For example, a note might offer direction or guidance about a particular segment of text.
4. Further reading	There is always more we can read about a topic. This section provides additional related articles that you may want to read, including sources outside Wikipedia.
5. External links	This section provides links to various websites that are relevant to the topic and located outside Wikipedia.

The sources provided in a Wikipedia article can be quite useful as starting points for a search for information or as a means of considering avenues to research. *See also* links can help to identify related topics and sources. The category *References* provides a list of items used in the creation of the Wikipedia article. Exploring this sort of information is referred to as *mining* the article for information. Figure 4.3 shows how these two elements of the sources area—*See also* references to related information and *References*—are displayed in Wikipedia. In each case, blue links can be selected to take you to a particular item.

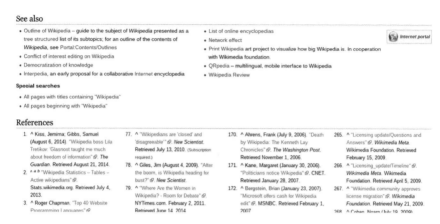

Figure 4.3 Sources area of a Wikipedia page: *See also* and *References*.

In addition, as shown in Figure 4.4, the sources area includes the categories *Notes* and *Further reading*, which may also be mined for information about your topic. The Notes section provides citations to particular points in the text of the Wikipedia article, letting you know where particular pieces of information were found. Further Reading is the next heading on a Wikipedia page; this section provides additional sources that you might explore to learn more about the topic discussed in the Wikipedia article.

Figure 4.4 Sources area of a Wikipedia page: *Notes* and *Further reading*.

Finally, a Wikipedia article may contain a list of *External links* to other content, as shown in Figure 4.5. Again, this information may provide valuable information about sources you might explore for your own research.

External links

- Official website ⚓ (Mobile ⚓) – multilingual portal (contains links to all language editions)
  - Wikipedia ⚓ on Twitter
  - Wikipedia ⚓ on Facebook
- Wikipedia ⚓ at DMOZ
- Wikitrends: Wikipedia articles most visited today
- Wikipedia ⚓ collected news and commentary at *The Guardian*
- Wikipedia ⚓ topic page at *The New York Times*
- Video of TED talk by Jimmy Wales on the birth of Wikipedia ⚓
- Audio of interview with Jimmy Wales about Wikipedia in general ⚓ on the EconTalk podcast
- Wikipedia and why it matters ⚓ – Larry Sanger's 2002 talk at Stanford University; video archive ⚓ and transcript of the talk
- "Intelligence in Wikipedia" Google TechTalk ⚓ on YouTube, describing an intelligence project utilizing Wikipedia, and how Wikipedia articles could be auto-generated from web content
- *Community Performance Optimization: Making Your People Run as Smoothly as Your Site* ⚓, talk presented at OOPSLA 2009 by the Wikimedia Foundation's senior software architect and former chief technology officer Brion Vibber, comparing the challenges of a large community of editors with those of a large community of software developers
- WikiPapers ⚓ – compilation of conference papers, journal articles, theses, books, datasets and tools about Wikipedia and wikis
- Open Wikipedia Ranking ⚓

Figure 4.5 Sources area of a Wikipedia page: *External links*.

4.4 HOW DOES WIKIPEDIA WORK?

Wikipedia is a relatively new encyclopedia. In 2001, Jimmy Wales and Larry Sanger launched Wikipedia in a wave of participative opportunities that were developing. As a source that actually allowed everyone, regardless of background or experience, to add and edit content, Wikipedia quickly curried favour with the public as a source by the people for people. There are now 287 language editions of Wikipedia; the English Wikipedia was the first and is the largest, with more than 4.6 million articles (English Wikipedia, n.d.; Wikipedia, n.d.).

The idea for Wikipedia was simple. Information is not static. It is constantly changing, being created, and being repackaged for new purposes. An encyclopedia that allowed the general public to shape content and to craft the encyclopedia that they envisioned offered a revolutionary change to this type of information tool. Traditional encyclopedias had always provided access to short, factual articles created by subject experts, and this process of generating a formal, recognized source of information helped us trust a given encyclopedia as a source. However, traditional encyclopedias did not reflect new and developing information; new editions were known for being published annually, and this meant a significant lag in time before content was updated.

Wikipedia turned this model on its head. Suddenly, information could and was updated instantly. And *anyone* could make changes or contribute new content. This notion of collaborative authorship offered an exciting new approach to interacting with information.

4.5 WHO IS BEHIND THE ARTICLES ON WIKIPEDIA?

As noted above, Wikipedia is based on the concept of collaborative authorship. This practice of co-authorship, or really multiple-authorship, involves co-creation and consultation between participants. Under collaborative authorship, the group, rather than the individual, becomes the author. As a result, instead of naming individual authors for creation of content, collaborative authorship enables multiple participants to share creation without necessarily listing contributors.

In Wikipedia, the effect is a means of producing content through a community of authors. The idea of community sourcing extends collaborative authorship to a community-based activity. Wikipedia (n.d.) boasts over 22 million accounts, and of these, 73,000 are active editors. Some editors progress within the Wikipedia community to higher administrative roles and may participate in decision making that is relevant to the wider Wikipedia project.

While Wikipedia is based on the notion of the collective participation of the public, the majority of content creators in Wikipedia are actually scholars and subject experts. In a recent study of how online communities produce content, Laniado and Tasso (2011) found "a nucleus of very active contributors, who seem to spread over the whole wiki, and to interact preferentially with inexperienced users." The authors found that these "elite" community members interacted with less experienced members, as opposed to with each other. They refer to this phenomenon as "one of the constituting characteristics of the Wikipedia community."

4.6 HOW DO I KNOW IF THE INFORMATION IS ACCURATE?

In 2005, the journal *Nature* published an article, in which accuracy of information in two encyclopedia giants, Wikipedia and Britannica, was compared (Giles, 2005). Controversially, the two encyclopedias performed similarly. The article sparked a fresh debate about Wikipedia. Britannica responded to refute the study. *Nature*, in turn, responded to Britannica's assertions. The dispute focussed attention again on the potential of collaborative authoring, casting doubt on the argument that established encyclopedias, such as Britannica, whose reputations were based on providing content written by subject experts, were superior information sources.

Given the outcome of the study published in *Nature*, we might wonder whether and why the producer of information still matters. To do this, we need to consider how we have traditionally identified credible sources. Credibility is an essential characteristic of information you may wish to use for assessment. When asked to evaluate the credibility of a source, we would normally look for evidence of the following questions.

1. **Who wrote this piece?**

   The author has traditionally been a key identifier of the quality of information. Is the author a known subject expert? What are this person's credentials? Understanding authorship can provide insight into potential bias (e.g., political beliefs) in the source.

   In the case of Wikipedia, however, this use of authorship to establish the reliability of information is not so clear. Remember that the foundation of Wikipedia is collaborative authorship. There is no particular author credited for a given Wikipedia article. Our evaluation of authorship must be determined differently. Instead of considering the author as an individual entity to be evaluated for perspective and subject knowledge, we need to consider the author as a community and consider authorship on that basis. Wikipedia has been criticized for bias and acknowledges a variety of issues that affect content, including those concerning authorship (Wikipedia: Systemic Bias, n.d.). For instance, the majority of editors in the English Wikipedia community have been found to be white men (Wikipedia: Systemic Bias, n.d.).

2. **Where was the source published?**

   A similar issue surrounds the notion of publisher. When we look for credible sources to use in an academic setting, we normally would turn to peer-reviewed sources as a gold standard. *Peer review* refers to a part of the publication process in which a piece is evaluated by experts in the field to ensure it meets scholarly publication standards.

   Wikipedia articles do not undergo this formal peer review. Instead, the Wikipedia community itself polices the encyclopedia. This approach is also debated. There is an inherent bias in not having external evaluation. Wikipedia continues to try and overcome this issue by expanding and diversifying its community of editors. In addition, research focussed on the accuracy of Wikipedia as a source has elevated the encyclopedia's reputation to some degree, particularly with favourable comparisons to sources such as Britannica, which have long been recognized as reputable sources and publishers of information.

3. **How current is the source?**

The currency of information can be extremely important. Current sources are essential for assessment, demonstrating exploration of current thinking around a given topic. This is not to say that older sources are never useful; however, sources with older publication dates are usually chosen for assessment to reflect landmark research in a field.

Wikipedia articles may or may not be accompanied by a last updated note. Community monitoring and editing of Wikipedia content is intended to provide continuously updated information. Wikipedia editors have particular areas of content to monitor.

This model of ongoing updating has proven particularly useful for information about current affairs, celebrities, and so on. This information is frequently updated in Wikipedia as quickly as it appears in news feeds. Wikipedia has an advantage here over more traditionally published encyclopedias, which have to wait for a new edition of the encyclopedia to update information or have to wait for the information to undergo an editorial process before inclusion.

4. **Who is the intended audience for the tool?**

The intended audience for a source is very useful for determining how and why to adopt the source. Wikipedia's intended audience is the general public. While not specifically known as an academic tool, the information provided in Wikipedia may still be useful for exploring the basics or a background summary of a topic. Wikipedia is intended for use by the general public, and the information is presented for that audience in terms of both depth and expression of content. As for any encyclopedia, the purpose of an entry is to inform the wider public, not to provide in-depth research and information about a topic.

5. **What sources does this tool use?**

Checking the sources used in any tool can reveal clues about the credibility of the tool. Because Wikipedia is an encyclopedia, it is essential to remember that the tool follows the encyclopedia model, including factual information about a topic. Wikipedia generally includes information that can be verified by available sources. As a result, newspapers, freely accessible articles, and so on may be found among citations in Wikipedia. Information that must be purchased to be used is unlikely to be found in Wikipedia. Again, the purpose of Wikipedia is to provide a general secondary information tool, as opposed to an in-depth exploration of topics with extensive primary documents.

6. **Who funded this publication?**

The source of funding for any publication can offer an indicator of potential bias in the tool. For instance, biographical dictionaries may have particular bias where the inclusion of summaries of people's lives is based on their payment for inclusion. Individuals paying to be represented in the tool may decide to "airbrush" their life stories, omitting details they would prefer not to have published. Similar to other tools, including encyclopedias, the means by which a publication is enabled can help to determine the usefulness of a tool for fact gathering and suggest the need for exploring alternative sources to establish a balance of information.

Wikipedia is funded through public donations. Anyone can donate to Wikipedia. Funds are gathered and processed by the Wikipedia Foundation in support of the encyclopedia.

7. **What potential bias does the source have?**

No source is without some potential bias. Wikipedia acknowledges several potentially limiting factors (Wikipedia: Systemic Bias, n.d.). Some examples include the pool of actual contributors to Wikipedia. While the encyclopedia is open to public participation, not everyone contributes, and even individuals within the Wikipedia community may participate to varying degrees and at different levels. Although neutrality of content is a goal of Wikipedia, the result of a smaller authorship circle is that content may potentially reflect the views of that smaller group.

Other issues, such as gender bias because of the larger ratio of men to women editors, may also influence the tone and inclusion of content. Western-world bias is a concern, in particular where potential contributors may have limited opportunities to participate, because they live in areas of the world lacking Internet access (Wikipedia: Systemic Bias, n.d.).

Many issues may introduce bias in a source. Remember to explore each Wikipedia article carefully for possible bias. For instance, control over editing for a particular article may both promote and inhibit the accuracy of information. People who vandalize entries may not only deliberately introduce inaccuracy into articles, but also may add malicious or, at best, mischievous content. The Wikipedia community is generally quick to respond to and correct vandalism, but the issue remains damaging to content, if only temporarily, and to the encyclopedia's reputation. Limited editing access to some Wikipedia articles has provided one way in which institutions, famous individuals, and others with pages that seem to attract vandalism have countered this problem. For instance, if you check your university's entries in Wikipedia, you will most likely find that these articles are closed to public editing. In this way, Wikipedia contains potential vandalism issues before they begin. On the other hand, while this approach may halt the addition of misinformation by others, it also allows for that person or company to airbrush their article content, just as they might do in any source.

In general, it is wise to keep in mind that anyone can add new content or modify existing Wikipedia content. Remember to exercise caution when using this information tool. Always maintain a critical awareness as you read, just as you would when considering the information found in any source.

4.7 BUT WIKIPEDIA PROVIDED GREAT REFERENCES. CAN'T I USE THEM?

A reference list should instil confidence that the information provided in a given text has been found using specifically identified sources and has been accurately documented. The reference list at the end of a Wikipedia article offers a potential wealth of information. The references help to explain the origin of content and are usually linked to specific points in the article text, either as a numbered referral to a reference in the text or as a hyperlink.

While references may exist, they should not replace your own research. They may not be complete or they may be missing for some parts of the article. Wikipedia often adds a note to the top of articles requiring verification. However, it is best to check all references found in Wikipedia before using them, as you would with any source.

4.8 HOW CAN I USE WIKIPEDIA FOR ACADEMIC ASSIGNMENTS WITHOUT GETTING PENALIZED?

Wikipedia now claims to be the largest and most popular reference tool on the Internet (Wikipedia, n.d.). Indeed, Wikipedia is quite popular among university students. In a Web survey of university students, Lim (2009) found that about a third of participating students reported that they used Wikipedia for their studies. Common uses included looking for factual information and background information on a topic. Head and Eisenberg (2010) found that university students use Wikipedia, but not as often as they used other sources, such as course readings and Google. Interestingly, the authors found that students commonly used Wikipedia in conjunction with other sources

(Head & Eisenberg, 2010). If Wikipedia may be useful and compatible with our studies, how can we best utilize this tool to support academic tasks?

First, let's consider your instructor's point of view. Your instructor may have asked you not to use Wikipedia. Instructors are familiar with Wikipedia and may use the source themselves (Eijkman, 2010). However, your instructors also want you to find the many academic sources applicable to your research that you might not otherwise consider if you limited yourself to Wikipedia. In addition, they know that collaborative information cannot be taken at face value; it must be verified and evaluated carefully before use. In the realm of urban legends, instructors have been known to make these points clear. For example, one story holds that an instructor warned students not to use Wikipedia for an assignment and then created the ideal page in Wikipedia for the assignment, riddled with incorrect information. Students who used the fake page, whether they cited the page or not, were caught out and learned a lesson about misinformation the hard way.

However, not all instructors simply ban Wikipedia from the classroom. Wikipedia is now recognized by some educators as a valuable learning tool. For instance, Wikipedia has been put forward as a useful tool for learning and practising academic writing. Tardy (2010) suggests Wikipedia as a useful forum for helping second-language students to develop academic writing skills; however, creating and editing content in Wikipedia can help every student understand the importance of writing clearly and succinctly, gathering information from appropriate sources, and referencing sources.

The best approach for you, as a user of Wikipedia or any source, is to think critically about all information you find. As tempting as using Wikipedia for researching assessment may be, basing your work on information found in Wikipedia may not provide a particularly helpful strategy for your studies. Wikipedia is an encyclopedia, and encyclopedias can be highly useful for locating general or introductory information about a given topic. You can then follow up with more detailed and subject-specific research sources to develop an overall picture of your topic. Your university education is directed at training you to think critically about information, so be sure to verify information as you would when using other sources.

4.9 COULD I CONTRIBUTE TO WIKIPEDIA ARTICLES?

The beauty and danger of Wikipedia is that almost anyone, including you, can add content. To begin, you need to sign up for a free Wikipedia account, and then you can start contributing.

Wikipedia does have some restrictions around content creation and editing. While originally open to anyone to edit, some areas of Wikipedia have placed some limits around content creation and modification; Wikipedia gives the example of the English language Wikipedia, the largest of the Wikipedia family, which allows only registered users to create new articles (Wikipedia, n.d.). Pages that are prone to vandalism—that is, the purposeful posting of misinformation—may also be protected, so that only approved editors or only administrators can alter those pages (Wikipedia, n.d.).

That said, it is still possible for you to become a contributor to Wikipedia. In particular, it is helpful to start out by editing existing articles. For example, you might help check factual accuracy or correct spelling. Participating in the Wikipedia community will help you understand how the community works and how collaborative authorship functions there. Once you have mastered editing contributions, you might move on to the more advanced creation of a Wikipedia article.

You may also find that your instructors are providing structured learning experiences through Wikipedia, in which whole classes contribute to Wikipedia content. A number of higher education institutions and Wikipedia are coordinating various efforts to encourage wider participation. For instance, Wikipedia champions, in the form of *campus ambassadors*, may facilitate the connection with Wikipedia. A campus ambassador may be, for example, a librarian, and this person may provide training to faculty and other staff to adopt and use Wikipedia in learning. Students can also act as ambassadors, similarly supporting others on campus as they develop educational opportunities around Wikipedia. If you want to get involved, see Wikipedia's entry for *Wikipedia: Education Program/Ambassadors* (n.d.), located at: https://en.wikipedia.org/wiki/Wikipedia:Education_program/Ambassadors.

4.10 SETTING UP AND USING A WIKIPEDIA ACCOUNT

To get you started, below are instructions for setting up a Wikipedia account and adding content. Set up your account now and get started!

4.10.1 Open Your Wikipedia Account

In your Internet browser, go to the URL: http://www.wikipedia.org.
1. Select *English*.
2. Select the lines icon to see options.
3. Select *Log in*.
4. Select *Create Account*.

5. Enter a username, password, and email address, and follow the security code instructions to create an account.

Note: You must be logged in to your Wikipedia account to make changes to Wikipedia content.

4.10.2 Edit an Article

1. Select an article to edit.
2. Select the pen icon.
   The article will appear with coding.
3. Select the settings icon (a wheel).
4. Choose *Edit* from the drop-down menu to edit information in the article.
5. Modify content.
6. Select the *Next* button at the top right of the screen.
   You will be asked how you have improved the article. Add a brief comment or leave blank.
7. Select the *Save* button at the top right of the screen.
   The article will now appear as it does to readers. You will also see a line indicating that you have edited the piece.

Note: Follow the icons at the top of the article to bold or italicize text, to add links, and to add references/citations to back up information added.

4.10.3 Create an Article

1. Select *Sandbox* from the top right of your main page.
2. Add content to be published now or saved as a draft for later publication.

Also, see and follow the detailed instructions provided in *Wikipedia: Your First Article*, Available at https://en.wikipedia.org/wiki/Wikipedia:Your_first_article.

4.10.4 Monitor Article Development

1. Select the star icon on the Edit page to add an article to your watch list. You can then monitor the development of this article.

4.11 FURTHER INFORMATION

Wikipedia provides a great deal of information to help you become proficient as a content creator and editor. Be sure to explore the resources on this site thoroughly!

4.12 CHALLENGES

Now that you have explored some of the inner workings of Wikipedia, it's time to put what you've learnt into action as a user and contributor to the encyclopedia.

1. As a user of Wikipedia:
   a. Search for an article about spices.
   b. Identify the list of contents for this article.
   c. Identify the references cited in this article.
   d. Find the See also reference(s) associated with this article.
   e. Under the subheading *Production*, a table of countries and their spice production is listed. Is this information credible?
   f. How might you use this article fully or in part for academic purposes?
2. As a content contributor to Wikipedia:
   a. Create your own Wikipedia account using the instructions provided in this chapter.
   b. In the English Wikipedia, find the article called "List of Historical Anniversaries."
   c. Select a date from the table.
   d. Edit the article by adding a year and event to the existing list.
   e. Remember to save your work!
   f. In the English Wikipedia, find the article called "Desserts."
   g. Select a dessert from the list provided.
   h. Find and add a fact to this article.
   i. Remember to save your work!
   j. Following the instructions provided at *Wikipedia: Your First Article*, found at https://en.wikipedia.org/wiki/Wikipedia:Your_first_article, start an article of your own.

REFERENCES

Eijkman, H. (2010). Academics and Wikipedia: reframing Web 2.0+ as a disruptor of traditional academic power-knowledge arrangements. *Campus-Wide Information Systems*, 27(3), 173–185.

English Wikipedia. (n.d.). In *Wikipedia*. Retrieved 06.08.15, from http://en.wikipedia.org/wiki/English_Wikipedia.

Giles, J. (2005). Internet encyclopaedias go head to head. *Nature*, 438, 900–901.

Head, A. J., & Eisenberg, M. B. (2010). How today's college students use Wikipedia for course-related research. *First Monday*, 15(3), Retrieved from http://firstmonday.org/article/view/2830/2476.

Laniado, D., & Tasso, R. (2011). Co-authorship 2.0: Patterns of collaboration in Wikipedia. In *Presented at ACM Hypertext 2011, 22nd ACM conference on hypertext and hypermedia, June 6–11, 2011*. Retrieved from http://airwiki.ws.dei.polimi.it/images/2/23/Coauthorship2.pdf.

Lim, S. (2009). How and why do college students use Wikipedia? *Journal of the American Society for Information Science and Technology, 60*(11), 2189–2202.

Tardy, C. M. (2010). Writing for the world: Wikipedia as an introduction to academic writing. *English Teaching Forum, 48*(1), 12–19, 27.

Wikipedia. (n.d.) *In Wikipedia*. Retrieved 06.08.15, from http://en.wikipedia.org/wiki/Wikipedia.

Wikipedia: Education program/ambassadors. (n.d.). In *Wikipedia*. Retrieved 06.08.15, from https://en.wikipedia.org/wiki/Wikipedia:Education_program/Ambassadors.

Wikipedia: Systemic bias. (n.d.). *In Wikipedia*. Retrieved 06.08.15, from http://en.m.wikipedia.org/wiki/Wikipedia:Systemic_bias.

CHAPTER 5

Judgement Day

5.1 THE DILEMMA: 'WHEN I FIND INFORMATION ON THE WEB, HOW CAN I TELL IF IT'S OKAY TO USE IT FOR COLLEGE ASSIGNMENTS?'

Today, you, as students, are spoiled for choice. Whether you are completing coursework assignments, carrying out research, or looking for information to handle a personal issue, you have access to more information—and in a more diverse range of formats—than at any time in history! From traditional print to video, animation, infographics, websites, e-books, slideshows and podcasts, the choices seem to be unlimited. However, choice can be challenging, particularly if you are not sure how to filter out the information that you do not need. In 1989, Richard Wurman coined the term *information anxiety*, in his book of the same name. Wurman defined information anxiety as 'the black hole between data and knowledge', which describes the challenges people face in obtaining the precise *knowledge* they need from information or data that is all around them. How do *you* make judgements about which sources to use and which to discard?

This chapter suggests different criteria that you can use to assess the quality of information on the Web, as well as rubrics and checklists to use when you are uncertain about whether particular sources can be used for a college assignment. The question of format is also addressed, including the appropriateness of non-textual and various multimedia resources (e.g., images, videos and infographics) for academic assignments.

In this chapter, you will:

- reflect on *how* you make decisions about which digital sources satisfy your information needs and which sources to discard.
- consider the special qualities of digital information, in particular web-based information, that make evaluation especially important.
- become familiar with two frameworks for evaluating digital sources.
- explore a range of criteria for evaluating digital sources, including *instant clues* for when you are in a hurry and more *in-depth clues* for when you have more time to consider sources.

Digital Detectives
ISBN 978-0-08-100124-0

5.2 HOW DO YOU SELECT DIGITAL RESOURCES TO USE IN YOUR COURSEWORK?

Take a moment to reflect on your own information behaviour and consider the following questions:

- What makes you click on or download a particular online source when you first encounter it? What makes you decide *not* to click on a link?
- How do you decide whether a source is *good* or *bad*?
- What do you think are the signs or clues that a source is not to be trusted?
- What kinds of online sources do you think your instructors want you to use for your assignments?
- What kinds of resources do you think would cause you to *lose* marks if you included them in your coursework?

A US-based study found that the top five student criteria for evaluating web-based information for coursework are *currency* (e.g., publication date), the *author's credentials*, the *URL*, the *interface design* and *external links* (links to other sites that are listed on the website) (Head & Eisenberg, 2010). When evaluating websites for information used in *personal* situations, however, the design of the website and students' familiarity with the website from previous use were the most important factors students considered. This study also showed that students tended to ask friends and/or family when they needed help with evaluating sources for personal use, but they turned to their instructors for help with evaluating course-related research materials found on the Web or through the library. What do *you* do?

This chapter will help you to ramp up your digital detective skills, with tips for figuring out how to distinguish useful and trustworthy information on the Web from sources that are of poor quality, biased, unsuitable for college work and misleading.

5.3 WHY EVALUATE DIGITAL SOURCES?

While it has always been important to evaluate the quality of the sources that you use for college work, the World Wide Web has made this both essential and incredibly complex. For you as a student, evaluating information works on two distinct levels:

1. **Relevance:** You must determine whether information is *relevant* to your needs. Will it help you to solve your information problem? This requires a critical analysis of your task and an ability to filter out information that is not directly related to your objective.

2. **Quality**: You must assess the *quality* and *authority* of information sources. Can you trust the information? Is it a suitable source for a college assignment? This requires the ability to apply the appropriate evaluation criteria to each information source to decide whether it can be used for your assessment.

Evaluating information takes time—something that you may not always have. As digital detectives, you must be able to make rapid judgements about the quality of information sources. This means becoming so familiar with the key quality criteria that you can apply them almost automatically as you search for and download online sources, in much the same way as you read road signs and markings and can operate a car's controls when driving. You do some of this work beforehand when you devise a search strategy that is as efficient as possible, applying the limiters and filters that we discuss in Chapters 3 and 8. When it comes to viewing and selecting sources, however, there are certain issues you need to consider, and we discuss them here.

5.4 WHAT IS DIFFERENT ABOUT INFORMATION ON THE WEB?

The almost unlimited and uncontrolled availability of information on the Web has increased the need for expert evaluation skills. Unlike the traditional formal publication process (see also Chapter 7), which is generally under editorial control, much of the information on websites is posted without undergoing any sort of quality control at all. Now, it is easy to post, whether you are blogging, tweeting, developing your own website, or uploading photos and videos. Getting the word out to a wide, and even global, audience has never been more straightforward. Let's explore some of the reasons why evaluating online information is one of the key skills of the twenty-first century.

- The Web is a vast resource. It is simply impossible to use everything you will find, even from a single search. According to Eli Pariser, the author of *The Filter Bubble*, 'if you recorded all human communication from the dawn of time to 2003, it'd take up about 5 billion gigabytes of storage space. Now we're creating that much data *every two days*' (2011, p. 11). A typical Google search can retrieve results numbered in the *millions*. Developing the ability to effectively filter this information is a top priority for you as a student.

- Anyone with the appropriate equipment and know-how is free to publish on the Web. The checks and balances of the traditional publishing process are frequently not applied to the information that is posted. One of the strengths of the Web is the platform it provides for free speech and expression. Paradoxically, this is also one of the Web's greatest challenges, especially if you are looking for information that is accurate, objective and unbiased.

- A lot of scholarly information is not freely available; it is hidden behind paywalls and subscriptions. While there is a lot of *information* available about any topic you care to mention, the kind of high-quality academic information that you need to write essays and papers often cannot be obtained without payment. Academic publishers collect sizeable profits from selling journal subscriptions and books to academic institutions and individuals, and making this information freely accessible to all is not on their agenda. As digital detectives, you need to know *when* it's time to move on to different sources if the Web is not able to solve your information problem. Never be tempted to settle for information that is not good enough simply because it's convenient.

- A lot of the information on the Web may be misleading, biased, or simply false. Experienced digital detectives can determine very quickly whether the information they encounter is objective; perhaps the information has been posted to sell a product or, from a more sinister perspective, to trick you into providing some personal information that might enable fraudulent activity to take place. Even from a more innocent standpoint, an individual's personal convictions may have led them to select only arguments that support their point of view and to ignore others that contradict them, leading to a lack of balance in the information they post.

5.5 MODELS FOR EVALUATING DIGITAL RESOURCES

To begin to develop your digital detective skills for discerning trustworthy and untrustworthy information online, it is useful to examine frameworks that have been created by experts to help students make judgements about the quality of the sources they encounter. Two frameworks that you might find helpful are the *twenty-first century information fluency* model (available at: http://21cif.com/rkitp/assessment/v1n4/evaluation_wizard.html) and the Cornell University Library webpage 'Introduction to Research' (available at: www.library.cornell.edu/research/introduction#2Findingbooks,articles, andothermater). While both frameworks cover similar criteria, the Cornell model is particularly interesting because it suggests a strategy for the *initial* appraisal of resources, that is, when you might not have much time to evaluate the information and you need to make a quick decision. Let us explore the criteria for ourselves.

5.6 CLUES FOR EVALUATING DIGITAL RESOURCES

In a similar way to the Cornell framework, it is helpful to examine the different criteria in terms of how much *time* you have to perform your evaluations. For that reason, it makes sense to look at *instant clues* noted first, that is, the criteria that you can quickly apply when you encounter an online source. The more often you do this, the more it will become an automatic behaviour when you are trawling the Web for information.

5.6.1 Instant Clues for Evaluating Digital Resources

What are the first things you notice about an online source when you encounter it? Are there particular characteristics that make you feel more or less confident about selecting a source for your college work? This section looks at the characteristics of digital information that you typically notice straight away when examining a source. Critical thinking will help you to be smart about evaluating these characteristics and making a choice about whether to use a source or not.

5.6.1.1 Document Type

The first and most obvious question to ask is, '*What type of document is this?*' When you click on a link, for example, you may not know at first whether you are dealing with a journal article, a book chapter, a blog post, a newspaper article, a magazine profile piece, a blurb on a webpage or even a paper from an academic conference. Choosing the right kind of document is central to your quest because certain types of documents, typically those from popular sources, are unsuitable for college work. However, when content on the Web is posted in text form, different document types can look similar; for example, an article published in a freely available e-journal may not be scholarly, but it might resemble the online version of an article from a prestigious academic journal. Table 5.1 offers some quick ways to identify different document types online.

5.6.1.2 Author or Creator

Good-quality information sources always provide clear information about the author or creator of the material, as well as their credentials, that is, the attributes that make them *qualified* to write about a topic. In the case of scholarly material, the author's academic qualifications, current position, place of work or affiliation and contact details are the key pieces of information to look for. You can usually see this information at a glance if the source

Table 5.1 Features of Document Types on the Web

Book	Scholarly Journal Article	Other Journal Article	Blog Post	Web Article
Chapter headings or numbered sections (e.g., 2.2, 3.4).	Contains an abstract summarizing the article's contents.	Usually contains an abstract summarizing the article's contents.	Entries are dated and often time-stamped. Blog entries are usually quite short.	The text is part of the webpage. You do not have to download anything. There are no section numbers or chapters.
Table of contents and index are available.	Usually provides publisher information (e.g., Sage, Emerald).	The article usually is not published by a well-known academic publishing house.	There are often readers' comments at the end of each entry.	The page may be sponsored by a specific organization.
Can sometimes resemble a *scanned* or PDF version of the printed book, if not an open textbook.	Usually provides information about how to download or purchase the full article. Full text is often not freely available.	Full text of the article is usually available with no cost or requirement to subscribe.	There is usually a sidebar with several widgets and a *blogroll*. Advertisements may appear on the page.	There are often banner or sidebar advertisements on the page, and there may occasionally be pop-ups when you click on links.
Pages may have sections missing; for example, Google Books cannot publish full books if they are still under copyright.	Contains a list of scholarly references, often with links to the resources in question.	Usually includes a list of references with links to the sources in question. The references may not all be scholarly in nature.	Style is often personal and conversational, with no references. There is often a strong viewpoint evident in the writing.	Style is often informal, and the article may or may not include references or links to other sources.
The authors' names and credentials are clearly indicated. There is usually a short author biography.	The author's credentials and affiliations are clearly indicated, and there is information about when the article was submitted, reviewed, revised and accepted.	Author's credentials and affiliations may or may not be included. There may be no mention of peer review of the article.	The author's real name or even just screen name is listed, but sometimes no other information about the author is provided. Bloggers are sometimes anonymous.	There may or may not be an author's name. Sometimes the names of very specific products or companies are mentioned in the article.

is reputable. For example, scholarly journals post all of this information on the first page of each article, in a sidebar or at the top or bottom of the first page of the article. Online versions usually provide a direct link to the author's email address. A source that does not identify the author nor offers any substantial background information about its author is to be treated with caution. If you are looking for trustworthy, expert information on a serious topic, an author who has a PhD, works at a well-known university and is listed as a lecturer or professor is a better sign than one who has a basic bachelor's degree and works for a commercial company.

You can also check for mentions of the work of a particular author by other reputable authors in their publications. This is known as *citing* an author and is a good indication of how well-regarded someone is in a field of research and how important their work is considered to be. One easy way to do this is to search for a given author's name in Google Scholar (available at: http://scholar.google.com/). Google Scholar shows you a list of an author's publications, as well as the number of other authors who have referred to their work and included the author's publications in the list of references at the end of their own papers. If you have access to academic databases through your university library, a more formal way of searching for an author's citations is through the *Web of Science* research platform, which provides access to a number of *citation indexes* (e.g., *Social Science Citation Index*, *Science Citation Index*, *Arts & Humanities Citation Index*); these are specialized academic databases that allow you to discover, among other things, the number of times a particular paper has been cited by other authors or the number of times an author has been cited overall in formal academic publications. These databases also tell you which papers have cited the author, so that you can read them as well. Sometimes, following a *citation trail* is an excellent method for discovering the major influences or theories in a particular field. Academics use the *metrics*, or measurements, generated from the analysis of citation patterns to calculate the relative popularity or influence of their work within a field. This process is known as *bibliometrics*, which is defined as 'a statistical analysis of books, articles, or other publications' (OECD, 2013). An important factor is the journal in which an article is published; some journals, such as *Nature* in the field of science, are considered extremely prestigious and are read by millions of scholars and researchers worldwide. Having an article published in such a journal is an important ambition of researchers and indicates that their work is highly respected. The Web of Science, through its annual *Journal Citation Reports*, allows you to discover the academic journals with the greatest impact in their fields.

5.6.1.3 Publisher

In the traditional publishing process, quality is controlled through strict editorial processes applied by the publishing houses, which build their reputations by publishing the most up-to-date, well-researched books and articles written by respected practitioners and scholars in their fields. Well-practised digital detectives can make a rapid judgement about the quality of a source by identifying the publisher. The more you explore digital information sources, the more familiar you will become with the major academic publishing houses and reliable organizations that make material available on the Web. For instance, you may discover that John Hopkins University Press, in existence since 1878, is a respected academic publisher with more than 80 journal titles in history, science, literary studies, political science and medicine. As such, this publisher is probably a good choice for college work. In reputable sources, information about the publisher should be clearly displayed, with a link provided to the publisher's homepage, if appropriate.

5.6.1.4 Date or Currency

For digital detectives, the year in which the information was published or the specific date on which it was last updated are key clues that should also be available at a glance. For certain types of information (e.g., medicine, computer science), currency is essential because the state of knowledge in the field changes so rapidly. In formally published sources, such as books and journals, this information is presented very clearly; for example, the date of publication is included on the *title page* of a book or on the first page (and at the foot of each page thereafter) of a journal article; however, it can be more difficult to locate this information in online sources. The usual trick is to scroll down to the very bottom of the webpage, where the *last updated* information is usually posted. Another clue to the currency of a source is the number of *dead links* on a page, that is, links to sites or pages that no longer exist. A source that contains several dead links is probably not updated on a regular basis. You should err on the side of caution. If there is no date provided and you are uncertain about the source overall, either discard it or try to verify the information by cross-referencing with another trustworthy source.

5.6.1.5 Writing Style

A quick read of any information source gives you an instant clue to its quality; poorly written content, with grammar and punctuation errors or the inclusion of *text-speak*, is an obvious warning sign. Scholarly information is written in a clear, articulate style, which sounds quite formal. Often, you will encounter technical terms, or *academic jargon*, specific to the topic in question. In this case, you may have to consult a dictionary or glossary to decipher these terms.

5.6.1.6 Appearance (e.g., Images, Colours)

Scholarly journal articles, even in online format, are free from advertising; there will be no pop-ups, sidebars, embedded Flash presentations, unrelated videos or any other eye-catching widgets to draw your attention away from the content. Such documents simply contain plain text, supplemented by any diagrams, graphs, photos, images or tables that are necessary to enhance the written content. With the exception of images and photos, most of the content will be in simple black-and-white. Less trustworthy sources may be awash with advertising and an overzealous use of colour, different fonts, images and other visual or audio effects.

5.6.2 Domain-Specific Clues

The next set of clues is linked to the actual Web addresses themselves and what they can tell you about quality. You may not have considered this before, but the *address* of a website, particularly the domain, reveals a lot of information about the source.

5.6.2.1 Reading a Uniform Resource Locator

Skilled digital detectives can read the address or *uniform resource locator* (URL) of a website like a book. One glance is enough to provide sufficient information to make a very quick judgement about the probable quality of the information on the site. However, you have to know what to look for. How do you dissect and analyze a URL? Consider the example in Figure 5.1.

Digital detectives should play close attention to the part of the URL that comes after the *http://*, which contains the *domain* information. This includes the host organization and the top-level domain name, identifying the type of organization. Top-level domain names offer clues as to the possible quality of information that is hosted by the domain. Consider some of the domain names that you will often come across:

- **.com**: Probably the most familiar domain name, '.com' denotes sites that are hosted by *commercial businesses*. If you are using a .com site, be aware of potential bias, since their principal concern may be selling goods or services. Similar UK-based commercial sites may be identified as *.co.uk*.

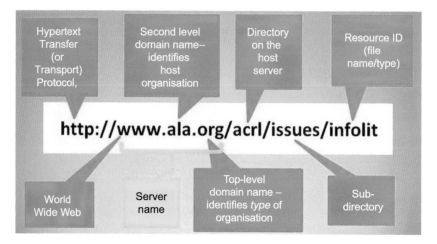

Figure 5.1 Reading a uniform resource locator (URL).

- **.edu:** This domain identifies US-affiliated institutions of higher education. In the United Kingdom, academic institutions are denoted by *.ac.uk*. Academic institutions are likely to be a trustworthy source of information. As a result, an .edu or .ac.uk domain name is usually a promising sign.

- **.gov:** This domain refers exclusively to US government sites. In the United Kingdom, the corresponding domain is *.gov.uk*. Government sites typically contain formal or official documents, which by nature are factually accurate and have been monitored for errors. However, with government information, the date of publication or last update should *always* be checked in case there have been new developments that have not yet been added to the site.

- **.net:** This is a general-purpose domain name that was originally intended to be used by organizations involved in networking technologies; now, however, it is used for many different kinds of sites, including Internet service providers, organizations and individuals. Caution should be applied when using material from a .net site because there are no particular restrictions associated with its use. In the United Kingdom, *.net.uk* is slightly different; it is restricted to Internet service providers and network companies.

- **.org:** This domain name was originally intended to be used by nonprofit organizations, but it is now often used by schools, open-source projects and communities, as well as for-profit entities. Information on .org sites should be carefully evaluated, particularly in terms of bias.

You should also examine the *host institution*. In the example in Figure 5.1, the ALA is the American Library Association and, as such, is recognized as a reputable information source. Treat the name of the host institution as you would an author's or publisher's name, and look for any credentials that signal to you that the information hosted by this institution is likely to be trustworthy.

5.6.2.2 Links to a Website

The *links to* a website tell a story all of their own. You might recall from Chapter 3 that the main factor in determining the ranking of websites on Google's results page is the quality of the websites that link *to* the page you are examining: the *incoming links*. High-quality sites are likely to link to other high-quality sites; thus another tool of the digital detective is to review those linking sites. To find them, simply use the search function *link: <name of website>* in a search engine and explore the list of sites that appear, evaluating them for quality in the same way you judge any website.

5.6.2.3 Links from a Website

Similar to *links to*, you should also consider the *links from* a website to other websites or sources, if there are any. For example, trustworthy articles always include accurate references, and many of these are likely to include links to the online versions of these sources, even if some of them are behind paywalls. If you are unsure about the quality of a source, spend some time checking out the links from a website to help with your evaluation. One particular thing to check for is that the outbound links are not just links to different pages *within* the same domain, since this will not offer you any additional information about the resource's quality. For instance, a webpage of a commercial business ('name.com') that provides links only to other pages within the same 'name. com' domain is not offering any additional clues as to quality with its outbound links, and they are all basically from the same source.

5.6.2.4 Checking Legitimacy

If a URL seems unusual in some way or if you are uncertain about it, there is a way to check whether it is a legitimate site. The site Whois (http://www.whos.com/whois), allows you first and foremost, to determine whether a particular domain name has already been taken. This is a useful tool if you are setting up your own website. However, Whois also gives you information about the owner of the domain name, the type of organization, the date the name was registered, renewal of ownership and so on. This information may help you decide whether the source can be trusted.

5.6.3 Digging Deeper: Content Clues

If you are still hesitant about using a particular resource, even after considering the instant quality clues, you need to dig deeper into the content to determine whether it meets the standard necessary for college work. The following criteria allow you to carry out a thorough evaluation of a resource.

5.6.3.1 Intention or Purpose

What do you think was the author's purpose in creating the resource? Some purposes that might affect the quality of the information in a resource include the following:

- Providing factual information about something (e.g., a school, university admissions, government policies)
- Communicating the results of research
- Selling a product or service
- Advocating for a cause for altruistic purposes
- Providing entertainment
- Giving an opinion or proposing a particular point of view
- Promoting an individual or an organization
- Socializing with others or contributing to a conversation

The *intention* of the authors in posting particular information provides you with yet another clue as to the potential quality of a source for your coursework. Opinion pieces or commentaries, for example, are likely to be one-sided, but they can give you an insight into prevailing public opinion on an issue, whereas research reports or articles, if they have been written to appropriate research standards, generally provide you with reliable information. Commercial sources, which aim to *sell* products and services, are usually not appropriate for college work, whereas advocacy pieces promoting a particular cause can introduce interesting points of view to your own research.

5.6.3.2 Intended Audience

The tone and language of the information in the resource give you an idea of the creator's intended audience. Text that is very technical and includes a lot of jargon and specialist terms is typically aimed at academic or professional audiences. A more simplified style that is easier to read and in which terms are clearly explained is usually for a general audience.

5.6.3.3 Coverage or Scope

If you are using a particular source for your coursework, you need to be sure that it provides coverage of your topic that is sufficient for your information need. For example, if you are researching a particular topic for an essay, does the source address just one perspective, or does it present counterpoints to the main argument or theory? If you are examining a topic from a historical perspective, does the source go back far enough in time? You must also make sure that you are able to see *all* of the information in the source. For instance, does the site provide just a *taster* of the full document, with the remainder located behind a paywall? Google Books is an example of a resource that *seems* promising; however, when you start to scroll through a book in Google Books that is still under copyright, you discover that many pages are missing and that, if you want the full text, you have to purchase it or, if you have access to a library, borrow it.

5.6.3.4 Accuracy and Evidence

When reading through an online resource, try to establish whether the information is presented as opinion or fact; for example, does the author use phrases like '*In my opinion*', '*I believe*', or '*From my point of view*'? Information that is presented as fact must always be supported with evidence, typically in the form of citations to other reliable sources. If an article seems to contain many unqualified statements, always check whether the author has included any evidence to support their assertions and whether the evidence presented is of a high quality. This is especially the case when dealing with information on scientific, medical and general health topics; avoid using sources that include phrases such as '*Recent research has shown*' or '*Researchers have found that*' without giving full details of the studies that underpin the statements or statistics in the piece you are reading. If it cannot be backed up, back off! The importance of strong evidence is emphasized by the creators of sources, such as Wikipedia, who have ruled that the information in each entry *must* be supported by trustworthy external references; without this, the information has no credibility, and a lack of trustworthy evidence is a major warning sign for any information source. A recent infographic published on the *Compound Interest* blog belonging to Andy Brunning, who creates chemistry-related graphics, displayed the following list of criteria designed to enable you to spot *bad science* in publications (http://www.compoundchem.com/2014/04/02/a-rough-guide-to-spotting-bad-science/):

- Sensationalized headlines
- Misinterpreted results
- Conflict of interest

- Mistaking correlation for causation
- Speculative language
- Sample sizes that are too small
- Unrepresentative samples
- No control group used in the study
- No blind testing used in the study
- Cherry-picked results
- Results that cannot be replicated
- Non-peer reviewed material

5.6.3.5 Bias

To detect bias, digital detectives must again focus on the tone of the *language* used in an article, as well as in the purpose of the piece and the background of the author. Words and phrases that are *personalized* and designed to appeal to the emotions are an indicator of bias, although this can have both a positive and negative effect, depending on context. For example, a piece advocating for an important cause (e.g., seeking volunteers or donations) might use strong emotive terms, images, videos or examples to persuade readers to get involved. For example, consider the following passage from the website of Focus Ireland, an agency that works to help those affected by homelessness in the Irish Republic:

> *You see, living in one room in a B&B or hotel, often far from home and family supports—like grandparents and schools and all too frequently with nowhere to cook or for children to play or do homework—places huge stress on young families. What happens so often in situations like this is that the parents are forced to spend what little money they have on transport and food, with the result that the family very quickly find themselves sinking deeper into poverty.*
>
> **Focus Ireland (2013)**

Although powerful, the lack of supporting evidence in this statement means that this source is probably unsuitable for a college assignment. However, sources with bias can be used to provide insight into prevailing or controversial viewpoints, challenges and perspectives, depending on what topic you are researching.

5.6.3.6 Relevance

Deciding whether a particular source is *relevant* to your task is a question of critical evaluation and judgement that only you can exercise. Analysing your information problem or question is the first step. Say, for instance, that you are writing a paper on a topic that is fiercely debated in the literature, as well as in the popular media. A paper discussing the 'right to die' is one example. When evaluating sources, you should ask yourself the following questions:

- Does this source contain information that directly addresses this topic or answers my question? Is my topic the main issue discussed in the resource? To determine this initially, without reading the whole piece, you can examine the title, abstract, subject headings and table of contents of the resource.
- Is the information in the source the *same* as information that I have already gathered from another source?
- Is this item considered a *seminal* or important piece on the topic?
- Does the information contained in the source agree with or refute my main arguments? Do I have answers for the arguments that go against mine?
- Does the source introduce any *new perspectives or insights* on the topic that I have not considered before and could include in my paper?

For major assignments, such as dissertations, it is a good idea to categorize or bookmark the sources you gather in terms of the major themes they cover and how they relate to your work. For example, you might have one online folder containing downloaded sources that argue in favour of the right to die and one containing source that argue against it. You might create another folder in which to store items that describe interesting case studies or outlines of the legal situation with regard to the right to die in different countries. Categorizing sources helps you to be more careful about the sources you select, to think about whether each source is relevant and, if so, to consider where each source fits your paper outline.

5.7 EVALUATING DIFFERENT MEDIA FORMATS

Most of the criteria described above can be applied to all digital information sources, regardless of format. However, over time, new information formats have appeared that may be a little trickier to judge or that have specific criteria to consider when deciding whether they are suitable for you to use. This section looks at three popular types of information sources that you will undoubtedly come across when carrying out research for your college work.

5.7.1 Infographics

What is an infographic? Chances are that you have seen them, laughed at the humorous ones, possibly used one to obtain information or maybe even created one—but you may not actually be familiar with the term.

An infographic is simply 'a visual representation of information or data, e.g., as a chart or diagram' (Oxford Dictionaries, 2015). The aim of those who create infographics is to take very complex information and data, which may be difficult to read if presented in text form, and make it easier to interpret through more simplified or attractive presentation. *Data visualisation* is another term for the creation of infographics. Although the concept of infographics is not new, they have increased in popularity during recent years as a result of the availability of easy-to-use web-based tools, which allow non experts to create and disseminate them. Examples of infographics with which you are almost certainly familiar include *weather charts*, which use icons of clouds and the sun, arrows for wind direction and pressure bars to represent current conditions. The famous map of the London Underground subway system is another example. Infographics are used for a variety of different purposes, including presenting survey data, providing instructions for how something works, comparing two different situations or phenomena, explaining complex concepts, raising awareness of an issue in a striking way, entertaining and presenting factual information in an interesting format.

A good infographic is professionally presented and rates highly on the criteria listed below:

- Has a clear objective. The infographic should have an obvious purpose and should not be just a random collection of facts or numbers. The infographic should *inform* the viewer. You should have a clear *take away* from it and feel you gained something from reading it.
- Presents data effectively, with good use of charts (e.g., pie charts, bar charts).
- Tells a story. The infographic flows well and builds to a conclusion.
- Has a clear and engaging design. The infographic is well organized, easy to follow and uncluttered.
- Draws attention to important points, which are clearly highlighted.
- Uses relevant icons, for example, an icon of a human figure to represent populations.
- Uses trustworthy sources. Not surprisingly, this is the most important criterion, especially when you are trying to decide whether you should use this information for a college assignment. The data represented in the infographic should be robust and drawn from credible and authoritative sources—you should always check the original publications that the infographic is based on. If there are no references provided for the data, discard the source.

5.7.2 Videos

You have probably noticed that when you search for a topic on the Web, more and more the search results page includes *videos*, most often from You-Tube but also from news sites, educational institutions or commercial companies. The ubiquity of personal video-recording devices and the affordability of high-quality professional-standard cameras mean that video has become an important channel for the distribution and dissemination of information in all contexts. Whether you are uploading an eyewitness account of an event to your Facebook page or streaming a news report on your tablet, video is challenging the previous dominance of text in the online world of information. The statistics are incredible. YouTube reports that they have *one billion* users who watch hundreds of millions of hours of video, generating billions of views. Added to that, 300 h of video are uploaded to YouTube every *minute* (YouTube, 2015). Another video website, Vine, reports that more than 8000 videos are shared by their users per *minute*, whereas 100 million users watch Vine videos each month (Smith, 2015). With all of this information circulating on the Web, it is more crucial than ever for you to know how to filter out poor-quality videos and how to choose the best ones for your purpose. While many of the evaluation criteria for video remain the same as for other sources (e.g., creator or publisher, accuracy, currency, quality of presentation), you should consider some questions that are specific to the medium.

- **Is it possible to identify the creator(s) of the video?** High-quality videos always provide information about the individuals or organizations that created, commissioned or sponsored them, either at the start of the video or in credits at the end. Once the creator has been identified you should apply the same evaluation principles as you would for textual sources.
- **Is the video legitimate, or has copyright been violated by uploading it?** The issue of illegal uploading or embedding is serious, and the owners of such material generally request that the videos be removed from a given site. People do not give up their rights by sharing their videos on websites such as YouTube. They remain the copyright holders of the material and have the right to decide how that material is used and distributed. Videos may only be embedded in non-creator sites with the explicit permission of the owner. If you are using a video for your college work and list it in your bibliography, you need to be certain that it will not disappear suddenly because of copyright violation. Always check whether a video has been posted by its creator or with the

permission of its creator. Alarm bells might ring if you notice that the person who has shared or uploaded a video is not the same person as the creator. If you are uncertain, you should try to find the original video posting and use that instead.

- **What is the quality of presentation in the video?** Depending on context, a well-made, professional-looking video is a good sign—for example, one that is smoothly edited, with good lighting and sharp definition, clear audio and captions or possibly subtitles. However, you should still pay close attention to the content or message that is conveyed in the video, rather than make a judgement solely on the visual presentation. Professional videos can be biased, error-strewn or deliberately misleading, whereas some videos that seem more amateur can be incisive, balanced and useful sources of information.
- **What is the quality of content in the video?** As with other information sources, you should ask yourself a number of questions about the content. For example, is there a central theme and narrative structure in the video? What seems to be the purpose of the video? Is it biased in any way? If people are interviewed in the video, think about why they might have been chosen. Are they proposing a particular viewpoint or a balanced point of view? Is the video edited in a way that is designed to support a certain perspective? All the usual checks and balances should also apply to this format.

5.7.3 Blogs

High-quality blogs typically display a number of characteristics. You should look for the following things when deciding whether to use a blog for a college assignment:

- The author of the blog is clearly identifiable, ideally using their real name rather than just a screen name. However, the use of just a screen name does not necessarily indicate that a blog is of poor quality; you must evaluate carefully according to all relevant criteria.
- The author possesses some degree of expertise in the area, and this is clearly indicated, typically in the author biography. There should be a link(s) that supports the information in the bio, for example, a link to the author's workplace profile, articles or books they have published or other more official sources.
- The blog is updated regularly and is topical and current.
- The comments under each blog posting are intelligent and analytical, promoting a lively discussion. Commenters are themselves knowledgeable in the area under discussion.

- There are many *links to* the blog from other reputable blogs and websites. Most blogs have a *blogroll* in the sidebar that provides a list of this sort of link.

5.8 CHALLENGES

1. **Snap judgement**
   Spend no longer than 10s evaluating each of the following web-pages. Be strict and time yourself—we are looking for the instant judgements you make about digital resources. Answer the questions that follow.
   Basic Information about Fluoride in Drinking Water: http://water.epa.gov/drink/contaminants/basicinformation/fluoride.cfm.
   NoFluoride.com: Citizens for Safe Drinking Water: http://www.nofluoride.com/
   a. What was the first thing you noticed about each resource? What *jumped out* at you?
   b. To what parts of the screen were your eyes mainly drawn?
   c. What *feeling* did you get when you looked at each source?
   d. Which resource do you think is the most trustworthy? Why?

2. **In-depth challenge**
   You have been tasked with writing a paper on the pros and cons of *gene therapy*. Using the criteria described above, carry out an in-depth evaluation of the following websites and assess their suitability for this assignment.
   GenoChoice: http://www.genochoice.com.
   National Cancer Institute, Biological Therapies for Cancer: http://www.cancer.gov/cancertopics/factsheet/Therapy/biological
   a. What did you notice about each website?
   b. How did you make your final decision about which to choose for the task at hand?

3. **Research challenge**
   Find one *suitable* and one *unsuitable* digital resource in each of the following formats for a college paper on the topic of *Internet privacy*. Explain your reasons for choosing each format.
   a. Blog
   b. Video
   c. Online journal article
   d. Podcast
   e. Newspaper article

REFERENCES

Focus Ireland. (2013). *Roisin's story: The new face of homelessness*. Retrieved from https://www. focusireland.ie/about-homelessness/customer-and-staff-stories/roisin-s-story.

Head, A. J., & Eisenberg, M. B. (2010). *Truth be told: How college students evaluate and use information in the digital age. Project information literacy progress report*. Retrieved from http:// projectinfolit.org/images/pdfs/pil_fall2010_survey_fullreport1.pdf.

OECD. (2013). *Glossary of statistical terms*. Retrieved from http://stats.oecd.org/glossary/ detail.asp?ID=198.

Oxford Dictionaries. (2015). Retrieved from http://www.oxforddictionaries.com.

Pariser, E. (2011). *The filter bubble: What the Internet is hiding from you*. London: Viking/ Penguin Press.

Smith, C. (2015). *By the numbers: 25 Amazing vine statistics*. Retrieved from http://expande-dramblings.com/index.php/vine-statistics.

Wurman, R. S. (1989). *Information anxiety*. New York: Doubleday.

YouTube. (2015). *Statistics*. Retrieved from https://www.YouTube.com/yt/press/statistics.html.

CHAPTER 6

Finders Keepers

6.1 THE DILEMMA: "NO PASSWORD? NO PROBLEM! IF I CAN DOWNLOAD IT, I CAN USE IT AND SHARE IT, RIGHT?"

The online environment often presents challenges around copyright and intellectual property. Information presented online may seem to have no obvious author and, therefore, seem as though it does not require referencing. Journal articles stored in open repositories may be easily downloaded without payment, but does "free" mean the material is no longer anyone's intellectual property? Regardless of the sort of information located online or elsewhere, all information we adopt for our own purposes must be appropriately attributed.

In this chapter, we explore the ethical use of material that appears online. Issues, such as open access, Creative Commons publishing and restricted use, the use of images and videos, as well as the necessity of accurate attribution, are included here. We examine means of locating information that is safe to use and how to recognize the different forms of licensing that govern the use of online material.

In this chapter, you will:

- explore copyright and intellectual freedom in the online environment.
- consider ethical uses of online materials.
- learn about licensing of online materials.
- learn to attribute different forms of digital materials appropriately and accurately.
- explore bibliographic management software for creating and managing references.

6.2 WHO OWNS DIGITAL INFORMATION?

Digital information can be extremely malleable and, as such, easily sampled, copied, and pasted to other digital spaces and published elsewhere. Tracing authorship under these circumstances can be a challenge. In

Digital Detectives
ISBN 978-0-08-100124-0

addition, crowd-sourced information may not reveal a single author, as we have discussed in this text with regard to sources, such as Wikipedia (see Chapter 4).

The same principles that govern copyright in the paper environment apply to the online world. Always give credit to the creator(s) of information you wish to use, regardless of where you locate the information. Where no author can be determined, the source itself should still be cited appropriately. If you did not create the information you wish to use yourself, the use of this information without appropriate attribution is theft.

In university, failure to attribute sources is called "plagiarism," and the penalties may be severe. Depending on the nature of the plagiarism, consequences may include the loss of a grade on a component of assessment, loss of credit for an overall course, or even expulsion from a program or institution. The risk associated with plagiarism is high; it is better to cite sources carefully, rather than to underestimate the abilities of tutors or computer software to spot potential issues. Most importantly, ensuring appropriate attribution helps you to maintain your intellectual integrity, both on- and offline.

6.3 HOW DO PEOPLE PROTECT THEIR DIGITAL CREATIONS?

Sending work out into cyberspace is a potentially risky venture. Once any item is online, it can be picked up, modified, and repackaged. Creators of information may take different approaches to protect their work. First, they may publish their work through formal channels, as they would in a nondigital environment. For example, peer-reviewed journals may offer prepublication versions of articles in advance of publication of the final journal issue. A digital marker known as a *DOI*, or digital object identifier, provides a permanent link to the article in its pre- or final publication state. Copyright applies to the article at all stages of this process, and appropriate attribution must be made to use the piece. Monographs or books may also follow a formal pathway to publication, which involves a unique identifier called an ISBN or international standard book number. All books, whether in hard copy or electronic formats, are assigned this form of identification, if they have been published through this formal process.

Creative Commons licensing is often used to protect material that is published more informally, rather than through the traditional formal publication process. Creative Commons (http://creativecommons.org) is a nonprofit organization that provides standardized copyright licensing for digital information to promote sharing of information. Creative Commons explains that their service does not replace copyright, but rather works with copyright to protect content creators' work, including music, video, scientific material, and so on, though not software nor hardware.

There are six license types offered through Creative Commons:

1. **Attribution**
   This license lets others distribute, remix, tweak, and build on your work, even commercially, as long as they credit you for the original creation. This is the most accommodating of licenses offered, and it is recommended for maximum dissemination and use of licensed materials.

2. **Attribution-NoDerivs**
   This license allows for redistribution, both commercial and noncommercial, as long as it is passed along unchanged and in whole, with credit to you.

3. **Attribution-NonCommercial-ShareAlike**
   This license lets others remix, tweak, and build on your work noncommercially, as long as they credit you and license their new creations under the identical terms.

4. **Attribution-ShareAlike**
   This license lets others remix, tweak, and build on your work, even for commercial purposes, as long as they credit you and license their new creations under the identical terms. This license is often compared with "copyleft" free and open source software licenses. All new works based on yours will carry the same license, so any derivatives will also allow commercial use. This is the license used by Wikipedia, and is recommended for materials that would benefit from incorporating content from Wikipedia and similarly licensed projects.

5. **Attribution-NonCommercial**
   This license lets others remix, tweak, and build on your work noncommercially, and although their new works must also acknowledge you and be noncommercial, they don't have to license their derivative works on the same terms.

6. **Attribution-NonCommercial-NoDerivs**
   This license is the most restrictive of the six main licenses, only allowing others to download your works and share them with others as long as they credit you, but they can't change them in any way or use them commercially.

(Creative Commons, n.d.)

The content creator selects a preferred license type to suit their needs. With a Creative Commons license, the work may be used but with attribution to the creator.

6.4 HOW DO I ETHICALLY USE THIS INFORMATION
   IN MY WORK?

A recent Facebook trend involved account holders changing their profile pictures to a cartoon. Many Facebook users found and posted pictures of their favorite cartoon action heroes, for instance. The cartoon profile pictures helped the account holder make a personal statement and to feel part of a wider group of like-minded people, but nearly none attributed the source of the pictures posted. Technically, these postings could be said to have violated copyright and were, at a minimum, unethical because of the failure to recognize the work of another person(s).

Similarly, copyright breaches have been common in other popular digital contexts, including Pinterest and YouTube. While businesses, such as these, monitor participant activity for copyright issues, it is always possible for copyrighted content to slip through, if it is posted temporarily and removed when identified as breaching copyright. As a result, as users and creators of content, it is essential to be vigilant in the online environment.

Ensuring that you have behaved ethically with digital information can be a challenge. The first step toward ethical use is to acknowledge that information found on the Internet may be owned and covered by copyright legislation. While copyright legislation is common, different countries may have slightly different copyright restrictions; it is important to understand what is and what is not considered to be permitted use in your region. In general, copyright usually allows university students to use copyrighted materials for their own education and research purposes. However, photocopying or downloading the text of entire books, for instance, is usually not permitted. Your university library most likely has paid subscriptions to e-books and journals, and the terms of subscription agreements allow for the downloading of a set amount of material. The full text of a journal article may be downloaded; however, e-books may permit users to download or print only a set number of pages per visit. It is essential that you familiarize yourself with copyright and publishers' restrictions around the use of materials. You, as an individual student, are responsible for abiding by copyright.

Once you have located content for assessment, you must ensure that you use that material ethically. Plagiarism—that is, using another person's ideas or their work without attribution—is a constant problem in the university environment. Universities invest significant time and effort communicating to students the perils of plagiarism, yet this form of cheating continues to exist. Plagiarism may result in disciplinary action by the university, including loss of grades, removal from courses, and even expulsion from the institution. The stigma associated with plagiarism should be a strong deterrent from active cheating.

However, plagiarism can be unwittingly committed by students who amass materials and draw from these without appropriate attribution. To ensure that you do not plagiarize, take care with the following steps:

- **Add quotation marks " " to any text you copy.**
  Taking this step will remind you that you have downloaded or recorded material that must be appropriately attributed, if used.
- **Paraphrase content.**
  To paraphrase means to "express the meaning of (something written or spoken) using different words, especially to achieve greater clarity" (Oxford Dictionaries, 2015). Essentially, to paraphrase is to reword content in your own words. It is good practice to paraphrase content. This will help you think about and reflect on the message found in the material you have used.
- **Note complete reference details when you locate material.**
  Record the reference details with the content you find. By keeping this information together, there is less risk of forgetting that some content belongs to someone else. In addition, you will avoid the stressful scramble to locate references for a bibliography as your assessment deadline looms.
- **Take an antiplagiarism course.**
  Universities often offer some sort of training around the issue of plagiarism; for instance, the institution's library may run workshops for students. Take advantage of this sort of help as soon as you register at the university. An antiplagiarism seminar will serve you well for your entire university career, and you may even be awarded credit for taking the course.
- **Adopt a referencing style.**
  First, check with your instructor for the referencing style used in your school or department, for example, APA (American Psychological Association), Chicago, Harvard, and MLA (Modern Language Association). Styles vary by discipline.
  Second, once you know the referencing style you must use for assessment, ensure that you understand the peculiarities of that particular style. A reference normally requires information about the author, title, and source, but what other information might be needed? For a digital

source, what information is needed about the e-location of that material? A style guide, either in hard copy or as information presented via the Internet, will be indispensable as you prepare citations in your text and a reference list for the end of your work. If you have questions, remember that your instructors or the staff in your university library will be able to assist you.

6.5 WHERE CAN I FIND INFORMATION THAT I CAN USE FREELY?

Finding material online that is not copyrighted can be a challenge. However, this is an important aspect of using material to protect both yourself and the creator of the material. Scholarly articles and books are more familiar to us with regard to clear statements of author, title, and source information. However, what should we do with a scholar's webpage? How can we be certain that an image is free to use?

Information found online should be treated in the same way as formal scholarly publications. Content, including a report published online, conference papers, presentation slides, and research project pages, should all be inspected for the usual author, title, and source information and then attributed accordingly. Inspect webpages closely for clues about publication date; the *last update* for the webpage may become critical information in the absence of other publication detail. Likewise, check the *About* tab on any webpage for information about the creation of the content provided on this site.

Images, including photographs, drawings, or any visual depiction, represent a tricky form of information, and discerning whether they are protected can be a challenge. Even trademarked content (words or symbols) within an image may be subject to restrictions. Paintings are also covered by copyright.

There are different categories of usage rights for images.

* **Public domain images**

   These images are generally free for anyone to use. Examples include images explicitly labeled as free to use and images downloaded from government websites. Take care when identifying images as free to use. All images have an association with copyright since someone created them; however, copyright may have lapsed for older images. An explicit indication of free use will allow you to use particular images without fear of breaching copyright.

- **Royalty-free images**
  Images that are royalty-free are not necessarily free to use. An initial royalty license fee may need to be paid, after which the image may be used. There may be restrictions around how many times the image may be used. Multiple customers may pay to use the same image; in other words, you are not paying for exclusive use of the image.

- **Rights-managed images**
  Images that are rights-managed require payment of a fee for each use of the image. Paid use may be exclusive to the individual who paid the fee or open to multiple customers paying to use the same image.

A variety of sources for images can be used freely. Watch for Creative Commons licensing, which may be provided to explain restrictions, if any, around a given image. A small sample of sources of images for free use in the digital environment includes the following:

- **Flickr Commons** (www.flickr.com/commons). Flickr is a social media site for uploading and sharing photographs, and the Commons area holds images from various libraries and museums. While images in Flickr Commons are generally in the public domain, institutions specify terms for referencing images when used.

- **Free Images** (www.freeimages.com) provides images uploaded by site members. Images are largely free to use, although there are some restrictions around nature of use; for example, images may not be used as part of a trademark.

- **Google Images Advanced Search** (http://www.google.co.uk/advanced_image_search) enables you to specify the type of image by license or restriction. Under the search filter *Usage Rights*, select one of the following: "not filtered by licence," "free to use or share," "free to use or share, even commercially," "free to use, share, or modify," or "free to use, share, or modify, even commercially."

- **Image Source** (http://www.imagesource.com/royalty-free) provides royalty-free and rights-managed images, which can be identified by search filter.

- **Wikimedia Commons** (http://commons.wikimedia.org/wiki/Main_Page) is an image database in Wikipedia, providing images that may be used freely.

In addition, a number of institutions are making collections available digitally in the public domain for use. For example, public institutions, such as the British Museum, the New York Public Library, Library of Congress, and NASA, provide digital images for free noncommercial use via their websites.

Even individuals are posting collections. For example, computer programmer Liam Quin has posted digital copies of engravings, illustrations, and so on from old books for which copyright has expired on a website called *Liam's Pictures from Old Books* (www.fromoldbooks.org). Use sites created by individuals with caution, taking note of copyright restrictions applicable in your region and any implications for materials you wish to use.

6.6 HOW DO I ATTRIBUTE A SOURCE TO ITS CREATOR?

As students prepare a reference list for the final page of an essay or other assessment, they are often quick to provide references for physical texts. For some reason, however, digital content often poses a stumbling block, and students miss recognizing the need for references for digital materials, as well as the appropriate content for those references. For example, website uniform resource locators (URLs) may be provided, but without a full reference. Just as you would reference hard copies of items used for assessment, it is essential to provide appropriate in-text citations and reference lists for digital content.

To begin, gather the necessary information to prepare a reference. Ask yourself the following basic questions to ensure you attribute digital content appropriately:

- Who created this work? If there is no obvious author, is it possible to determine the author(s)?
- Who published this work? Where was this work published?
- When was this work created or published?
- Where is the digital location of this work? Is this location permanent? That is, is there a DOI, URL, or other identifier?

Next, select the appropriate style guide for your discipline to prepare references. Remember that different disciplines use different referencing styles. For instance, the APA style is used not only in psychology but also in other social science subjects. MLA style is used in humanities subjects, for example. Equally, your discipline or university school/department may use the *Chicago Manual of Style* or Harvard referencing. Check with your instructor before you begin preparing references.

Once you have identified the appropriate style guide to follow, start preparing references. Let's explore referencing and the peculiarities of referencing digital items. For the purposes of illustrating how to reference particular types of items in digital format, in this book we use the APA style guide. You will find the *APA Style Guide to Electronic References* available as a

PDF download at https://library.bowdoin.edu/phebe/protected/apa-guide-to-electronic-references.pdf; this manual provides essential reading.

6.7 REFERENCING TRADITIONAL SCHOLARLY ITEMS IN DIGITAL FORMATS

The digital scholarly sources that you will use for assessment, namely, academic books and journal articles, must be referenced just as the printed formats would. However, a reference to a digital item takes account of format. As a result, referencing style guides provide particular rules for attributing digital materials to ensure that references include complete information about an item.

6.8 IN-TEXT REFERENCES

In APA style, the general format of an in-text reference is as follows:

(Author, Year)
Example: (Gui & Argentin, 2011)

Use this across types of information you need to reference within the text of an assignment. In cases where there is an element missing, consult the *APA Style Guide for Electronic References* for a substitution; for example, when no author is provided with an item, use the title of that item instead.

Example:
("Global Digital Literacy Council Charter," n.d.)

Online information sources, including websites and social media, can present unique challenges, because information creators and posters sometimes post anonymously. Where there is no author noted, use the screen name of this individual, for example:
- **YouTube video**
  (Surname of person who posted video OR Screen name, Year)
- **Blog post**
  (Author Surname OR Author screen name as it appears on the blog, Year)

6.9 A WORD ABOUT DOIs IN REFERENCING

You will see throughout our referencing examples the use of a *DOI*, a permanent means of identification assigned to digital publications. Because a DOI is permanent, it is preferable to a URL in a reference. For instance, journals may publish online early versions, as well as a final version, of an article; as a result, the DOI is critical for identifying the penultimate version of the article at this moment.

The DOI, used alone, can also be used to locate the associated content; for example, if you enter into your search engine http://dx.doi.org, followed by the DOI of the item, you can locate the item; for example, use http://dx.doi.org/10.3402/rlt.v22.21440 to locate the 2014 article called "Defining a self-evaluation digital literacy framework for secondary educators: the DigiLit Leicester project." You can also use the *Resolve a DOI Name* website (http://dx.doi.org) to search for an item with just the DOI as your search information.

6.10 REFERENCES TO e-BOOKS

When a book is published as or used in e-book format, references to this item follow various formulae under APA style.

6.10.1 Whole e-Book

In the list of references at the end of your essay, there are two ways to refer to an e-book in its entirety:

1. Author Surname, Initial(s). (Date). Title of e-book. Retrieved from URL

    Example:
    Fulton, C. (2010). *Information pathways: A problem-solving approach to information literacy*. Retrieved from https://rowman.com

2. Author Surname, Initial(s). (Date). Title of e-book. http://dx.doi.org/ xxxxxxxxxxxx

    Example:
    Lee, N. (2014). *Facebook Nation: Total Information Awareness*. http://dx.doi. org/10.1007/978-1-4939-1740-2

6.10.2 Chapter in an Edited e-Book

Specify the chapter, as well as information about the editor, in your reference for this item. Again, APA provides two formats for references to chapters in edited e-books with multiple contributors to chapters:

1. Author Surname, Initial(s). (Date). Title of chapter. In Initial(s). Editor Surname (Ed.), *Title of e-book* (pp. xx–xx). Retrieved from URL
2. Author Surname, Initial(s). (Date). Title of chapter. In Initial(s). Editor Surname (Ed.), *Title of e-book* (pp. xx–xx). http://dx.doi.org/ xxxxxxxxxxxx

Example:
Galbraith, J. (2011). E-books on the Internet. In S. Polanka (Ed.), *No shelf required: E-books in libraries* (pp. 1–18). Retrieved from https://www. alastore.ala.org/detail.aspx?ID=2902

6.11 REFERENCES TO ARTICLES

6.11.1 e-Journal Articles

The reference format for an e-journal article is similar to that for a printed journal article:

Author Surname, Initial(s). (Year). Title of article. *Title of Journal, Volume,* Pages. http://dx.doi.org/xxxxxxxxxxxx

Example:
Pieri, M. (2014). An e-learning Web 2.0 experience at the university. *International Journal of Digital Literacy and Digital Competence, 5,* 1–9. http://dx.doi.org/10.4018/ijdldc.2014010101

6.11.2 Newspaper Articles

Newspaper articles can be very useful for historical and current events research. Reference a newspaper article as follows:

Author Surname, Initial(s). (Year, Month Day). Title of article. *Title of Newspaper.* Retrieved from URL

Example:
Lewin, T. (2012, November 2). Digital natives and their customs. *New York Times.* Retrieved from http://nytimes.com

6.12 REFERENCES TO SOCIAL MEDIA

The explosion of information in various forms in social media offers a new challenge in referencing. Some areas of social media easily lend themselves to the form of attribution that is familiar to us; others seem more complicated to reference. Remember to keep in mind the essential elements of any reference that we discussed above, and let these help guide you, if you are uncertain of what information to gather for referencing social media.

The general reference format for websites, message boards, electronic mailing lists, and social media is as follows:

Author, Initial(s). (Year). Title of document [Format]. Retrieved from URL

Using this general reference format, we created some examples of how to reference commonly used social media below.

6.12.1 Facebook, Twitter, and Google+

Referencing these three communication tools is still new. However, the both the *APA Style Guide to Electronic References* and the APA blog (APA Style. Quick Answers, n.d.) offer advice on how to proceed. First, the APA blog explains that social media are not really used in academic writing just yet. The APA Style Guide to Electronic References (2012) reminds us that technology changes rapidly and, as a result, the rules around referencing social media are "an ongoing process." However, the *APA Style Guide to Electronic References* does offer an array of examples for citing information found on social networking tools. Remember to consult the *APA Style Guide to Electronic References* and the APA blog for updates.

Example: Facebook page
Digital literacy and skills. (2010). Study calls for stronger focus on IT and
    entrepreneurial skills in schools [Facebook page]. Retrieved August
    20, 2015, from https://www.facebook.com/DigitalLiteracyAndSkills

Remember to consult the APA guide for substitutions when part of the reference information is missing; in this case, the title of the Facebook page was used in the absence of an author.

Example: Twitter update or tweet
DML Research Hub. (2015, August 1). Digital literacy: Unlocking tech-
    nology's potential bit.ly/1AyniTl [Tweet]. Retrieved from https://
    twitter.com/dmlresearchhub/status/627541954826518529

6.12.2 YouTube and Other Social Media Video-Posting Tools

Video content is increasingly a common feature of learning. While YouTube is very well known, there are other video-hosting sites on the Web, for example, TEDx Talks and Video Jug. When we use a video, we must reference it appropriately. APA style provides the following general reference guidelines for YouTube videos and videos posted via other social media tools:

Author Surname, Initial(s). [Screen Name]. (Year, Month Day). Title of
    video [Video file]. Retrieved from URL

Example:

TEDx Talks. (2012, March 22). The essential elements of digital literacies: Doug Belshaw at TEDxWarwick [Video file]. Retrieved from
https://www.youtube.com/watch?v=A8yQPoTcZ78

It should be noted that, in this case, the APA guide refers to both the
author and poster of the video as the same person for retrieval purposes.
When only the screen name is known, provide this name without brackets;
when both the poster of the video and the screen name of this individual
are known, provide both with the screen name in square brackets.

6.12.3 Blogs

A more developed area of referencing social media pertains to blogs, a digital form of a diary or journal. Referencing a blog includes the usual points
of attribution information we have discussed; in the case of blogs, an author's
screen name can be used when the author's name is not provided. References to a blog are arranged in this order:

Author, Initial(s). OR Author screen name as it appears on the blog. (Date).
Title of blog post [Format]. Retrieved from URL of specific blog post

Example:

McAdoo, T. (2015, August 4). How to cite online maps in APA style [Blog
post]. Retrieved from http://blog.apastyle.org/apastyle/2015/08/
how-to-cite-online-maps.html

Note, here, that the title of the blog is *not* italicized. The APA Style Blog
(Lee, 2010) explains that titles of content produced by online communities,
such as blogs, newsgroups, and forums, should not be italicized.

6.13 REFERENCING OTHER DIGITAL INFORMATION SOURCES

As you will recall from your reading of other chapters in this textbook, there
are additional digital sources of information that may be useful. Because all
sources of information must be cited, it is important to consider how to
approach references for sources that may seem less formal or ephemeral.

6.13.1 Webpages

Should you use a webpage in your assignment, you must provide an appropriate reference for this information. For example, you might need to cite the

webpage of a commercial organization for an economics or business report you are writing, The general APA reference format for websites is as follows:

> Author, Initial(s). (Year). Title of document. Retrieved from URL of webpage

> Example:
> National Telecommunications and Information Administration. Digital literacies. Retrieved from http://www.digitalliteracy.gov

Note that the format of an item is only added for unusual items; a website is considered a routine item that does not require a format description.

In-text references to websites differ from other in-text references. The APA style permits you to use the URL alone in parentheses for example, (www.dropbox.com).

6.13.2 Digital Images

Images can add interest to an assignment. For instance, NASA offers public access to digital images that you may find useful for assessment; however, it remains essential to reference this material. NASA provides information and links to information regarding how posted royalty-free images may be used; referencing is important, and this agency explains when to attribute content (NASA, 2015).

> The general format for a reference to a photograph is as follows:
> Artist, Initial(s). (Copyright Year). *Title of Work* [Medium]. Retrieved from URL

> Example:
> NASA. (2015, July 13). *Recent Measurements of Pluto and Charon Obtained by New Horizons*. [Photograph]. Retrieved from http://www.nasa.gov/image-feature/recent-measurements-of-pluto-and-charon-obtained-by-new-horizons

In this case, there is no photographer listed with the photograph; the photograph is attributed to NASA.

6.13.3 Infographics

Infographics, often found posted in various social media venues, such as Pinterest, or included in newspaper articles, are classified under social media for the purposes of referencing by the APA blog (Lee, 2013). Reference an infographic as follows:

Author, Initial(s). (Year, Month Day). Title of infographic [Format]. Retrieved from URL

Example:
TheVisualCommunicationGuy. (2014). Can I use that picture? The terms, laws, and ethics for using copyrighted images [Infographic]. Retrieved from http://infographics.custominfographics. org/2015/06/17/sample-reference-list-apa-style-subject-guides-at-murdoch-1-a975e58bdafe88f3.jpg

In this example of a reference to an infographic, only the year of copyright is provided.

6.13.4 Wikipedia Articles

In Chapter 4, we explored the potential uses of Wikipedia, an online encyclopedia, as an information source. Remember that not all instructors allow the use of Wikipedia for assessment. If you can and do use Wikipedia, it is essential to provide an appropriate reference. Because Wikipedia authorship is collaborative, that is, community-based as opposed to attributable to a single author, it is unlikely that you will be able to provide author information. However, there will be a title, revision date, and other information by which you can identify this information source. Cite a Wikipedia article as follows:

Wikipedia article title. (Date). In *Wikipedia*. Retrieved Month day, year, from URL

Example:
Digital identity. (2015, July 29). In *Wikipedia*. Retrieved August 5, 2015, from https://en.wikipedia.org/wiki/Digital_identity

6.13.5 Online Lecture Notes or Other Slide Presentations

APA referencing distinguishes between lecture notes and presentations that are only available to you from your instructor and lecture notes and presentations that are available to the general public. For example, your instructor may post their notes or lecture slides online in the digital teaching space or learning management system (see Chapter 12) for your course. Always ask your instructor if it is appropriate to use their slides as a source for your assessment. If they agree, then be sure to reference your use of this material. Lecture slides are treated as a form of *personal communication* for the purposes of referencing. In this case, you would provide *only* an in-text reference to the lecture notes or presentation, and you would *not* include this in your reference list.

You may also wish to use lecture notes or slide presentations that are posted publically on the Internet, for example, on *SlideRocket* or *SlideShare*. The general APA reference style for a slide presentation that is accessible by the public looks like this:

> Author, Initial(s). (Year). *Title of presentation* [Lecture notes or PowerPoint slides]. Retrieved from URL

> Example:
> Kemp, S. (2015). Digital statshot China: Key statistical indicators for Internet, mobile, and social media usage in China in August 2015 [PowerPoint slides]. Retrieved from http://www.slideshare.net/wearesocialsg

6.13.6 E-mail Message or SMS/Text Message

E-mail messages and messages sent as text or instant messaging (e.g., WhatsApp messages) are treated as *personal communications* for the purposes of referencing. Again, consult with your instructor before you decide to include this type of information in your assessment. Instructors may allow some or no personal communication in formal assessment, depending on the nature of the assessment. If you are permitted to cite these forms of communication in assessment, follow the rules for referencing personal communication and include an in-text reference only.

6.14 BIBLIOGRAPHIC MANAGEMENT SYSTEMS

A bibliographic management system (BMS) is a form of software that enables the collection and management of materials for the purpose of preparing in-text citations and reference lists in varied citation styles. A BMS generally supports the importation of content manually or directly from online journals and websites. Once citation data have been entered into a BMS, references can be generated in the citation style required for a given piece of assessment (e.g., APA, Harvard, MLA).

Your university may subscribe to a particular proprietary BMS, such as Endnote, Papers, Flow, or RefWorks. There are also several BMSs online that are free to access and use. For example, CiteULike (http://www.citeulike.org) is a common BMS that offers free web-based bibliographic data management. Wikipedia maintains a list of various free and proprietary BMSs, including software comparisons that may help you consider the product best suited to your own needs and preferences (https://en.wikipedia.org/wiki/Comparison_of_reference_management_software).

There are also various citation generators available free online. This form of service provides a space for you to enter essential citation information and then generates a citation in a particular style. For example, Citation Machine (http://www.citationmachine.net) generates references in APA, Chicago, Harvard, MLA, and Turabian styles. BibMe (www.bibme.org), Cite This For Me (www.citethisforme.com), and EasyBib (http://www.easybib.com) also generate references for multiple styles. When using any of online reference generator, take care to check the version of the style guide used and ensure that this matches the requirements of your assessment.

REFERENCES

American Psychological Association. (2012). *APA style guide to electronic references*. Retrieved from https://library.bowdoin.edu/phebe/protected/apa-guide-to-electronic-references.pdf.

American Psychological Association. (n.d.). *APA style. Quick answers – References*. Retrieved from http://www.apastyle.org/learn/quick-guide-on-references.aspx.

Creative Commons. (n.d.). *About the licenses*. Retrieved from https://creativecommons.org/licenses.

Lee, C. (2010, November 18). *How to cite something you found on a website in APA style [Blog post]*. Retrieved from http://blog.apastyle.org/apastyle/2010/11/how-to-cite-something-you-found-on-a-website-in-apa-style.html.

Lee, C. (2013, October 18). *How to cite social media in APA style (Twitter, Facebook, and Google+) [Blog post]*. Retrieved from http://blog.apastyle.org/apastyle/2013/10/how-to-cite-social-media-in-apa-style.html.

NASA. (2015). *Media usage guidelines*. Retrieved from http://www.nasa.gov/audience/formedia/features/MP_Photo_Guidelines.html.

Oxford Dictionaries. (2015). Retrieved from: http://www.oxforddictionaries.com.

CHAPTER 7

In Too Deep

7.1 THE DILEMMA: "I CAN HARDLY FIND THE FULL TEXT OF *ANYTHING* FROM MY CLASS READING LISTS ON THE WEB. WHY IS THIS?"

In a recent report, the researchers from Project Information Literacy in the United States found that university students almost always turn first to course readings for academic assignments (Head & Eisenberg, 2009, p. 15). This suggests that, despite the popularity of Web sources like Google, reading lists are still a trusted and important source for students like you, since they are directly linked to your college courses and assignments and have been identified by your instructors as relevant or important.

This chapter has three main objectives. First, to provide a context for the discussion, we explore the differences between popular and scholarly information and explain why you need to be discerning in terms of the type of information to use in your college assignments. Second, we introduce you to the *Deep Web* and reveal how the full texts of scholarly and formally published information resources may not show up in general Internet searches because they are locked behind subscription paywalls or are otherwise inaccessible to general Internet users. The final aim of the chapter is to show you how scholarly search engines, such as Google Scholar and Microsoft Academic Search, can be used effectively to locate scholarly information, follow citation trails, identify key authors, and so on.

In this chapter you will:

- learn about the differences between popular and scholarly information resources.
- discover how the scholarly publishing process ensures that academic publications, such as books and journal articles, meet the high standards that are expected in academia.
- find out about the "deep Web" and the reasons why the information that you need might not be available by searching the Web.
- become familiar with the specialized academic Web search engines that you can use for your college work.

Digital Detectives
ISBN 978-0-08-100124-0

- understand when you *need* to use specialized scholarly resources instead of the Web to complete your research.
- discover what open access (OA) resources are and how they differ from the traditional scholarly publishing model.

7.2 READING LISTS

When you enter higher education, you experience a different kind of learning from that in secondary school. For one thing, you are expected to be much more independent and self-motivated. Your college professors will not check up on you as much as your teachers did! Second, the way you are expected to learn about different subjects also changes. You may no longer be asked to purchase one single textbook that contains all of the information you need to understand a topic; rather, you will find that, in addition to lecturing and running seminars, your professors probably supply a list of *required and recommended readings*, and then send you out to obtain these items yourself. They do this for a number of reasons, but the most important one is to provide you with a *sense of direction* or a framework for engaging with a field of study, about which you might know very little at the start. Typically, the lists that you receive in the early years of your college education contain primary or *seminal* readings about the subject in question, with the aim of introducing you to the most influential authors and key principles or theories in the area, since it might take too long for you to figure this out yourself. However, it is also true that many professors hope that the reading lists will spark a lively and enduring interest in students and inspire them to go deeper and to seek out further material, which will expand the topic for them even more. Some students are very enthusiastic and gladly read extensively around a topic. However, a study by Stokes and Martin (2008) uncovered a belief among instructors that students actually look at a very limited number of items on their reading lists and are unwilling to go beyond that. In particular, some of the instructors felt that students only wanted to use the *Web* for their college work, rather than other kinds of resources: "I [the instructor] expect that they [students] go to the library and seek information from books/journals. The reality is, that they want to sit in front of a monitor and get information from a Website" (Stokes & Martin, 2008, p. 117). Is this true for you? How many of the items on a reading list will you actually read? And do you agree with the belief that students want only the most convenient, easily accessible resources? This chapter explores some of these issues.

Nowadays, the reading lists that you receive typically consist of a mix of resources in multiple media formats. For instance, references to journal papers, book chapters, Web documents, videos, blog entries and documentaries are all examples of the items that might appear. They are often now referred to as "resource lists," rather than reading lists. In many cases you will be given a direct clickable link to some of the items on the list, for example, a YouTube video or blog. For other types of resources, however, direct access is not so straightforward, and you need to do a little detective work to lay your hands (or eyes) on the full text of the item in question. If you attempt to access all of your reading list items on the Web, you may wonder why you keep running into barriers that prevent you viewing whole documents; you might get a tantalizing view of a few pages, or the abstract of a document, but then find you can go no further. Why? To answer this question, we are going to explore the world of scholarly resources on the Web and to understand the difference between scholarly and popular information, which is at the root of this issue.

7.3 SCHOLARLY VERSUS POPULAR INFORMATION

In Chapter 5 we discussed how information on the Web is often posted with no checks or balances. Anybody with the know-how and access to the appropriate infrastructure is free to post what they wish and to make that information available for all to view. As you may recall, highly developed evaluation skills are now absolutely crucial, particularly for students like you, who need to find the best information for your college assignments. When deciding which resources to choose for your papers or projects, you need to consider carefully the *type* of information resource you are dealing with and whether it is appropriate for use in an academic assignment. In short, as a first step, you need to be able to distinguish between *popular* and *scholarly* information resources.

What do you think you know about this already? To test your knowledge, take a look at these two resources, which are more or less about the same topic:

1. Crean, R. D., Crane, N. A., & Mason, B. J. (2011). An evidence based review of acute and long-term effects of cannabis use on executive cognitive functions. *Journal of Addiction Medicine, 5*(1), 1–8. Retrieved from http://www.ncbi.nlm.nih.gov/pmc/articles/PMC3037578/.

2. Utton, T. (n.d.). How cannabis use can destroy mental skills. *Daily Mail.* http://www.dailymail.co.uk/health/article-149937/How-cannabis-use- %09%09destroy-mental-skills.html.

Which of the two documents do you think would be more suitable for a college assignment? What features of each document led you to this conclusion? Popular information sources differ from scholarly sources with regard to a number of important attributes that are indicative of the quality and credibility of the information they contain.

7.3.1 Popular Information Sources

What does the term *popular* mean to you? The *Oxford Dictionary* defines it as an adjective, which is used to describe activities or products that are "intended for or suited to the taste, understanding, or means of the general public rather than specialists or intellectuals" (Oxford Dictionaries, 2015). When applied to persons, it signifies those who are "liked or admired by many people or by a particular person or group." Describing an information resource as *popular* gives you valuable clues as to the nature and quality of the content, as well as the intentions of the creators, which can help you make a decision about whether you should use it for your college work. To summarize, popular information resources typically display the following characteristics:

- They are designed to appeal to a *general* audience, rather than an audience consisting of specialists, experts, academics, and professionals. The tone, level, and presentation of the information in these resources reflect this.
- The topics written about in popular sources are usually not concerned with research or highly specialized, theoretical, or technical issues, but instead are focused on general-interest issues such as human-interest news stories, entertainment, sport, hobbies, health and nutrition, and so on.
- The authors or creators of these resources are usually journalists, professional writers, or sometimes amateurs with well-developed knowledge of a topic.
- The style and language used in these resources are tailored to the general public; for instance, popular resources would not contain any specialized or technical language, diagrams, graphs, or other information that could not be easily understood by members of the general public.
- In popular resources, articles are usually shorter and snappier than those in scholarly sources.
- Authors or creators of popular information sources frequently do not provide full citations for the sources they quote, paraphrase, or refer to—it can be difficult to track down the original sources of facts or assertions

that are made in popular-type articles. This is a major warning sign with regard to the credibility and trustworthiness of information in this type of source.

- The articles published in popular sources are, at most, reviewed only by the publication editor, and sometimes not at all.
- The aim of popular sources is generally to inform or entertain the readers.
- To attract as many buyers, subscribers, or "clicks" as possible, popular sources are often glossy and slick, with color images and photographs, and high production values, or, in the case of digital resources, full of engaging whizz-bang widgets, videos, or other hooks designed to gain the attention of readers.
- Popular resources, both print and digital, often display advertisements for products and services that may be related to the topics of the articles or tailored to the expected audience of the piece.

7.3.2 Scholarly Information

Scholarly publications, by contrast, are those in which "the content is written by experts in a particular field of study—generally for the purpose of sharing original research or analyzing others' findings" (University of British Columbia Library, n.d.). When it comes to carrying out research for academic assignments, scholarly information resources should be at the top of the pile. Let us explore some of the characteristics that define scholarly sources.

- Scholarly publications are typically aimed at *specialist* audiences—for example, academics, researchers, and professionals such as doctors, lawyers, engineers, and technical specialists. As a result, there is no attempt to make them understandable to the general public; a certain level of expert knowledge among the readership is assumed.
- Similarly, the authors of scholarly pieces are usually academics, researchers, or experts in the particular area, who possess a broad spectrum of basic disciplinary or professional knowledge, coupled with a specialization in a particular area.
- The style of the publications reflects the knowledgeable or expert status of the readers; typically, they are written in very scholarly or technical language, with extensive use of *jargon* or technical terms.
- Scholarly articles are usually much longer than popular ones, sometimes including extensive footnotes or endnotes.
- There is always an abstract included at the beginning of a scholarly paper.

- Scholarly papers that report research must always include a *Methods* section, which describes in detail the methods of data collection and analysis that were used in the study.
- In scholarly publications, authors must include full citations for the sources they quote, paraphrase, or refer to. There usually is an extensive bibliography included at the end of each article so that readers are able to assess the quality of research for themselves and to follow up with any sources they find interesting.
- Most important, scholarly publications are almost always *quality controlled*—articles are reviewed by other specialists, as well as an editor, before being published; books are subjected to editorial assessment. The peer-review process for scholarly articles is described below in our discussion of the traditional versus newer publishing processes.

7.4 TRADITIONAL PUBLISHING VERSUS WEB PUBLISHING

A key difference between information that appears in traditional academic sources and that which is freely available on the Web lies in the formal processes that lead to publication. Let us consider for a moment how academic books and journal articles come to be published officially.

7.5 TRADITIONAL PUBLICATION PROCESS FOR ACADEMIC BOOKS

In the beginning, an author might have an idea for a book and approach a selected publisher themselves, or, alternatively, they may be actively recruited by a publisher for their expertise on a subject or reputation in a field. Publishers often send out targeted emails, which aim to encourage prospective authors to publish with them. This, in a way, is the first line of quality control to ensure that reputable authors are recruited. Once an author has been recruited, a contract is negotiated between author and publisher, outlining the terms and conditions under which the manuscript will be prepared and submitted, as well as the royalties that will be due from any sales, and other formal issues that need to be established. The author submits a completed manuscript, although it is common practice to send individual chapters to the publisher so that quality can be monitored on an ongoing basis. The publisher then facilitates the production of the physical book, including copyediting, proofreading, printing the physical copy or developing the e-book, distribution, marketing, and publicity. Strong editorial guidance is provided throughout the process to ensure that the book meets the required standards. Finally, the book is given a unique ISBN (international standard book number) and placed on the market. Book reviews in the appropriate channels (e.g., scholarly journals) serve as an additional indicator of quality following publication, as well as sometimes at the prepublication stage.

7.5.1 What Are ISBNs?

An ISBN is a "13-digit number that uniquely identifies books and book-like products published internationally" (ISBN.org, 2014). The purpose of an ISBN is to support effective universal bibliographic control by identifying *one title* or *edition of a title* from one specific publisher; it is a unique identifier that prevents confusion with other books, perhaps with similar titles or by the same author. ISBNs are assigned to publishers by an ISBN agency; a publisher receives a publisher prefix and an associated block of numbers, which it can then assign to publications for which it holds the publishing rights. Publishers that can request ISBNs are not just publishers of traditional print books, but also include e-book publishers, audio cassette and video producers, software producers, and museums and associations with publishing programs. When publishers assign ISBNs to publications, they should then be reported to R. R. Bowker as the database of record for the ISBN agency.

7.6 TRADITIONAL PUBLICATION PROCESS FOR JOURNAL ARTICLES

Journal articles typically undergo an even more rigorous quality control process, especially for journals that are considered to be prestigious and receive a large number of manuscripts from prospective authors. Most of the time, it is the authors who initiate the process; they wish to write about their cutting-edge research or practical experiences and to have this information disseminated in the appropriate literature so that their colleagues and counterparts in other countries are aware of what they are doing. Publishing articles in highly ranked journals is important for academics because it establishes their reputations in their field and increases their prospects of attaining tenure (secure, permanent jobs) at their institutions or of being awarded prestigious research grants. Therefore, authors will select the most appropriate journal for their topic and write their paper, adhering to the author guidelines (word count, format, etc.), which are provided by the publisher. Sometimes, as with books, reputable authors are actively recruited to write about specific topics, for example, if a special issue of the journal, focusing on a particular area, is to be published. The submitted paper undergoes a rigorous *peer-review process* (explained below), after which it may be rejected, accepted with modifications, or accepted outright. The paper is then published in the journal, both digitally and in print, although some journals are now only available in digital format. The peer-review process is at the heart of quality control in scholarly journals. Let us consider the process and how it ensures that the information you read in scholarly journals is of a high standard and can be trusted.

7.6.1 Peer Review

Peer review is defined as "a standard procedure in scholarly publishing, whereby a prospective publisher submits the manuscript of an article to experts in the research field for their critical scrutiny, under conditions of anonymity, with the aim of assuring quality and reliability of findings" (Brown, 2007). To put it simply, it is other academics who ultimately decide whether a submitted article is worthy of publication. When a journal editor receives a manuscript, they send it out to two or more reviewers who are experts in the subject area. These reviewers consider the manuscript against a list of criteria, as well as their own expertise, in order to determine whether the content and style meet the appropriate standard to merit publication in this particular journal. The reviewers often suggest revisions to improve an initial manuscript. Revisions are communicated to the author, who may then choose to amend the manuscript and resubmit. Articles that are deemed below standard may be rejected outright. The process is generally anonymous, although this is not always the case. There are two types of peer review: the first is *blind review*, where the authors' names may appear on the piece under review, but the author does not know the identity of the reviewers; the second is *double blind review*, where neither authors nor reviewers know each other's identities. The peer-review process is essential in ensuring that the information published in journals is accurate, trustworthy, and original. This is not always the case with web-based information.

7.6.2 How Can You Tell Whether a Journal Has Been Peer-Reviewed?

There are certain clues to look for, and strategies that you can adopt, to determine whether a journal article is from a peer-reviewed journal. Finding materials that have been peer-reviewed is essential if you wish to use these items for college work. Try the following approaches to ascertain that an item has been peer-reviewed:

- Look for clues on the first page of the article itself; for example, can you see dates that indicate when the article was originally submitted by the author, revised, and then finally accepted for publication?
- Check the homepage of the journal on the Web to see if there is a statement regarding their peer-review policy. Another clue is to look for any reference to an *Editorial Board* on the journal website; the presence of an editorial board may indicate that the articles in the journal have been peer-reviewed, but you should always cross-check by additional means noted in this list.
- Limit your search to peer-reviewed journals only when searching certain scholarly databases. Examples of journal databases with this function include Ebsco and ProQuest, which include a box you can tick to ensure that only peer-reviewed items are retrieved for your search. Databases are discussed in greater detail in Chapter 8.
- If your library provides you with access to the *Ulrichsweb Global Serials Directory* (http://ulrichsweb.serialssolutions.com/login), you can search for a specific journal. In the case of *Ulrichsweb*, the appearance of a particular icon beside the journal name—a sporting image of a referee's jersey—indicates that the articles in it are peer-reviewed or *refereed*, which is another way of describing the same process.

7.7 PUBLISHING ON THE WEB

One of the strengths of the Web is the platform it offers for freedom of expression to those who have access to the appropriate infrastructure, software and hardware, and skills and know-how to post information online. New forms of information production and distribution have emerged with the evolution of the Internet, and we have gradually become familiar and more comfortable with media, such as blogs, podcasts, videos, discussion boards, and social networking sites, as sources of information. However, the means by which much information appears on the Web and the traditional publishing processes described above differ greatly. What we gain in scope, variety, and breadth we sometimes lose in quality. In many cases, the means by which information is "published" on the Web are subject to none of the checks and balances described above. While information on the Web may be free and convenient to access, it may be less suitable for your college assignments than scholarly information, which is normally *not* free. The information on your reading lists is typically scholarly in nature. Let us explore the issues around accessing scholarly information on the Web and find out why you need to go beyond basic Web searching to find the items you need.

7.7.1 Where and What Is the Deep Web?

Before explaining the *Deep Web*, it helps to first understand what is meant by the *surface Web*. Essentially, the surface Web consists of all the data that search engines, such as Google and Bing, are able to find or to *crawl* (it might help to refer to Chapter 3 here)—in other words, static webpages that remain relatively stable over time and are linked to other pages. If you recall, search engines work by sending out Web *spiders*, which crawl through webpages, sending data back to the search engine index, where it can be searched by users. However, because not all information on the Web is static, stable, or freely accessible, search engines, such as Google and Yahoo!, are unable to "see" certain types of resources. "A serious limitation of popular search engines is that the 'surface' Web they cover (or 'crawl') is a fraction of the total amount of information actually available in digital form" (Eells, Vondracek, & Vondracek, 2012, p. 4).

The Deep Web, by contrast, is another world. Also known as the *hidden Web* or the *invisible Web*, the Deep Web "is the set of websites and their documents that cannot be accessed via crawler-type search engines such as Google" (Deep Web Technologies, n.d.). Although difficult to quantify, it is estimated that the size of the Deep Web could be around *500 times* the size of the surface Web (Kumar, 2012), so it is something that you need to be familiar with.

"Deep Web content typically lives inside of *databases* and is accessed through search forms" (Deep Web Technologies, n.d.). Another way of describing the Deep Web might be "content in searchable databases that only produce results dynamically in response to a direct request" (Bergman, 2001). More simply put: Think of when you search a database, for example, a library online catalog, or when you wish to book flights through an airline's flight database online. The page that appears when you enter your search terms *is only created in response to your particular query.* The information is pulled together for that one time only. There is no webpage with a list of specific results just waiting around to be crawled by a spider, which means that the information that is contained in this page specifically can never appear in the search engine's index. The information is effectively buried beneath the surface of the Web that you can search, and you need to know the specific systems, access points, and permissions to be able to retrieve that information.

7.7.2 Deep Web versus Dark Web

The information in the Deep Web is, for the most part, not hidden. It is just not possible for current search algorithms to locate and index it. It is important that you do not confuse the Deep Web with the more sinister subcategory, the *DarkNet* or Dark Web, although the effect of difficult-to-access information is the same. In the DarkNet, however, information is intentionally concealed, often to enable illegal activity to take place. Untraceable communication is at the heart of the DarkNet. It is described as "a routed allocation of IP address space that is not discoverable by any usual means… The purpose is to hide not only the communications themselves but the fact that information is being exchanged" (Rouse, 2011). Those wishing to access the DarkNet must download special software, providing access to an anonymous network of nodes, effectively masking the user's internet protocol address and protecting their privacy. A great deal of illegal trading takes place on the DarkNet, including drugs, weapons, fake identifications, contraband, and other products and services. Bitcoin is often used in place of hard currency, which further conceals the activity. The positive side of the DarkNet, however, is that it allows communication to take place in closed regimes, where freedom of expression is not considered a basic human right; for example, journalists in countries where there is extreme censorship can access the DarkNet to exchange and disseminate information about political or human rights issues that they would otherwise be unable to share.

7.7.3 Deep Web Characteristics

Deep Web content typically has the following characteristics:
- The content of databases, which is accessible only by direct query.
- Nontext files, such as multimedia, images, software, and documents in formats including portable document format (PDF) and Microsoft Word. However, as search algorithms become ever more sophisticated, this category is becoming smaller.
- Content available on sites that are protected by passwords or other restrictions (e.g., fee-based content, content on company Intranets). A good example here is a commercially available scholarly database, which contains the full texts of journal articles. This material is not freely available to the general public.

- Special types of online documents that do not exist as actual webpages, for example, full texts of journal articles or books.
- Dynamic content that changes constantly because it is updated so often, such as stock market information and flight arrivals and departures.
- Communication that takes place on social networking sites, such as Facebook and Twitter, bookmarks and citations stored on social bookmarking sites, threads on discussion boards, among others.
- Pages that have no inbound or outbound links.

7.7.4 Scholarly Search Engines

How is the Deep Web relevant to your reading lists? Most reading lists contain chiefly scholarly information, such as peer-reviewed journal articles, book chapters, and technical reports. Although more and more quality information is appearing online with no cost attached, the vast majority of scholarly items are not cost free and must be purchased, either through buying the item itself or obtaining a subscription or license to permit access to the information. So, much of the information that you need is buried in the Deep Web, and all you can find via Google are seemingly popular information sources that you are not sure whether you should use for your college work. Are there *any* search engines that you can use to find the scholarly information that is primarily located in the Deep Web? In short, the answer is yes. Over the past few years, there have been many attempts to categorize and provide access to scholarly information on the Web, and while you still mostly need access to the library resources of an educational institution to gain access to full text, the availability of specialist search engines and websites has made academic research a lot easier.

7.7.4.1 Google Scholar

The best known of the scholarly search engines is *Google Scholar*, which "provides a simple way to broadly search for scholarly literature" and to "search across many disciplines and sources: articles, theses, books, abstracts and court opinions, from academic publishers, professional societies, online repositories, universities and other websites" (Google Scholar, n.d.). Although it retains the familiar features of the general Google search engine, it is focused primarily on retrieving scholarly information, such as journal articles and conference papers, rather than sources that might fall into the "popular" category.

To search Google Scholar, enter https://scholar.google.com/into the address bar of your browser, and press the Enter button on your keyboard. The homepage will appear as shown in Figure 7.1.

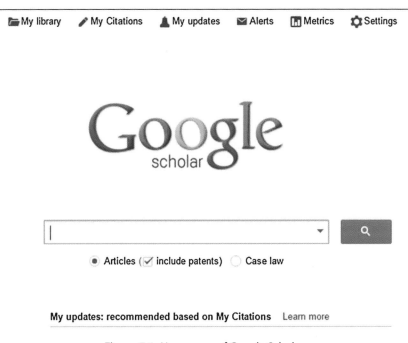

Figure 7.1 Homepage of Google Scholar.

From here, you can enter a simple word or phrase search, just as you would do when using the basic Google search box. On Google Scholar's main search page, you can also specify whether you want the search to include patents and case law. However, if you click on the arrow at the right hand side of the search box, a selection of advanced search options will appear. Select an advanced search feature to refine your search for more precise results, such as Boolean operators (AND, OR, NOT), author's name, journal title, and publication dates, which are similar to the search features discussed Chapter 3.

When you enter one or more search terms into Google Scholar, the results page offers you further options to refine your search. Consider the example in Figure 7.2, which shows the results page following a search for the phrase *digital literacy*.

You can specify a time range and sort your results according to relevance or publication date; for instance, it might be useful to view only the most recent articles on a topic by specifying results from the current year. You might also notice the *My library* option on this page. If you enable this function, you can then build a personalized collection of relevant resources by clicking *Save* underneath a reference that you deem important. Equally, if you want to be notified when new items relating to your topic appear, you

Google

Scholar

"Digital Literacy"   🔍   ✏️ My Citations

About 43,000 results (0.04 sec)

Articles

Case law   [PDF] from ncsu.edu
My library

[BOOK] **Digital literacy**
P Glister, P Gilster - 1997 - ncsu.edu
This century has been one of change and growth, and media and communication have been
among the most rapidly developing. At the turn of the last century, theatre, the telegraph, and
the newspaper entertained and informed us. By the 1930s, movies replaced theatre as ...
Cited by 998   Related articles   All 6 versions   Cite   Save   More

Any time
Since 2015   [HTML] from galegroup.com
Since 2014   Full text - MIT Libraries
Since 2011
Custom range...

[HTML] **Digital literacy**: A conceptual framework for survival skills in the digital era
Y Eshet-Alkalai - Journal of Educational Multimedia and ..., 2004 - go.galegroup.com
In light of the rapid and continual development of digital technology, individuals are required
to use a growing variety of technical, cognitive, and sociological skills in order to perform
tasks and solve problems in digital environments. These skills are referred to in the ...
Cited by 315   Related articles   All 15 versions   Cite   Save   More

Sort by relevance
Sort by date

[BOOK] Digital **literacies**: Concepts, policies and practices
C Lankshear, M Knobel - 2008 - books.google.com
... Printed in the United States of America Page 7. ❖ I Contents Acknowledgments vii Introduction:
Digital Literacies—Concepts, Policies and Practices 1 COLIN LANKSHEAR AND MICHELE
KNOBEL 1: Origins and Concepts of **Digital Literacy** 17 DAVID BAWDEN 2: Functional ...
Cited by 259   Related articles   All 11 versions   Cite   Save   More

✓ include patents
✓ include citations

[BOOK] Popular culture, new media and **digital literacy** in early childhood   [PDF] from libsyn.com
J Marsh - 2005 - books.google.com
This book offers a range of perspectives on children's multimodal experiences, providing a
ground-breaking account of the ways in which children engage with popular culture, media
and **digital literacy** practices from their earliest years. Many young children have extensive ...
Cited by 160   Related articles   All 4 versions   Cite   Save   More

☑ Create alert

Figure 7.2 Search results for *digital literacy* on Google Scholar.

can click on the *Create alert* link, which you can see in the lower left-hand corner with the envelope icon in Figure 7.2, and enter your details; new references will be emailed directly to you.

7.7.4.1.1 Does Google Scholar Reveal the Deep Web?

The most important question you might have about Google Scholar is whether it gives you access to the full text of all of those hard-to-find items on your reading list? In other words, is Google Scholar a portal into the hidden Web? The answer is both yes and no. If you look again at the screen-shot in Figure 7.2, you will notice links to the right of some of the search results. These are the direct links to the full-text PDFs of the items in question, which you can access straight away. Remember to check to see whether the items are peer-reviewed!

However, some of the items do not have these links. Is there a way of gaining access to these documents also? If you are enrolled in an academic institution, Google Scholar offers a very convenient means of finding out whether your educational institution holds these resources or has a subscription providing access to the full-text of these items and, if so, can take you directly there.

7.7.4.1.2 Google Scholar: Library Links

The Library Links feature connects the Web to the resources in your institution. To set up this feature, click on *Settings*, which you can access from the homepage of Google Scholar. On the Settings page, you will see a link called *Library links* on the left-hand side of the page. Click on Library links, and you will arrive at the page shown Figure 7.3.

This page allows you to set up a *library access link* for up to five libraries of your choice. When you subsequently perform a search on Google Scholar, the search engine will provide you with a direct link to your library's electronic resources for each item retrieved, so that you can see at a click whether your library can facilitate access to the full-text item. In Figure 7.4, you can see the direct links to the full-text of items in MIT Libraries. Clicking on these links brings you to the records for each item that is held in your library. You will, of course, be required to log into your institutional account before you gain access. However, if you are using the Web to carry out research for your college assignments, Google Scholar is the best place to start, rather than the general Google search page, which does not prioritize scholarly items and offers no way for you to check the availability of items in your institutional library.

Google

Scholar Settings

Search results	Show library access links for (choose up to five libraries):
Languages	
Library links	[ ] 🔍
Account	*e.g. Harvard*
Button	

Online access to library subscriptions is usually restricted to patrons of that library. You may need to login with your library password, use a campus computer, or configure your browser to use a library proxy. Please visit your library's website or ask a local librarian for assistance.

Save   Cancel

To retain settings, you must turn on cookies

About Google Scholar   Privacy   Terms   Provide feedback

Figure 7.3 Google Scholar Library links.

7.7.4.1.3 Google Scholar: Other Useful Features

Google Scholar has a number of other features that you may find useful for research. One potentially useful function in Google Scholar is the *Cited by* link, usually followed by a number, that you will see underneath each search result. This tells you the number of other publications that have referred to and have included the item you are looking at in their bibliographies. When you click on the link, you are brought to a list of all of those publications. This is a very useful function if you wish to access items that are similar to the one in your search results list. The relative popularity of an item is also indicated. If the citation number is high, this may, in turn, be a potential indicator of quality. Following a *citation trail* in this way can enable you to go deeper into a topic and uncover some of the important works in the area.

The *Related articles* link brings up sources that are similar to the one you are looking at. Select *More*, and you will see the *Library Search* link. This link performs a search in *OCLC WorldCat* to identify the libraries that hold or provide access to this item. You can specify your location and instruct the system to include only libraries physically located near to you.

7.7.4.2 Microsoft Academic Search

Another popular scholarly search engine is Microsoft Academic Search (MAS), which you can access at this link: http://academic.research. microsoft.com. Like Google Scholar, MAS indexes millions of scholarly

Google

"Digital Literacy"

Scholar   Page 3 of about 43,000 results (0.04 sec)

✎ My Citations

Articles

Case law

My library

Can we teach digital natives digital literacy?
W Ng - Computers & Education, 2012 - Elsevier
In recent years, there has been much debate about the concept of digital natives, in particular the differences between the digital natives' knowledge and adoption of digital technologies in informal versus formal educational contexts. This paper investigates the ...
Cited by 87   Related articles   All 7 versions   Cite   Save

[PDF] from researchgate.net
Full text - MIT Libraries

Any time
Since 2015
Since 2014
Since 2011
Custom range...

Changes over time in digital literacy
Y Eshet-Alkalai, E Chajut - CyberPsychology & Behavior, 2009 - online.liebertpub.com
Abstract The current study is a follow-up on the 2002 empirical study by Eshet-Alkalai and Amichai-Hamburger, which investigated digital literacy skills among different age groups. This study explores changes through time in digital literacy among the same participants 5 ...
Cited by 50   Related articles   All 5 versions   Cite   Save

[PDF] from researchgate.net
Full text - MIT Libraries

Sort by relevance
Sort by date

✓ include patents
✓ include citations

Instant messaging, literacies, and social identities
C Lewis, B Fabos - Reading research quarterly, 2005 - Wiley Online Library
... lives. Grounded in theories of literacy as a social and semiotic practice, this research asked what functions IM served in participants' lives and how their social identities shaped and were shaped by this form of digital literacy. ...
Cited by 435   Related articles   All 10 versions   Cite   Save

[PDF] from uconn.edu
Full text - MIT Libraries

☑ Create alert

Digital skills of internet natives: Different forms of digital literacy in a random sample of northern Italian high school students
M Gui, G Argentin - New Media & Society, 2011 - nms.sagepub.com
Abstract This article outlines the main results and methodological challenges of a large-scale survey on actual digital skills. A test covering three main dimensions of digital literacy (theoretical, operational and evaluation skills) was administered to a random sample of 65 ...
Cited by 68   Related articles   All 4 versions   Cite   Save

[PDF] from unimib.it
Full text - MIT Libraries

Figure 7.4 Library links for MIT Libraries.

publications; in addition to this, MAS endeavors to "display the key relationships between and among subjects, content, and authors, highlighting the critical links that help define scientific research" (Microsoft Academic Search, 2013). It should, however, be noted that the search engine is classified as *beta*, which means that it is not quite at the final stage of development. It is effectively still a work in progress and is in the *testing* phase. In fact, Microsoft refers to it as an "experimental research service." While this does not mean that it is of poor quality and should not be used, you should be aware of its status as an experimental service and understand that it might not receive the same level of attention and maintenance as products that have been officially released.

In addition to a basic search box, similar to Google Scholar, the homepage of MAS displays rankings of the top *authors, publications, conferences, journals, keywords*, and *organizations* in different fields of study by means of clickable links; these links can serve as a map to a field for novice researchers. For instance, if you are new to a topic, it might be helpful to identify the major authors in a field (those whose publications have been cited most frequently by other authors and in the most prestigious journals) and use their work as a springboard to explore the topic further. If you need more cutting-edge information on a particular subject, having access to the top conferences in the field can help to lead you to the most up-to-date research papers.

Searching on MAS is similar to searching on other search engines. In addition to the basic search box, you can click on *Advanced Search*, which allows you to search by *author, conference, journal, organization, year*, and *DOI*. The DOI, or *digital object identifier*, which you learned about in Chapter 6, is a unique alphanumeric string assigned to a digital item that provides a stable link to its location on the Internet. Because URLs are unstable and can disappear, this identifier ensures that the item can always be located. DOIs are used frequently for digital versions of journal articles when it is important to have a reliable way of accessing them.

Ranking of search results on MAS is calculated according to the relevance of the user's query, as well as by a static rank value for each item; this calculation "encompasses the authority of the result, which is determined by several details, such as how often and where a publication is cited" (Microsoft Academic Search, 2013).

An interesting feature of MAS is its search features for authors, conferences, journals, and so on. If you click on an author's name, for example, you are brought to an author profile page. This page lists the number of publications by that author that have been indexed by the search engine, as well as the number of times he/she has been cited by other authors. This information is also displayed in a graph, showing the changes over a number of years. Links to the publications themselves are also included (although you may not be able to access the full-text versions), as well as links to the publications *that cite* the author's papers.

Searching for a particular journal retrieves a list of publications from that journal. You then have the option of limiting the results by year of publication (e.g., specifying papers that were published since 2000 or since 2014). Similarly, if you search by *conference*, a list of papers from that specific conference are retrieved, which you can again limit by publication date. Searching by *organization* retrieves a list of papers written by authors affiliated with that particular organization or institution. You can also combine the various search parameters using Boolean operators to refine your searches; for example, you might combine the organization "University College Dublin" with author "Claire McGuinness" using the operator AND. A list of papers by one of the authors of this book will be retrieved!

You should note that, unlike Google Scholar, MAS does not offer a *Library Links* feature, so there is no way of directly accessing your library's resources from the search results page to see whether full-text items are available to you. MAS does, however, give you the opportunity to explore different fields of study in a way that Google Scholar does not: by identifying the important authors, key journals, major conferences, and organizations that constitute the *map* of the particular field that interests you. If you are new to a subject area and are struggling to get started in research, MAS can offer a useful starting point, although it should never replace resources, such as subject pathfinders in your library, LibGuides, or reading lists provided by your instructors.

7.7.4.3 Other Scholarly Search Engines

While Google Scholar and MAS are the most popular academic search engines on the Web, there are many other options you can try. Here are some examples:

- **BASE** (Bielefeld Academic Search Engine): Maintained by Bielefeld University Library, BASE is a multidisciplinary search engine that specifically covers academic OA Web resources and index resources, such as e-journals, institutional repositories, and electronic libraries. It is a vast database, providing access to more than 60 million documents from over 3000 sources. You can access BASE at this link: http://www.base-search.net.

- **DOAJ** (Directory of Open Access Journals): The DOAJ is an online direc-tory that provides access to OA, peer-reviewed scholarly and scientific journals. OA journals do not charge readers for their content, which means that full-text articles are available to the general public. An advantage of the DOAJ is that all articles indexed *must* be peer-reviewed and are therefore of high quality, even though they are free to download. You can access the DOAJ at this link: http://doaj.org.
- **ERIC** (Education Resources Information Center): ERIC is a world-renowned academic resource that has been available in different formats for half a century. This database provides access to literature in the field of edu-cation. ERIC holds more than 1.5 million records and provides access to hundreds of thousands of full-text resources dating back to the 1960s. The database covers sources such as scholarly journals, reports, conference pro-ceedings, and reference works. Where available, links to the full text of docu-ments are provided. You can access ERIC at this link: http://eric.ed.gov.
- **PubMed**: PubMed is a publicly accessible search engine that provides access to the *MEDLINE* database, maintained by the US National Library of Medicine. Through PubMed, you can search an index of more than 20 million high-quality journal articles from over 5000 schol-arly journals in the fields of biomedicine and health, including elements of the life sciences, behavioral sciences, chemical sciences, and bioengi-neering. PubMed is a vast and sophisticated resource, with links to many full-text articles. It includes an index of *clinical queries*, which are designed to assist practitioners with their on-the-spot information needs. You can access PubMed at this link: http://www.ncbi.nlm.nih.gov/pubmed.

7.8 OPEN ACCESS PUBLISHING

While most of the academic resources we have discussed in this chapter are available only via subscription or direct purchase, there is a growing body of scholarly information that is based on the removal of the traditional access bar-riers put in place by commercial publishers and the delivery of high-quality, cutting-edge research directly to audiences at no cost. OA literature is "digital, online, free of charge, and free of most copyright and licensing restrictions" (Suber, 2015). While scholarly publishing has always been based on the willing-ness of scholars and researchers to make their work publicly available without receiving monetary payment for it, intended readers have always faced price barriers to accessing this work because it is published in subscription journals and closed-access books. According to the Budapest Open Access Initiative (2002), removing these barriers will "accelerate research, enrich education, share the learning of the rich with the poor and the poor with the rich, [and] make this literature as useful as it can be." The definition provided by the Budapest Initiative offers a clear overview of what OA literature should comprise:

By "open access" to this literature, we mean its free availability on the public internet, permitting any users to read, download, copy, distribute, print, search, or link to the full texts of these articles, crawl them for indexing, pass them as data to software, or use them for any other lawful purpose, without financial, legal, or technical barriers other than those inseparable from gaining access to the internet itself.

Budapest Open Access Initiative (2002)

Supporters of OA believe that peer-reviewed scholarly literature should be accessible online without cost to readers; however, the fact that publication of information is never entirely without cost has led to a reconsideration of the cost models behind scholarly publication and an overall rethink of the economics of scholarly communication.

There are two ways of supporting OA publishing: (1) self-archiving/OA repositories and (2) OA peer-reviewed journals, referred to as "Green OA" and "Gold OA" respectively. With self-archiving, or Green OA, contents are not always peer-reviewed, but are made freely available to the world through deposition in repositories, frequently by the authors themselves. These resources might include unrefereed versions of articles before printing (the versions submitted to a journal before peer review), refereed versions after printing, or both, as well as dissertations, course materials, departmental databases, data files, audio files, and video files. The repositories frequently are situated in institutions, such as university libraries or research organizations. Authors do not need publisher permission to deposit their articles before printing, and even after the articles have been officially published, most publishers will permit their authors to archive the final version.

OA journals, or Gold OA, perform the same functions as subscription journals in that content is peer-reviewed before publication, the manuscript is prepared for publication by the journal, and the manuscript is then published on their own server. To fund this process, some OA journals are subsidized by universities or professional societies; others charge a processing fee to their authors or authors' sponsors to have the article published once it has been accepted as suitable.

Some examples of OA portals include the following:

- **The Directory of Open Access Journals**, mentioned above, provides access to more than 10,000 OA journals covering science, technology, medicine, social science, and humanities. You can access this portal at https://doaj.org.

- **Project Gutenberg**, which has existed since 1971, when its founder Michael Hart created the first Project Gutenberg e-text by digitizing a copy of the US Declaration of Independence. Since then, the project has continued with its mission "to encourage the creation and distribution of e-books," and now provides access to over 49,000 free e-books. It can be accessed at http://www.gutenberg.org/.
- **The Online Books Page**, which is "a website that facilitates access to books that are freely readable over the Internet" at the University of Pennsylvania. It is available at: http://onlinebooks.library.upenn.edu.index.html.
- **PLOS (Public Library of Science)**, which is a nonprofit publisher and advocacy organization, has to date published more than 140,000 peer-reviewed articles in its range of OA journals. Titles include *PLOS One*, *PLOS Biology*, and *PLOS Medicine*. It can be accessed at http://www.plos.org/.
- **Harvard University Library Open Collections Program (OCP)** was established in 2002 to provide access to Harvard's many collections developed over centuries. The OCP currently facilitates access to over 2.3 million digitized pages, including more than 225,000 manuscript pages. It can be accessed at http://ocp.hul.harvard.edu/.
- **OpenDOAR** is a directory of academic OA repositories that allows users to search for repositories or to search repository contents. The aim of OpenDOAR, which is maintained by the University of Nottingham in the United Kingdom, is "to provide a comprehensive and authoritative list of such repositories for end users who wish to find particular archives." The OpenDOAR search interface is flexible, allowing users to search by keyword, subject area, country, language, and content or repository type, among other fields. It is located at http://opendoar.org.

7.9 CHALLENGES

1. Classify the following items about *driverless vehicles* as either scholarly or popular. What are the reasons for your choices? Which items could you use to write a college paper?
   a. Wohltorf, J. (2015, June 17). Driverless cars are already here. *Tech-Crunch*. Retrieved from http://techcrunch.com/2015/06/17/driverless-cars-are-already-here/#.fm4cx2:IQId (31 July 2015).
   b. Urmson, C. (2015, June 26). Chris Urmson: How a driverless car sees the road [Video file]. Retrieved from https://youtu.be/tiwVMrTLUWg (18 August 2015).

    c. Carlson, M. S., Desai, M., Drury, J. L., Kwak, H., & Yanco, H. A. (2014, March). Identifying factors that influence trust in automated cars and medical diagnosis systems. In *AAAI Symposium on The Intersection of Robust Intelligence and Trust in Autonomous Systems* (pp. 20–27).

    d. Muller, J. (2012). With driverless cars, once again it is California leading the way. *Forbes 2012.*

2. The following are sample items from a resource list on *Internet privacy* that could be provided by a college professor. Which of the items on the list can be found in full on the *surface Web*, and which can be found in the *Deep Web* only? How did you come to this conclusion?

    a. Bull, M. (2013). Effects of social media on Internet privacy. Retrieved from https://mikebull94.com/articles/ethics-essay.pdf (15 August 2015).

    b. Singh, T., & Hill, M. E. (2003). Consumer privacy and the Internet in Europe: A view from Germany. *Journal of Consumer Marketing, 20*(7), 634–651.

    c. Luo, X. (2002). Trust production and privacy concerns on the Internet: a framework based on relationship marketing and social exchange theory. *Industrial Marketing Management, 31*(2), 111–118.

    d. Malhotra, N. K., Kim, S. S., & Agarwal, J. (2004). Internet users' information privacy concerns (IUIPC): the construct, the scale, and a causal model. *Information Systems Research, 15*(4), 336–355.

    e. Buchmann, Johannes, ed. (2014). *Internet Privacy: Options for adequate realisation.* Springer Science & Business Media.

3. Use the two main academic search engines, *Google Scholar* and *Microsoft Academic Search* (MAS), to search for items for the following college paper: *The Impact of Social Media on Marketing for Small Businesses.* Examine the first two results pages from each search engine and answer the following questions:

    a. Are there significant differences between the items retrieved by both search engines, or do both engines retrieve the exact same items and in the same rank order?

    b. Based on the first two search results pages from each search engine, which search engine do you think has provided the most useful and relevant results for your paper?

    c. If you wanted to narrow your search results to items that were published since 2012 only, do you have the option to do that?

    d. Can you access the full text of many of the items in the list of results?

    e. Which search engine do you think worked the best for this task? What are your reasons for this choice?

REFERENCES

Bergman, M. K. (2001). White paper: the deep web: surfacing hidden value. *Journal of Electronic Publishing*, 7(1). Retrieved from http://quod.lib.umich.edu/cgi/t/text/idx/j/jep/3336451.0007.104/–white-paper-the-deep-web-surfacing-hidden-value?rgn=main;view=fulltext.

Brown, D. (2007). *Scientific communication and the dematerialization of scholarship; glossary.* Proquest-CSA Discovery Guides. Retrieved from http://archive-com.com/page/1795906/2013-04-02/. http://www.csa.com/discoveryguides/scholarship/gloss_f.phph.

Budapest Open Access Initiative. (2002). *Read the Budapest Open Access Initiative.* Retrieved from http://www.budapestopenaccessinitiative.org/read.

Deep Web Technologies. (n.d.). *What is the deep Web?* Retrieved from http://www.deepwebtech.com/company/resource-center/faqs/#deepweb.

Eells, L., Vondracek, R., & Vondracek, B. (2012). Fishing the deep Web: the search for information. In C. A. Jennings, T. E. Lauer, & B. Vondracek (Eds.), *Scientific communication for natural resource professionals.* Bethesda, Maryland: American Fisheries Society. Retrieved from http://www.fisheriessociety.org/proofs/sci/eells.pdf.

Google Scholar. (n.d.). *About Google Scholar.* Retrieved from https://scholar.google.com/intl/en/scholar/about.html.

Head, A. J., & Eisenberg, M. B. (2009). *Lessons learned: How college students seek information in the digital age.* Project Information Literacy First Year Report with Student Survey Findings University of Washington's Information School. Retrieved from http://projectinfolit.org/images/pdfs/pil_fall2009_finalv_yr1_12_2009v2.pdf.

ISBN.org. (2014). *FAQs: General questions.* Retrieved from http://www.isbn.org/faqs_general_questions.

Kumar, M. (2012). *What is the deep Web? A first trip into the abyss.* The Hacker News. Retrieved from http://thehackernews.com/2012/05/what-is-deep-web-first-trip-into-abyss.html.

Microsoft Academic Search. (2013). *About Microsoft Academic Search.* Retrieved from http://academic.research.microsoft.com/About/Help.htm.

Oxford Dictionaries. (2015). Retrieved from http://www.oxforddictionaries.com.

Rouse, M. (2011). *DarkNet definition.* TechTarget Network. Retrieved from http://searchnetworking.techtarget.com/definition/darknet.

Stokes, P., & Martin, L. (2008). Reading lists: a study of tutor and student perceptions, expectations and realities. *Studies in Higher Education*, 33(2), 113–125. http://dx.doi.org/10.1080/03075070801915874.

Suber, P. (2015). *Open access overview.* Retrieved from http://legacy.earlham.edu/~peters/fos/overview.htm.

University of British Columbia Library. (n.d.). *Scholarly vs. popular sources.* Retrieved from http://help.library.ubc.ca/evaluating-and-citing-sources/scholarly-versus-popular-sources.

CHAPTER 8

It's Only Words...

8.1 THE DILEMMA: SEARCHING IS SEARCHING, WHETHER YOU'RE ON THE WEB OR USING ONE OF THE LIBRARY DATABASES, RIGHT?

You know the story. Your professor has assigned a tricky research paper. You have been given strict instructions *not* to use Wikipedia, but to log in and explore the databases that are available via your Library's website. However, when you do, you are confronted by strange names, such as NEXIS, JSTOR, and ProQuest, as well as incredibly complex search interfaces, which talk about *fields*, *wildcards*, and *EarlyCite*—whatever they mean. You haven't a clue where to start. Perhaps your professor might not notice if you take a quick look at Wikipedia...

By now, you should be familiar with the strengths and limitations of the Web when it comes to your college work, and perhaps you feel more confident about what the Web can and cannot provide in terms of information that is suitable for a college assignment. Of course, the story does not end there; in some ways, it is merely the beginning. Part of being digitally literate involves understanding what *types* of resources to choose in different scenarios and contexts; as we know, the Web is not always the most appropriate route to take. There is evidence that college students like you are becoming increasingly savvy when it comes to planning an appropriate research strategy. For example, the *Project Information Literacy* study found that college students tend to use scholarly databases first and foremost for academic assignments because they perceive them to be more reliable than web-based sources and typically the kinds of resources that are recommended by their instructors (Head & Eisenberg, 2009). However, knowing when it is appropriate to select scholarly resources is one thing; it is equally important that you also are aware of the different features and functions that will help you to get the most out of the scholarly resources that you choose.

In this chapter we look at the type of scholarly resources that exist primarily in the Deep Web. Recall from Chapter 7 that the Deep Web refers to websites that cannot be accessed via crawler-type search engines, such as

Digital Detectives
ISBN 978-0-08-100124-0

Google, for a number of reasons; for example, they may require a subscription, be locked behind a paywall, or contain information that can be accessed only via direct query. Scholarly databases and discovery services are good examples of this kind of resource, which you will almost inevitably use during your time at college. We look at ways in which these types of databases differ from the vast resource *databases* that constitute web-based search services, such as Google and Bing. We also discuss the importance of effective search strategies, including Boolean logic, advanced searching, and other useful tricks of the trade, to ensure that you never miss an important document.

In this chapter, you will:
- Reflect on your own search strategies for college assignments.
- Differentiate between information searching and browsing, and when each approach is appropriate.
- Identify scholarly databases and use them instead of the Web.
- Differentiate between subject terms and keywords when searching databases.
- Build and refine a search strategy using Boolean operators.
- Finesse searching using the advanced features and functions of scholarly databases.

8.2 QUICK REFLECTION: THINKING ABOUT RESEARCH STRATEGIES

Before we begin this chapter, let us take the opportunity to reflect on how you usually approach college assignments. For example, if you were given the following assignment by one of your instructors, how would you go about it?

> *"Write a two-page synopsis of the most up-to-date research findings on the Internet of Things (IoT)."*

While this might seem like a straightforward task, you want to be certain that you are on the right track. Take a few minutes to answer the following questions, which might help to shine some light on your information searching behavior:
- What is the *first* thing you would do when you begin this assignment?
- Which resource(s) would you turn to first?
- How would you go about searching the resources you have chosen?

- What do you think would be the *perfect* way to approach this task?
Perhaps your answers to the questions go something like this:
- "I would usually start by entering the term *Internet of Things* into the basic Google search box and see what the first search results tell me; Wikipedia usually provides a good overview and is quite up-to-date, which is important for this assignment. I would then work through the first page of search results and start to build a list of relevant links."
- "I always use Google and Wikipedia, and then I would search the online library catalog for information on the Internet of Things, although a lot of what I find there seems to be quite advanced, with very technical-sounding titles, and I don't know how far I need to go with this. So, I usually end up sticking with the Web resources. I pass over anything that I can't get straight away, which usually means that I don't use books."
- "I might enter the full phrase *up-to-date research about the Internet of Things* in the search box, just to see if anything interesting comes up. Sometimes I can get lucky this way. Google especially seems to be good at figuring out what I'm looking for."
- "The 'perfect way' would probably mean being familiar with the highest quality resources to search, which would give me pretty reliable information that my instructors would be happy to see. But I think you need to be an expert, or at least fairly knowledgeable on that topic, to really know what the best sources are."

Perhaps you answered the questions differently and would start with the library's resources. The important point to make is that you must *stop* and *think* before you begin an assignment. It is not wise to dive directly into searching before you have considered what the assignment requires and how you should approach it. Before we discuss the specifics of searching, we are going to look at two information problem scenarios—both of which you are likely to encounter—to give you an opportunity to think about the personal search strategy that will serve you best, depending on the task you are required to complete.

8.3 DIFFERENT TASKS REQUIRE DIFFERENT APPROACHES

The search strategy that you construct and the resources that you choose are usually determined by a number of factors: availability, time, format, and convenience, to name but a few. In college work, however, there are two fundamentally different scenarios that call for different approaches to information seeking. Consider the following situations.

8.3.1 Scenario 1

You have a list of *specific items* you need to find for a class or an assignment, for example, references you have come across through browsing, items on a reading list, and lecturers' recommendations. For example, your politics professor might have suggested that you read the following two resources on the subject of democracy in the digital age. Where can you go to get your hands (or eyes) on these items?

- Hague, B. N. & Loader, B. D. (1999). *Digital democracy: discourse and decision making in the information age.* London: Routledge (book).
- Burroughs, S., Brocato, K., Hopper, P. F. & Sanders, A. (2009). Media literacy: A central component of democratic citizenship. *The Educational Forum, 73*(2), pp.154–167 (journal article).

8.3.2 Scenario 2

You have an *information problem* that needs to be solved or a question that needs to be answered, but have no specific items to retrieve yet. For example, you might have been given an essay to write or a research project to complete. You are not sure what you should search for. All you have is the topic of the assignment, but nothing else. For instance, your communications professor has assigned this paper:

> *"Informed citizenship is impossible without digital literacy. Discuss."*

How do you approach each task? Let's explore the different search strategies that you can apply to each scenario.

8.4 HOW WE SEARCH: INFORMATION SEARCHING (QUERYING) VERSUS BROWSING

The basic difference in approach can be summarized by comparing *information searching* or *querying* to *browsing.* What do these terms mean?

Information searching, also referred to as *querying*, refers to well-defined, targeted information seeking for a clearly articulated information need, that is, when you have a fairly clear idea of the kind of information you need. Scenario 1 above, with *specific items*, falls into this category. However, information searching can also encompass searching when you do not yet have specific items to find but have clearly identified your information needs and are relatively certain about the type of information that you require. Rowley and Hartley (2008, p. 114) identify three different types of searches that fall into the category of information searching:

1. **Known-item search**: When you have sufficient details about an item to be able to identify and locate it, for example, author's name, title, ISBN, journal title, volume, and issue number.

2. **Factual search**: When you require information about concrete facts, for example, the population size of Iceland or the year in which the Empire State Building was constructed.

3. **Subject search**: This involves searching for information on a topic that you might not be able to define fully. This is the most challenging type of search because you cannot specify precisely what you need and what you can safely reject. Rowley and Hartley (2008) note that when you are subject searching you are (1) trying to retrieve enough relevant information while at the same time trying to (2) avoid retrieving too much or too little information—or too much *irrelevant* information. Most of the assignments you receive in college will call for subject searching; therefore we will spend some time discussing it.

In contrast to searching, *browsing* is *nontargeted searching*, where your information need is ill-defined or very general, or you are unfamiliar with the topic that you are researching. Browsing allows you to get a *feel* for a topic area, which ideally will develop into a more targeted and precise form of searching after a time. The aim of browsing is *discovery*. You skim and flick through information in the hope of discovering information that will help you with your task. In effect, you are looking for information resources that *you do not yet know exist*. Information searching, by comparison, involves looking for resources that you know for sure, or at least strongly suspect, are out there somewhere. Browsing allows for serendipity, "the occurrence and development of events by chance in a happy or beneficial way" (Soanes, Waite, & Hawker, 2001). We browse in the hope of being inspired or of unexpectedly stumbling across the perfect source. Following links through the Web, scanning the shelves in a library, reading through the tables of contents in books, scrolling through menus on a website—these are all examples of browsing behavior. Sometimes we need to start broad and narrow our search until we find that perfect source.

Most electronic search systems now support both information searching and browsing behaviors. Think of a website such as Amazon: you can, for example, choose either to search directly for an item by entering keywords or authors' names in the search box or, if you are not sure what you want to find, to browse through different departments or genres. websites like Amazon acknowledge the importance of browsing and serendipity by providing lists of items similar to the one you just clicked on under the heading "*Customers Who Bought This Item Also Bought*." The same applies to the systems that you will use for your college work. Depending on whether your information need is clearly defined or vague and general, as digital detectives you must know how to select the appropriate resources to search and how to develop efficient search strategies that will enable you to complete high-quality assignments.

8.5 SUBJECT SEARCHING

Subject searching refers to searching for information on topics when you have not fully articulated a precise information need and are unfamiliar with the subject areas or fields in question—for example, when you don't know who the main authors or journals are or when you are feeling your way around a new subject. This form of searching is at the heart of much research that is carried out in higher education. This need has long been recognized in academic libraries, which organize their collections according to *subject area* first. Perhaps you are familiar with the *Dewey Decimal* or *Library of Congress* classification schemes, which provide numerical and alphabetical schemas for organizing information items according to subject discipline. This is the notation that you see on the spine of a book or in a catalog record on a screen; it indicates a specific item's place in the collection and where it is shelved in the library.

It is important, therefore, that the electronic systems that you use in college support the need for subject searching; after all, most students at the beginning of their college careers do not have any knowledge of the key authors or books in a subject area and need a way to become familiar with their field before they can become proficient researchers. In the following sections we see how scholarly databases serve this exact purpose and how you can learn to become expert searchers in your subject areas.

8.6 DATABASES

Although the format has changed considerably over time, from printed bibliographies and indexes to CD-ROMs to online systems, databases have been at the center of academic research for many decades now.

A database is defined simply as "a structured set of data held in a computer" (Soanes *et al.*, 2001), or as "any collection of data that can be retrieved using organized search procedures" (Badke, 2004, p. 19). The concepts of *structure* and *organized search procedures* are central to these definitions. To get the very best out of any database that you use, it is essential to have, at a minimum, a basic understanding of how they are organized, as well as an understanding of the search functions that enable you to mine the information effectively and retrieve the best information for the task at hand.

Subscription databases are simply electronic collections of published journals, magazines, reports, newspapers, dissertations, books, images, conference papers, book reviews, and even raw data that are not freely available on the Web. Usually, only people who are enrolled in a large institution, such as a university, will have access to a wide range of subscription databases. The cost is often prohibitive to small institutions and most private individuals.

In the context of academic work, databases provide you with either *direct* or *indirect access* to resources (Fulton, 2010, p. 18).

8.6.1 Indirect-Access Databases

Indirect-access databases provide you with information *about* and directions *to* the items you are seeking, but they may not provide direct access to the original, full-text documents. You might need to take some further steps before you obtain the information you need. Examples of this sort of database include the following:

- **Bibliographic databases:** These databases include bibliographic information about documents, which tell you what the items are about and enable you to locate them—for example, the titles of journal papers, journal volume/issue, and page numbers. *Abstracts* provide a summary of the content of items that allow you to make a decision about whether to seek out the full item.
- **Catalog databases** (e.g., library online public access catalogs (OPACs)): OPACs provide information on the collections of items *held by libraries* or to which the library provides direct access via subscription or license. The information in catalog records contains the *shelf-mark*, which tells you where in the library you need to go to obtain the item in question. However, OPACs also usually provide direct links to the full text of electronic items to which they hold a subscription, such as journal articles, reports, and e-books.

8.6.2 Direct-Access Databases

Direct-access databases provide immediate access to the full text of the information items you are seeking (e.g., articles, e-books). Examples include the following:

- **Directory-type databases** (e.g., *Golden Pages* or *Yellow Pages* online): This type of database is like a directory, containing information such as the contact details of services, private individuals, and organizations.
- **Numeric and text-numeric databases**: Also known as databanks or data files, these databases contain materials such as raw data sets, research reports, stock market quotations, statistics, and annual reports. These types of databases might be used for tasks such as economic forecasting or market research.
- **Full-text databases**: This type of database provides access to complete information items, such as journal articles, conference papers, reports, newspaper articles, and e-books. Examples include JSTOR, Sage Journals Online, Nexis UK (newspapers), and Safari Books Online (e-books).
- **Multimedia databases**: These contain information in a variety of different formats, including text, video, and audio, among others.
- **Institutional repositories**: These are digital services in academic institutions that contain "a wide range of material that reflects the intellectual wealth of an institution—for example, journal articles submitted for publication, articles (pre-prints) accepted for publication (post-prints), conference papers, working papers, doctoral theses and dissertations, data sets resulting from research projects, etc." (SPARC Europe, 2015). Typically, academics and research staff in an institution deposit their own work in the repository to make it available for other people who also belong to the institution and anyone who has access to the repository. The repository offers a way of sharing research that is being carried out and is a rich source of scholarly information.

8.7 DATABASE VERSUS WEB

Why should you choose a database over the Web? Although we discussed the limitations of the Web for college work in Chapter 7, it is helpful to compare the two resources with regard to a number of important criteria. Table 8.1 focuses on the attributes you should consider when planning your research strategy.

Table 8.1 Databases Versus the Web

	Databases	Web
Trustworthiness	Contain primarily authoritative, scholarly materials by qualified authors, most (although not all) of which have been peer-reviewed. The resources contained in databases are carefully selected for inclusion by professionals, in accordance with strict criteria.	Provides access to multiple information formats and documents, many of which come from unverified or unqualified sources. Anyone with the equipment and know-how can post information on the Web. The creators of Web documents may not be qualified or sufficiently knowledgeable to write or speak authoritatively on topics.
Organization	Databases allow you to search through collections of materials that are highly organized and controlled through the use of standardized subject headings, descriptors, and other relevant fields. When the available search functions have been mastered, searching is efficient and precise.	Information on the Web is not organized in a standardized manner, and there are many different ways to search. The lack of standardized subject descriptors means it is difficult to be certain that all relevant sources have been retrieved.
Search features	A Typical scholarly database offers extensive search features, allowing you to search multiple fields, to refine searches to a very precise degree, to save and export searches and documents, and to link to full-text items where they are licensed by your institution.	Depending on the search engine, search functions on the Web can vary from extremely limited single search boxes to advanced search options that allow a greater degree of refinement. Generally speaking, however, Web search engines lack the sophistication and flexibility of scholarly databases.

Continued

Table 8.1 Continued

	Databases	Web
Coverage	Databases provide for in-depth and wide-ranging coverage of topics; depending on the database, coverage can reach back many decades and include documents that are difficult to find, such as conference papers and low-circulation journals.	Coverage of topics varies widely; in-depth information on scholarly topics is problematic because much is contained in the "hidden Web" and not accessible via search engines. Many important documents may be missed if you rely on the Web alone.
Relevance	The strict criteria for inclusion of scholarly materials and the sophistication of database search features mean that it is possible to construct searches that will retrieve only the most relevant documents in manageable quantities. To some extent, this does depend on the skill of the searcher.	A basic search may retrieve thousands of results, ranked by the search engine algorithms according to a conceptualization of relevance unique to that search service. The task of filtering search results on the Web to identify the most relevant documents for academic work is a major challenge.
Currency	Databases are updated regularly, with the most recently published information included as soon as possible.	Information on the Web may be updated only sporadically or not at all.

8.8 CHOOSING A DATABASE

Before you start searching through databases, you should ask yourself some questions to ensure that you are choosing the correct resources for your particular task:

- What is (are) your *information need(s)*? Do you have a problem to solve, a paper to write, or do you have to find a list of specific items?
- What *type* of information do you require? For instance, is it factual, historical, analytical, news reports, theoretical, statistical?
- What *subject areas* are relevant to your topic?

- What resources do you actually have *access* to?
- How *up-to-date* must the information be, or how far back do you need to go?
- Do you have time to *request* delivery of items that are not instantly available, or must you have access to full-text items?

8.9 WEB-SCALE DISCOVERY SERVICES

When you log into the website of your institutional library, you might notice at first that there does not seem to be any distinction between the different databases to which the library subscribes and the library online catalog itself; rather, you may find that you are given the option of entering your search query into a single search box that seems to cover everything. What you are using in this scenario is known as a Web-scale discovery service (WSD). This is defined as a service that is "designed to provide a simple Google-like search box, which enables library users to search all of the library's resources with a single query" (IEEE, n.d.). Vendors who currently offer WSD platforms to libraries include EBSCO's Discovery Service, Ex Libris Ltd's Primo Central Index, Serials Solutions' Summon, and OCLC's WorldCat Local. Similar to a metasearch engine on the Web, a WSD service allows you to search a *consolidated index* of virtually all of the databases and resources in the library's collection, and then it presents the results to you in a single list, ranked for relevance. The introduction of WSD services reflects the influence of the Web on our search behavior and our expectations of how online searching should work; for instance, when most of us think of online searching, we might recall first the Google interface. A WSD mimics this type of searching, but with the reassurance that the information we retrieve is scholarly and reliable. You should be aware, however, that licensing agreements could mean that the WSD service in your library might not actually include everything that the library holds or to which it provides access. Some publishers do not permit their content to be included in the WSDs provided by certain vendors.

8.10 CREATING YOUR *GO-TO* DATABASE LIST

When you are new to an academic discipline, you are unlikely to be familiar with the databases that are relevant to that subject. As you begin to understand more about your topic, however, you will slowly begin to develop a familiarity with the key databases, authors, and journals that should be at the core of your research strategy. A list of *go-to* databases—that is, the main resources that you should turn to first when you have a task to complete—becomes essential. You can start to build your list in the following ways:

- Your university or institutional library will provide a list of the databases to which you have access. These databases will be classified and searchable by *subject*. This should be your first point of call. Which databases relevant to your subject field are accessible to you locally?

- It is likely that your university or institutional library also has special subject pages or access points on their website, which will consolidate the key resources for individual subject areas, including subscription databases, into one user-friendly portal. Some libraries also create subject *pathfinders*, which are specialized bibliographies designed to help people do research in a particular subject area. Explore what pathfinders your library offers.

- Many libraries are now using the *LibGuides* publishing platform to create user-friendly online research guides for a variety of topics; these contain textual information, links to databases, video tutorials, and more. You should check whether your library has created any LibGuides for your subject area that might be useful.

- If your library provides access to it, the *Gale Directory of Databases* is a useful resource that contains information on databases in all subject areas that are available worldwide. You can use this resource to find out which databases have the best subject and geographic coverage, for example, or what time period is covered in each database.

- A number of scholarly databases are multidisciplinary and can be a good place to start if you are not sure where to go. The following are examples of databases that are not restricted to particular subject areas:

  Academic Search Complete
  JSTOR
  Academic OneFile
  Project Muse
  WorldCat
  Books in Print

8.11 BUILDING AND REFINING A SEARCH STRATEGY

"An important feature of information searching in an electronic environment is the interactive nature of the searching; that is to say, the searcher can amend the search in the light of results achieved" (Rowley & Hartley, 2008, p. 114).

One of the enormous advantages of scholarly databases is the excellent search features that allow you to refine your search strategy to gradually narrow down your list of results until they are precisely what you need to solve your information problem. In effect, *YOU* control the search outcome as you use your knowledge and skill to increase the precision of your search and thereby the relevance of the documents you retrieve. In this section we examine some of the search functions and operators that enable you to develop the perfect search.

8.11.1 Controlled Vocabularies

In terms of searching, one of the most important differences between databases and the Web is the use of *controlled vocabularies* (controlled indexing languages) in databases to index records or items. A controlled vocabulary is defined as "an organized arrangement of words and phrases used to index content and/or to retrieve content through browsing or searching" (Harpring, 2010). Basically, a controlled vocabulary consists of a list of *predetermined terms* or *descriptors* that are assigned to records in databases by human indexers to describe the content of those information items. If you think this sounds similar to *tagging* items online, you are on the right track, except that this kind of indexing is carried out by trained information professionals, rather than being user-generated. The aim of controlled vocabularies is to organize records in electronic systems in a consistent and standardized fashion so that items that are about similar topics are organized under the same headings and will, therefore, be easier for searchers to retrieve. Popular controlled vocabularies that are widely used in database indexing include the *Library of Congress Subject Headings* and *MeSH* (Medical Subject Headings). For instance, imagine you have two items with very different titles, but each effectively deals with the same subject, such as the following two items:

- Brabazon, T. (2013). *Digital dieting: From obesity to intellectual fitness.* Ashgate.
- Carr, N. G. (2010). *The shallows: What the Internet is doing to our brains.* New York: W. W. Norton.

You can see that classifying these books by *title* alone would not be useful for the searcher. For a start, there are no words in common in the titles and therefore no clue that they are about more or less the same topic. Unless you are already familiar with the books, you are unlikely to search by the author's name. As a result, a person who is searching a database or catalog for information on how digital information formats and systems are affecting our information behavior and how our minds work might not find *either* of these books, depending on the search words they enter. However, if a controlled vocabulary is used, both of the items could be assigned the same descriptors, such as *digital literacy* or *digital information* and *information behavior*. Someone using these terms to search the system has a much better chance of retrieving both items in their results list.

To maximize the efficiency of your search and retrieve the best results from scholarly databases, it is a good idea to play by the rules and use the terms that the system presents as controlled vocabulary. The downside of this approach, however, is that the controlled vocabulary terms used in the system might not be the terms *you* would use to describe the subject. To help with this potential problem, most databases provide an online *thesaurus*, or list of *subject terms*, which allows you to identify the correct subject terms or descriptors that are used in the system before you search. When you enter a term—for example, *Internet*—in the thesaurus, you might retrieve an entry that looks something like this:

Internet
> **Notes**
> Use term for:
>> Information superhighway
> **Related terms**:
> Chat rooms
> Intranets
> Invisible Web
> World Wide Web

The thesaurus confirms that *Internet* is a valid subject term used to describe information items in the database and advises you that this term should be used instead of other terms, such as Information superhighway, which you might be tempted to use instead. You may also wish to consult the list of *Related terms* if you want to broaden or narrow your search. In this case, the system suggests *chat rooms, intranets, invisible Web*, and *World Wide Web* as terms you might also consider using. This is a way of trying to figure out your information needs, similar to the way that Google provides you with suggested search terms when you begin to enter your query in the search box. You should get into the habit of querying the online thesaurus each time you use a database, before you begin to search for your topics.

8.11.2 Keyword Searching

You should not, however, confuse controlled vocabulary searching with *keyword* searching; the latter is not controlled, but it perhaps is more in tune with your own natural vocabulary—the words and phrases used in conversation on a daily basis. *Natural language searching* is often an attractive search option. Unlike controlled vocabulary searching, a keyword search allows you to search for important words (*key* words) *anywhere* in a database record, rather than just in the subject heading or descriptor fields—for example, in the title, abstract, authors' names, publisher details, and so on. You should note, however, that this type of searching does not pay any attention to the *meanings* of the terms, nor to the context of your search. The database search engine simply matches the words you enter with exactly the same words where they are found in the database records. For example, there is no way of controlling for homonyms—words that are spelled or pronounced in the same way but have different meanings from the one you are searching for. An example of a homonym would be the words *band* and *banned*—although pronounced the same, they have entirely different meanings. Keyword searching can, therefore, produce many results that are unrelated to your topic.

However, from another perspective, keyword searching can add an element of flexibility to your search when subject descriptors are a little too restrictive and do not quite capture what you want to find. For example, when subject descriptors are not specific enough, combining a subject descriptor with a particular keyword might enable you find the exact sources you want to find.

When you have a paper to write, your research should always begin with identifying the keywords in the paper title you have been given, even if you intend to use the subject descriptors in the database. Breaking your title into keywords will help you start thinking critically about the topic. If the given terms do not yield sufficient or relevant search results, you may find that you need to identify alternative terms to the ones in the title. Recalling the essay title suggested earlier in this chapter (*Informed citizenship is impossible without digital literacy. Discuss.*), you might build the following list of keywords:

Main keywords in title:
    Citizenship
    Digital literacy
Alternative and related keywords:
    Information literacy
    Political engagement
    Civil rights
    Social media
    Digital skills
    Advocacy
    Activism

When you have finished your list of keywords, you can go one step further and perhaps create *mind maps* with your keywords, connecting related topics until you build a diagram showing the links between different concepts and themes. This will also help you to develop the arguments and discussion for your paper, as you are inspired to "think outside the box."

8.11.3 Smart Searching with Boolean Logic

"Search logic is the means of specifying combinations of terms that must be matched for successful retrieval" (Rowley & Hartley, 2008, p. 156). When you have settled on the subject headings or keywords you wish to use, the next step is to construct search strings that narrow or broaden your search, until you are left with the list of results that are most suitable for your task.

In Chapter 3, when we discussed Google's Advanced Search, we noted how the interface gave you the option to specify webpages that "Contain *all* of the words that you enter," "Contain *any* of the words you enter," and "Contain *none* of certain words that you specify." Although you may not have been aware of it, what you are doing here is applying *Boolean logic* to your search through combining and excluding specific terms from the search string that you are entering. The following are the main *Boolean operators* that allow us to expand and refine our searches:

OR: Combining search terms using the *OR* operator retrieves all items that contain *any* of the terms you have entered. If you enter three terms, results that contain only one or two of the words will still be retrieved, as well as those that contain all three. This search strategy *broadens* a search and is therefore a common starting point in any search, but it can mean that you may obtain items that are not really relevant to your topic. This operator is useful, however, when you are not sure what the correct term is for the topic you are researching; for example, do you say *digital* information or *electronic* information? What about *footpath* or *sidewalk*? The OR operator is often used to combine synonyms (different words that have the same meaning) to ensure that you don't miss out on an important item. A search string using the OR operator would appear as shown below and would retrieve any records in a selected database containing the phrases *digital literacy* or *digital skills*:

"digital literacy" OR *"digital skills"*

AND: Combining search terms using the AND operator retrieves all information items that contain *all* of the terms you have requested; that is, this approach *narrows* a search. You will not retrieve records that contain just one or two of the search terms you have entered. A search using AND would look like the example below, using quotation marks to specify that *digital literacy* should be treated as a phrase. This search will only retrieve items containing the terms *digital literacy* and *citizenship*; items that contain only one search term or the other will not be retrieved:

"digital literacy" AND citizenship

NOT: The *NOT* operator combines search terms to retrieve items which *exclude* items that you specify; that is, this operator *narrows* a search by getting rid of items that you do not wish to retrieve. Suppose you want to search for information on *social media*, but you want to exclude mentions of Twitter. Your search string would look like this:

"social media" NOT Twitter

8.11.4 Building Search Strings

If you want to build longer search strings, where you first broaden, then narrow, a search, for example, you can use parentheses or brackets to tell the search engine which operation to perform first. For instance, we could combine some of our previous searches as follows:

("digital literacy" OR "digital skills") AND citizenship

The operation enclosed in parentheses is always performed first, followed by the other operation in the search string. Here is another example:

((Facebook OR Instagram OR Pinterest) and "team communication") NOT Twitter

In this case, we use two sets of parentheses to tell the search engine what to do first, then second, and finally third. First, search hits for *Facebook OR Instagram OR Pinterest* are retrieved. This search result then is combined with the phrase *team communication*, and then the term *Twitter* is removed from this result.

Always ensure that you have used the NOT operator to appropriately exclude undesired terms. For example, compare the following two search strings:

(Facebook OR Instagram) AND photos NOT Twitter

((Facebook OR Instagram) AND photos) NOT Twitter

The order in which search operations are completed is as follows: NOT, AND, OR. In the first search string, the NOT operator is executed first: *photos NOT Twitter*. However, if your goal is to exclude Twitter from your entire search, then only the second search string will achieve this goal. As shown in the second search string, remember to use parentheses to ensure that search operations are executed in the order you want, as well as on the parts or whole of the search intended.

In most of the databases you use, you will not be required to enter long and convoluted search strings; instead, you will have the option of simply entering your chosen words and phrases into individual search boxes using drop-down menus to select Boolean operators, which can be combined as you wish. You can almost always *add a row* if your search is more complicated than just one or two terms. However, it is essential to understand what effect these combiners have on your search results when you use them.

8.12 ADVANCED SEARCH FUNCTIONS

For quick and easy reference, let's highlight some of the other search functions and notable features of databases to make your search strategy even more effective.

- **Phrase searching**: Phrase searching, noted by quotation marks surrounding the terms you wish to search as a phrase (e.g., "*digital literacy*") allows you to ensure that your search terms appear together in the document. This approach helps to narrow a search, excluding documents where both terms appear, but not together.
- **Adjacency or proximity operators**: These operators are used to specify where terms should be located, including *near, after, before, around,* and *adjacent* to a specified term. For example, the Google *AROUND* operator allows you to find webpages that include words or phrases near to each other by enabling you to specify the maximum number of words

that separate the two search terms. For example, you might have a search string such as *"digital literacy" AROUND(5) "European Union,"* which would retrieve only webpages that include the two phrases separated by five or fewer words.

- **Truncation**: This function enables you to search for variants of the same term, such as plural forms. Truncation symbols, such as ⋆ or *?*, are added to the stem of a term for searching; for example, *Librar⋆* will retrieve items containing the words *library*, *libraries*, *librarian*, and *librarianship*. Take care, however, with the stem you use; for example, if you want to search for *cats*, locating both singular and plural forms, you might think *cat⋆* would return the desired results. However, using truncation in this way will also retrieve items with the words *catalog*, *catastrophe*, *Catholicism*, and so on, as well as variants of these words. Some databases provide specific truncation marks for searching plural forms of terms; otherwise, it can be better to search for singular and plural forms of a term, for example, *cat OR cats*.

  It is important to be aware that truncation symbols can vary according to the database or search engine; for example, Google uses asterisks for *wildcard words* rather than for individual characters. Remember to check the search engine's online *Help* to determine the correct symbol to use.

- **Wildcards**: Wildcards work in a similar way to truncation in that a symbol is used to search for words that can be spelled in different ways. However, the symbol is usually inserted within the word to replace a single letter, rather than after the stem. A good example is searching for terms that have American and United Kingdom spellings, particularly when it comes to the letter *u*:

favo⋆rite

In this instance, the use of a wildcard retrieves *favorite* as well as *favourite*.

humo⋆r

The use of a wildcard here retrieves *humour* as well as *humor*.

In addition, you can use a wildcard to retrieve the singular and plural forms of some words, for example, *woman* as well as *women*:

wom⋆n

- **Search limiters**: Most databases allow you to select options to limit or narrow your search even further, for very precise results. For example, you almost always are able to limit your search by publication date(s); document type (e.g., article, book review); publication or source type (e.g., journal, book, newspaper); language; as well as by instructing the system to retrieve only items that are scholarly and have been peer-reviewed. Some databases permit you to limit a search to those items to which your library can provide access; most databases provide a direct link to your library's collections in order to search for the item you have selected.

8.13 OTHER DATABASE OPTIONS

- **Saving search results**: All scholarly databases offer you the option to save or export search results in some format; for example, you will be able to:
    Email database results to a specified email address
    Save to your device or to a memory stick
    Export your results directly into bibliographic management software, such as Ref Works and EndNote, for easy management
    Print your search results
- **Reference harvesting**: Also known as *snowballing*, this is a more advanced search process that involves "locating, tracking and chasing down references in the footnotes and bibliographies of articles and other documents" (HLWiki International, 2015) in order to expand a search. When searching databases, you can carry out a similar type of searching through examining the records of the references that you find useful. For instance, what subject descriptors were assigned to the article? Could you use them to carry out a better search in the database? Scanning through the list of references at the end of the article in question, then searching the database to locate the relevant ones is also a useful approach.
- **EarlyCite**: In some databases, you may find that you have an option to limit your results to "EarlyCite." This is a useful feature provided by the publisher Emerald, allowing you to access journal articles before they have been officially published in Emerald's journals. The articles may be available in their final proofed and edited publication form up to a full year before publication.
- **SmartText searching**: In EBSCO databases, SmartText searching allows you to search for as much text as you want, rather than for single words— for instance, a phrase, a sentence, paragraph, or even *whole pages* of items.

8.14 KEY DATABASES FOR SUBJECT DISCIPLINES

To round out this chapter, below is a useful list of some of the important databases that you can use for a few of the different subject disciplines that you may study in college. Do not forget the multidisciplinary databases we mentioned earlier! Remember to explore your institutional library's digital collection to see what is available to you there:

Business and Economics
ABI/INFORM Global
Academic Search Complete
Business Source Complete
EconLit
Emerald Management Xtra
Computer Science
ACM Digital Library
Computer and Information Systems Abstracts
Education
British Education Index
Education Index with Full-text
ERIC (Educational Resources Information Center) and ERIC International
Law
HEINOnline
Justis
Lexis Library
Westlaw UK
Sociology
International Bibliography of the Social Sciences
Sociological Abstracts
Social Sciences Full-text
STEM Subjects (Science, Technology, Engineering, Medicine)
American Chemical Society Journals
ArXiv
Biological Sciences Abstracts
Biosis Citation Index
British National Formulary
Cochrane Library
Ei Compendex
Construction Information Service (IHS)

DynaMed
Electronics and Communications Abstracts
EMBASE—Excerpta Medica
IEEE Xplore
MEDLINE (Ovid)
PsycINFO
Reaxys
ScienceDirect Journals
SciFinder Scholar (CAS)
Scopus
SpringerLINK
Technology Research Database
Web of Science

8.15 CHALLENGES

1. Using the resources available to you at your own institution, create a *go-to* database list for one of the following subject areas:
   a. Climate control
   b. Human-computer interaction (HCI)
   c. Psychology of addiction
   d. Democracy
2. Individually or in a group, create an outline of a *LibGuide* for your major subject or a subject area of your choice. Sample LibGuides can be searched at this link:http://libguides.com/community. What resources would you include in your LibGuide?
3. Plan a research strategy for the following essay topic by answering the list of questions below:

   "Social networking leads to an increased sense of isolation, rather than an enhanced sense of community. Discuss this statement, with reference to popular social networking sites of your choice."

   a. Select the database(s) available in your institution that you believe would be most useful for this topic. Why did you choose these databases?
   b. What keywords could you include in your search query?
   c. What subject terms or descriptors in your selected databases are most appropriate for this topic? Is a thesaurus available?
   d. What options do you have for Boolean searching in your selected database?

e. List 10 of the most suitable sources that you found for this essay by searching your chosen database(s). How did you determine the relevance of search results?

f. Which database produced the best results? Explain why.

REFERENCES

Badke, W. B. (2004). *Research strategies: Finding your way through the information fog.* New York: iUniverse, Inc.

Fulton, C. (2010). *Information pathways: A problem-solving approach to information literacy.* Lanham: Scarecrow Press.

Harpring, P. (2010). *Introduction to controlled vocabularies: Terminology for art, architecture, and other cultural works.* J. Paul Getty Trust. Retrieved from http://www.getty.edu/research/publications/electronic_publications/intro_controlled_vocab/index.html.

Head, A. J. & Eisenberg, M. B. (2009). *Lessons learned: How college students seek information in the digital age. Project information literacy first year report with student survey findings.* University of Washington's Information School. Retrieved from: http://projectinfolit.org/images/pdfs/pil_fall2009_finalv_yr1_12_2009v2.pdf.

HLWiki International. (2015). *Snowballing.* Retrieved from http://hlwiki.slais.ubc.ca/index.php/Snowballing.

Institute of Electrical and Electronics Engineers (IEEE). (n.d.). *Discovery services.* Retrieved from http://ieeexplore.ieee.org/Xplorehelp/#/tools/toolsForAdministratorsAndLibrarians/discoveryServices.

Rowley, J. E., & Hartley, R. J. (2008). *Organizing knowledge: An introduction to managing access to information.* Hampshire: Ashgate.

Soanes, C., Waite, M., & Hawker, S. (2001). *The Oxford dictionary, thesaurus, and wordpower guide.* Oxford: Oxford University Press.

SPARC Europe. (2015). *Institutional repositories.* Retrieved from http://sparceurope.org/repositories.

CHAPTER 9

All Play and No Work

9.1 THE DILEMMA: 'SOCIAL NETWORKING SITES ARE JUST FOR FUN AND FRIENDS. I CAN'T USE SITES FOR COLLEGE WORK, CAN I?'

This chapter introduces you to a plethora of tools, resources, and apps that fall under the banner of *social media* and explores the ways in which these social media tools can be used to support your learning and research. While social media are often primarily connected with leisure time and your social life, this chapter offers an alternative viewpoint: Formal learning can be enhanced dramatically through the effective use of a range of tools, including social sharing and bookmarking sites, collaborative authoring tools, blogging software, and many more. In addition, you will be asked to consider the issue of your own online presence and the digital footprint you leave behind when you spend time online. Strategies for managing your online reputation will help you to develop a positive digital image.

In this chapter, you will:
- consider the place of social media in academic settings.
- explore a range of social media tools for use in your academic studies.
- briefly consider your own digital footprint.
- develop an online presence to facilitate academic study and future workplace participation.

9.2 WHAT DO WE MEAN BY *SOCIAL MEDIA*?

Social media, now several years old, has become a household term. The phrase *social media* is used to describe a range of online tools that facilitate interactive and participative data sharing, creation and management, as well as social networking. You have likely used common social media tools, such as Facebook, Twitter, and Instagram to communicate and socialize. There is a multitude of social media tools, each created to offer a particular means of communication, networking, and sharing.

We may think of apps as social media. Apps are actually the software manifestations of social media tools. In other words, an app is a piece of

Digital Detectives
ISBN 978-0-08-100124-0

software that you can add to an iOS or Android platform. The app facilitates mobility, enabling you to use a particular piece of software on the go. For instance, you may rely on your personal computer to access a social networking site, such as Twitter, but an app installed on a tablet computing device, such as an iPad, allows you instant access in any location.

9.3 SOCIAL MEDIA FOR LEISURE AND LEARNING

While social media often are associated with leisure time, social media tools also have applications that are useful for work and academic study. For instance, social media tools have been applauded for having a potential positive impact on student learning. In fact, a study of first-year undergraduates revealed that students expect their instructors to integrate technologies, including social media tools, into their classroom learning (Gabriel *et al.*, 2012). However, this same study found that students use different technologies in (e.g., most often the Internet, email, word processing, math and science programs, mobile phones, and electronic databases) and outside (e.g., most often email, Internet, social media, SMS and talking on mobile phones, and instant messaging) the classroom, as well as for different purposes. For example, students used technologies in the classroom to collect, select, and store information, but they used technologies outside the classroom to communicate and socialize (Gabriel *et al.*, 2012). Clark *et al.* (2009, p. 56) similarly found what they termed a *digital dissonance*—a 'tension with respect to learners' appropriation of Web 2.0 technologies in formal contexts.'

It is clear that a variety of technologies, including social media tools, hold an important place in our learning, but how we effectively integrate these technologies to support our learning is a challenge. *Social media literacy* is increasingly becoming critical to our learning; Rheingold (2010) identifies five essential *literacies of social media* that accompany learning:

- **Attention**: This is an ability to know when and where to focus our attention, for example, on our mobile devices or classroom discussion or lectures. Without focus, we may become overwhelmed.
- **Participation**: This is an ability to participate effectively. Through positive participation, we can move from digital consumer to digital citizen.
- **Collaboration**: Social media can enhance wide social collaboration, connecting people who are geographically dispersed and including individuals of different age groups, social backgrounds, and so on. This

collaboration can enhance the social outcomes of activities, that is, progressing activities in ways that are not achievable by individuals alone.

- **Network awareness**: This refers to understanding how a social network works and the influence of these social networks in the digital context. Because membership in a social network can mean wide visibility, it is essential to develop literacy around how we can set network boundaries, for example, using privacy settings to set limits.
- **Critical consumption**: This refers to our evaluation of who to trust and what information to trust in the online environment. Critical consumption returns us to *Attention* and our selection of where to focus our attention, which Rheingold (2010) refers to as *sampling the flow* of social media.

Part of our task is to identify which social media tools can support our learning of the social media literacies described by Rheingold (2010). In some cases, tools are directly focussed on learning; other tools are more generic, but may be used in different life contexts for different purposes. Let's consider some of the tools you might adopt to support your learning needs.

9.4 USING SOCIAL MEDIA TOOLS AND APPS TO SUPPORT MY LEARNING

There are literally dozens of social media tools and apps that can support your learning. While you may already use some social media, now is a good time to explore further options and select the tools that best suit your learning. Remember that one tool is unlikely to address all potential learning needs. And social media tools, while covering a range of topics, are not well integrated—meaning that you need to select tools to cover different aspects of learning.

A key task in this section is to identify the various types of social media tools at your disposal to enable selection of particular tools that may be most useful for your educational purposes. It should be noted that some tools have overlapping functionalities. As a result, selection is not a straightforward task.

9.4.1 Selection Criteria: Your Learning Needs

Before exploring potential social media tools, it is essential to identify now how you want a given tool to assist you in university. To help you achieve academic excellence at university, three key areas of learning must be considered:

1. **Time management**: Managing your time effectively at university is central to juggling all of your academic responsibilities. Social media tools can help organize daily time commitments, including class scheduling, deadlines, and meetings with project and study teams, among others.

2. **Learning acquisition in and outside the classroom**: Social media tools that assist with note taking, information storage and management, reading articles, and so on can help you to process information in the academic context, both in the formal classroom and in your studies outside lecture time.

3. **Assessment**: Assessment may depend on your use of particular pieces of software, for example, statistical software for analysing numerical data. There are various social media apps that can help you, whether you need to analyze numerical or textual data, write essays or prepare visual presentations.

Make a list of the functions you require in a social media tool, given your academic needs, and compare those criteria against the features provided by each social media tool you examine.

9.4.2 Identifying Social Media Tools and Apps

To match learning needs to social media tools and apps, an understanding of the different types of tools and their function(s) is needed. Below is listed a range of social media tools and apps by function. The items noted represent examples only; new social media tools and apps are created continuously. We strongly advise you to start your selection process here, but then to continue to monitor for other software that may be useful for your studies.

9.4.2.1 Time Management Tools

Managing your time effectively is critical to your success at university. Ideally, a balance between academic and personal activities is desirable. Attending to your scholarly needs will help you to achieve good grades. And while a social life at university is often characterized as a more frivolous part of university life, social activities, including clubs and special events, can actually add value to your education, by helping you get to know other people, develop communication skills, and learn skills associated with particular activities. Your challenge is to juggle all of these academic and social commitments. Luckily, there's an app for that!

A first task here is to organize a calendar of events, deadlines, and commitments. Any calendar application will help, particularly something you can use via computer and mobile device. For instance, GWhizz is a free mobile app that links multiple social media tools in one venue, including Google Calendar, allowing you to move seamlessly from, for example, calendar to email to Google search to Twitter.

Google Calendar on its own has much to offer, integrating into your calendar information from other Google tools, in addition to the items you manually schedule. For example, Google Calendar draws on the information in your Gmail contacts to create automatic calendar dates for birthdays of your contacts and on your email message content to note things like flight times you have organized. In addition, Google Calendar enables you to create multiple calendars, each colour-coded and accessible to an audience you select. As you add events for meetings and deadlines, your classmates with collaborative access to a given calendar can simultaneously add events as well.

Whatever your favoured calendar tool, the important issue here is to create and maintain a calendar. Keeping track of assessment deadlines, lectures, and other events will help you to juggle all of the different university activities that demand your attention. Check your calendar daily. Use functions like Google Calendar's reminder to receive reminders for immediately scheduled events, as well as a daily digest of events to your Gmail account. Importantly, count backward from final deadlines to identify key points for completion of reading, draft assessment, and so on.

9.4.2.2 Social Networking Sites

Communication through social sharing and networking is at the heart of social sharing sites. Tools, like Facebook, Twitter, and Whatsapp, are great for keeping in touch with others, tracking current events, and sharing information. Although they provide social outlets, these tools can consume hours of valuable time, potentially eroding study time. Sometimes, use of these tools is forbidden in the classroom. Honestly assess your own use of these tools; to what degree is your focus on a task diminished when you are checking your account on these tools at varying intervals? Maintaining complete focus on the work at hand in the classroom or any learning environment is vital. However, this does not preclude incorporating these tools into your learning where appropriate.

Social media networking tools can actually prove quite helpful in particular learning situations. For instance, a Facebook group can be used effectively to manage team collaboration. Students also find the instant messaging offered through WhatsApp, for example, helpful in maintaining lines of group communication and quickly alerting each other to team project needs. Social networking tools are valuable for collaborative learning, because they enable immediate communication, even when team members are geographically dispersed. Free accounts and usage commonly associated with these tools make them even more popular.

9.4.2.3 Social Capturing and Sharing of Content

The content available online is diverse, often free to access and potentially informative. Capturing content varied in form and type and managing that content remains an area of interest among those trying to find the perfect information management system. The concept of personal information management described by Jones (2008) is helpful here. Personal information management embraces the organization and management of information at the individual level. In other words, we construct our own ways to sort, store, and keep or delete information as relevant to our own understanding and categorization of information. Social media tools can be very helpful to us, as we attempt to assert our own version of control over information.

Social bookmarking of websites and Web content has long offered a simple way to capture and organize content thematically. Delicious, formerly called del.icio.us, was founded in 2003 and represents an early social bookmarking tool that provided a means of collecting Web links and organizing this content. Pinterest, launched in 2010, is a more recent social content tool that focusses on the capture and organization of visual material. Following a thumbtack bulletin board approach, Pinterest members 'pin' content to 'boards' customized thematically by the user. One of the criticisms of Pinterest has been the frequent breach of copyright by pinners, who may not only post content without attribution to its creator, but also share or 'repin' this content throughout the Pinterest community. In an academic context, a social bookmarking tool may be useful for monitoring and collecting information on a given topic. Just take care with copyright; ensure you understand the source of the information you collect and reference it appropriately.

Collecting items in their entirety, as opposed to links to content, may be preferable for convenience, although sufficient storage space is needed to maintain this form of collection on your mobile device and elsewhere. Various reader devices, like the very popular the Kindle, and social media apps are available to assist you with managing your selected e-materials, ranging from news feeds to books. For instance, the Kindle reader is a mobile device that is commonly used to download and read e-books. However, the Kindle reader is not necessarily essential for reading books or articles; the Kindle app supports the same e-reading via Android and iOS devices. The choices do not end there. Other apps enable reading of various types of materials. For instance, Pocket allows you to collect, view, and organize news articles, videos and images. Even a commonly known and used software tool, such as the Adobe Reader app, facilitates reading of items in PDF format, as well as marking up text with coloured highlighting.

9.4.2.4 Collaborative Authoring Tools: Wikis
The wiki is a software tool that enables collaborative creation and management of content. Typically, wiki software provides a 'sandbox' area where one or multiple people can develop content together. Content creation in this environment is often called 'collaborative,' because authorship is shared; as a result, wikis are known also as collaborative authoring tools. Possibly the best known example of a wiki is Wikipedia. Wikipedia is an online encyclopedia for which authorship is collaborative and anonymous. We already explored Wikipedia as a space for participatory content creation and management, as well as its potential as a source of information for university work, in Chapter 4.

One of the tasks you might be asked to do during your university studies is to generate a specified piece of content with others in a team. If your university subscribes to an educational content system, such as Blackboard, you may use the wiki tool provided. Wikispaces also offers a standalone wiki tool that supports collaborative information generation. Wikispaces has useful and easy-to-use features, such as design templates that add colour to information and page linking to facilitate the organization of information. If you have the option to select the wiki tool you use, be sure to explore a range of wiki tools before settling on one. Wikipedia offers a helpful list of wiki tools at http://en.m.wikipedia.org/wiki/List_of_wiki_software; Wikipedia also provides a list of sites using wiki software at http://en.m.wikipedia.org/wiki/List_of_wikis, which is useful for thinking about the different ways in which you might choose to use a wiki.

9.4.2.5 Blogging Software
Blogging is a form of diary keeping that provides an electronic space for people to express themselves. Some use blogs to write about their own life events; however, blogs are also used for a wide array of purposes. For example, in business, blogs may be used to market goods and announce new

products. Journalists and writers may use blogs to document news, hobbies, and other far-ranging topics. For instance, a hobbyist who likes to knit may share projects, including step-by-step instructions and pictures, via a blog. A blog may provide useful learning support in an informal context.

Depending on the blog topic, audience, and reader interest, blogs may have significant followers, which can serve to raise the profile of a given blog. Some websites offer annual ranked lists of top blogs, both general blogs and blogs on particular topics, for instance, *eBiz/MBA: The eBusiness Guide* (http://www.ebizmba.com/articles/blogs). Some well-known blogs include, for instance, the Huffington Post (www.huffingtonpost.co.uk). To identify blogs in your area(s) of interest, try Google's Blog Finder search tool at www.google.com/blogsearch.

Blogs may be created via various software tools; for example, *WordPress* (https://WordPress.com) and Google's *Blogger* (www.blogger.com)provide free blogging tools; *Typepad* (www.typepad.com) and *Squarespace* (www. squarespace.com) offer subscription blogging services. Google's Blogger represents an early blogging tool specifically set up for blogging. Websites still provide a means of publishing a blog. A website has the advantage of giving the blogger complete control over site appearance and functionality, whereas blogging tools usually offer templates to customize a blog. Blogging software tools do vary in how appearance may be customized, although there are common functionalities across platforms. Experiment and opt for a blogging tool that meets your preferences.

Once you have set up your blogging space, your next task is to start blogging. Normally, a blog entry contains the following elements:

- **Header**: This is the title for your blog entry. Add a meaningful title for each entry. This is an important first opportunity to attract the reader's attention.
- **Blog Post**: This is the main area of your blog entry, where you create content. You may wish to include text as well as content, such as pictures or video.
- **Permalink**: This is the URL or Web address specifying the location of your blog entry on the Internet.
- **Date of posting**: This is the time stamp for your blog entry, documenting when you published the post.
- **Blog Comments**: This is a participative space in which you and your readers may comment on the content of your blog entry.

Figure 9.1 shows a sample blog entry, which has the usual characteristics of a blog outlined above.

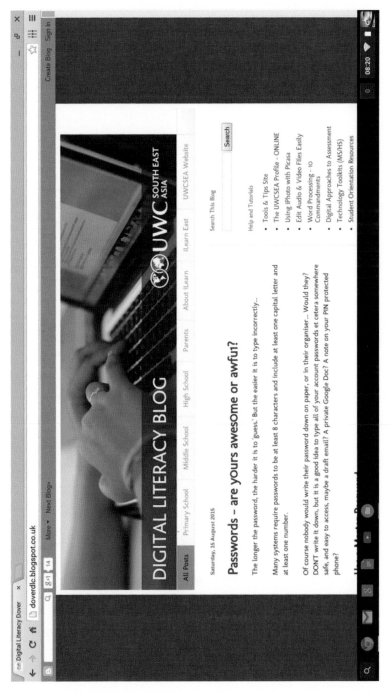

Figure 9.1 A sample blog post.

9.5 SOCIAL MEDIA APPS TO FACILITATE INFORMATION FINDING

Various information sources have set up apps to enable you to locate information on the move. With mobile devices, such as iPads and mobile phones, it is possible to keep a range of tools at your fingertips for quick reference. The key for you as a university student is to identify those apps, whether general apps or subject-specific apps, that support your studies.

To identify a core of information sources to support your academic work, consider the types of information needed in your subject area. For instance, film studies students will want the app for the *Internet Movie Database (IMDb)*, which, like the IMDb website, provides information about various performance media, including television and film. Economics and accountancy students may find XE.com's Currency app useful for working with financial information. Geography students have multiple choices, including *Google Maps*, available via website or app, Mobius's *Sky Map* of celestial bodies, disaster alert maps, travel guides, and so on. There are many apps for students studying languages, including translation websites and apps, sign language tutorials, and specific language-training apps. The possibilities for most subjects are endless.

9.5.1 General Study and Information Finding Tools

Every student should have close at hand a dictionary for study and assessment purposes; various apps provide dictionary access, such as *Oxford Dictionaries Quick Search*, by the well-known and trusted publisher Oxford University Press. The well-known TED Talks website and app provide video access to short talks and lectures by industry and scholarly experts on a host of topics.

9.5.2 File Management and Sharing Tools

Sharing information holds an important place in learning. For instance, you may wish to share a project between yourself and a co-author. You may also wish to co-edit material stored in the same file. File management and sharing tools facilitate the sharing and editing of files.

Two popular tools stand out among file management and sharing software frequently adopted as support tools: *Dropbox* and *Google Drive*. Both enable cloud storage of multiple file formats (that is, digital storage of material and access to that material from any location), organization of items by folder, and sharing with one or more individuals. Both offer varied services via computer login and mobile app; for example, Dropbox allows file sharing, but this function cannot be implemented via mobile app. Both come with free file storage; Dropbox encourages its members to earn space by inviting friends and colleagues to join. Both offer file sharing and editing by file members; Google Drive even allows simultaneous edits by different file members and saves changes automatically so that edits are not lost.

Why use these tools? Storing information *in the Cloud* or in a virtual location has advantages and disadvantages. This form of file storage offers the benefit of anytime, anywhere access, locally and via the Internet through your computer and via the Internet through your mobile device. There is no need to carry files with you on a memory stick or other physical storage device, which can be easily lost or broken. Remember, however, that computerized devices update Cloud files only when connected to the Internet, meaning that you need to connect to your Internet-based file storage space to ensure that you are working with the latest version of your work or to store the latest version in the Cloud.

9.6 BEST FOOT FORWARD: MANAGING YOUR DIGITAL PERSONA

There is currently a tendency for people to live their lives through social media, or so it would seem. While the technologies supporting an Internet presence encourage us to reveal information about ourselves, too many also give up that information without questioning this demand for access to our personal details. Research continues to show that students need and want guidelines around how to create and foster a professional online presence (e.g., Prescott *et al.*, 2012). With so many varied apps and software programmes, the process of establishing a personal comfort zone regarding privacy and access across the board can be a challenge. Your online presence leaves a trail; now is the time to take steps to manage your digital persona.

9.6.1 Controlling Your Digital Footprint

Protecting your online reputation is essential. While it may seem that pictures and posts distributed by you or your friends are harmless, this material can come back to haunt you in future. If you believe that content is lost as new posts push old posts down a viewing list, think again. Out of sight does not mean out of mind.

Some key things to think about **BEFORE** you press the POST button:

- **Consider who will have access to this content once you have posted it on the Internet.** Prescott *et al.* (2012) noted that students often leave default privacy settings in social media tools, such as Facebook, which leaves their content open to the public. Always review the privacy settings for each social media tool you adopt and revise them to protect your digital footprint.
- **Stop and reflect on how you may feel about your future self and this content.** How could this content potentially affect your future career prospects? While this may not seem important to you while you are a student, later you will be glad you critically assessed the nature of content before posting it.
- **Be vigilant about self-protection.** Once content has been posted, you no longer have real control over it. Think of all content as *forever posted* and be selective about what you post.
- **Give your posts a time out.** Use a social media tool, such as Buffer (www.bufferapp.com), to schedule your postings to other tools, such as Facebook, Twitter, and LinkedIn. By scheduling posts to occur in the future, you allow yourself time to pause and reconsider posts as necessary.
- **Choose the venue(s) for your posted content carefully.** It is possible to enhance your digital footprint through social media (e.g., Benson & Filippaios, 2010). LinkedIn (www.linkedin.com) provides a space in which you can develop your professional image. Remember that employers increasingly check prospective employees' Facebook and other social media spaces as well to double check their fit with the organization. Do not let yourself down by posting inappropriate content that may compromise your job prospects. And remember: your future employers know how to use Google, too! Even keeping your personal and professional online spaces separate does not prevent detection of your online trail.
- **Think about creating a positive digital footprint.** What does the content you wish to post say about you? Choose content that helps to develop a positive image of you.

Digital footprints and online reputation management are discussed more fully in Chapter 11.

9.6.2 Beware! Trolls are No Longer Confined under Bridges

While you are busy posting your thoughts, pictures, and other information to the Internet, others are potentially viewing and commenting on your content. Take care with whom you decide to share or grant access to your digital spaces and information. Trolls and cyberbullies exist and can pose a significant threat to your online persona.

Avoid strangers who are trolls and cyberbullies, by setting your privacy settings in all tools, so that access to your content is limited to people on your friends list. Remember that social media tools are not integrated, meaning that you must perform this action in every social media tool you use. In addition, take care with whom you accept on your friends list. Accept only people you actually know. Decline other friendship requests until you have explored their identities and have determined that you are not dealing with unscrupulous individuals.

Always address trolling and cyberbullying, reporting instances to group mediators or customer relations for a given social media tool. This includes inappropriate postings to your space or about you to other spaces. The issue is serious and can have severe, life-threatening outcomes. Legislation has begun to address some of these trolling and cyberbullying issues to help prevent social harm. For instance, in the United Kingdom, the Criminal Justice and Courts Act includes rules to enable prosecution of individuals who post *revenge porn* or inappropriate sexual content about others on the Internet (see, for example, Ministry of Justice, 2015).

9.7 CHALLENGES

Having considered various applications of social media tools in the academic setting, now select appropriate social media tools and identify how you might use them effectively to solve the following problems.

1. Locate and evaluate 10 top apps to add to your mobile device. Each app should support your work as a student, whether as a general information tool or as an application tool designed for your particular subject area. For each app you choose, note how you will use this app in your studies and how the app offers something critical and distinct from other similar apps.

2. You have been assigned to a team to complete a collaborative assessment. What social media tool might you suggest to the team for communication between team meetings? How would you integrate this tool into your project work?

3. You have been asked to write a reflection on your learning in the course of completing a particular piece of assessment. What social media tool

could you use to track your learning progress? How might you share your reflection with your instructor for grading?

4. You have been asked to prepare an assessment that will be graded online. Specifically, you must collect recipes for famous international dishes, linking the recipe instructions to visual content, including pictures and the geographic origins of the recipes. What social media tools might you combine to address the different aspects of your project?

REFERENCES

Benson, V., & Filippaios, F. (2010). Effects of digital footprint on career management: evidence from social Media in business education. Knowledge management, information systems. *E-Learning, and Sustainability Research Communications in Computer and Information Science, 111,* 480–486. Retrieved from https://kar.kent.ac.uk/28769/1/TECHEDU.pdf.

Clark, W., Logan, K., Luckin, R., Mee, A., & Oliver, M. (2009). Beyond Web 2.0: mapping the technology landscapes of young learners. *Journal of Computer Assisted Learning, 25*(1), 56–69.

Gabriel, M. A., Campbell, B., Wiebe, S., MacDonald, R. J., & McAuley, A. (2012). The role of digital technologies in learning: expectations of first year university students. *Canadian Journal of Learning and Technology, 38*(1), 1–18. Retrieved from http://www.cjlt.ca/index.php/cjlt/article/view/637/335 (19.08.15.).

Jones, W. (2008). *Keeping found things found: The study and practice of personal information management.* London: Elsevier Inc.

Ministry of Justice. (2015, October 12). *New law to tackle revenge porn.* Retrieved from https://www.gov.uk/government/news/new-law-to-tackle-revenge-porn.

Prescott, J., Wilson, S., & Becket, G. (2012). Students want more guidelines on facebook and online professionalism. *The Pharmaceutical Journal, 289*(August), 1–3.

Rheingold, H. (2010 September/October). Attention and other 21st-century social media literacies. *EducauseE Review.* Retrieved from https://net.educause.edu/ir/library/pdf/ERM1050.pdf (19.08.15.).

CHAPTER 10

Truth or Dare

10.1 THE DILEMMA: 'MISINFORMATION, SCAMS AND HOAXES ON THE INTERNET ARE EASY TO SPOT. I WON'T BE CAUGHT OUT, WILL I?'

In this chapter we address the extremely important and topical issue of personal protection in online spaces and take a look at the constantly evolving variety of scams, hoaxes and other risks that are associated with Internet use—these are an ever-present concern. As true digital detectives, you will learn how to recognize when information that is posted on the Web, or appears on your social media accounts or in your email inbox, may be false, deliberately misleading or designed to defraud you.

You will become familiar with strategies for protecting yourself from the consequences of fraudulent or hostile online activity, such as identity theft, phishing, malware and payment fraud. You will also reflect on the potential of the Web for rapid dissemination of false information, particularly in light of the availability of fast-moving social media sites such as Twitter, Facebook and discussion forums, where news items—both true and false—can go viral in a matter of minutes.

In this chapter, you will:
- discover how social networking has increased the speed at which misinformation can travel around the Web.
- learn about cybercrime and the different types of fraudulent activities that are perpetrated online.
- understand how to spot a scam and become familiar with the clues that tell you all is not what it seems.
- learn how to protect yourself against Internet fraud.

10.2 THE WILD, WILD WEB

As part of its annual review of the year at the end of December 2014, the BBC News website posted a top-10 list of strange, wonderful and poignant items (Lee, 2014); included among them were Ellen DeGeneres' famous '*Oscars selfie*', which was re-tweeted more than 3 million times, a video of a dog disguised as a spider, a singing priest, a bunch of goats playing on a

Digital Detectives
ISBN 978-0-08-100124-0

metal sheet, a video exposing everyday sexism experienced by women, and an image of the US-based reality television celebrity Kim Kardashian. A quizmaster in a particularly challenging quiz show might ask, What could all of these seemingly random items possibly have in common? The answer, of course, is in the title of the article on the website: '*The Top Memes and Viral Videos of 2014*'.

What is your understanding of the term *viral*? Although it obviously sounds health-related, in recent years another meaning has become attached to the word, and it is now included in the *Oxford Dictionary*. It is defined there as 'an image, video, piece of information, etc. that is circulated rapidly and widely on the Internet' (Oxford Dictionaries, 2015). No doubt you have heard of pictures, videos or memes 'going viral'. Perhaps you also are aware of the recent phenomenon of 'viral marketing'. The phenomenon of going viral is a testament to the unique power of Internet sharing and social media in spreading a message rapidly and globally, with unprecedented efficiency, reaching staggering numbers of Internet users. For example, the video that has become the most 'viral' in history is the Kony 2012 video by Invisible Children, which received 34 million views on the day it was uploaded in 2012 and reached 100 million views within *6 days*. Another very famous example, although not as rapidly spreading, is Psy's 'Gangnam Style' music video, which has become YouTube's most-watched video of all time, with more than 2 billion views since it was released in 2012.

The speed at which information on the Internet can now travel around the globe is unprecedented. Thanks to social media sites such as Facebook, Twitter, Snapchat, WhatsApp, Reddit, YouTube and many more, articles, pictures and videos can pass from person to person at an astonishing rate, and simple hashtag phrases can spread awareness of an issue like few other media. This can be an undoubtedly positive phenomenon; if you think of the role played by social media in raising awareness and spreading the message for social movements such as the Arab Spring (from 2010 to 2012) and Occupy Wall Street (from 2011), you will understand how going viral can be harnessed as a force for good. More recent examples include the *#BringBackOurGirls* Twitter campaign, when 300 Nigerian schoolgirls were kidnapped by the Boko Haram terrorist group in 2014, and the *Ice Bucket Challenge* of summer 2014, which raised millions in donations for charities supporting those afflicted with motor neurone disease.

However, there is also a downside to 'going viral'. The absence of checks and balances with regard to information on the Web means that the videos, photos and articles that are circulated so rapidly from person to person might not be what they seem. Social media has also made it possible for false or inaccurate information to reach all parts of the globe before it has been properly verified. The ease with which information can be deliberately altered or falsified underscores the need for extra vigilance when engaging with social media sites:

It's going to get much worse because technical rules to stop it are often almost impossible to implement. When you send a jpeg, you may have photoshopped it but there's no way of the recipient determining what has been photoshopped. You could just say it has been cropped rather than that the content has been changed – somebody taken out of the picture, someone else put in – but it is almost impossible to prove. Increasingly, you can't tell truth from lies in the digital age.

(Viktor Mayer-Schönberger, quoted in Jeffries, 2011)

The 'Twitter hoax' is a good example of the role played by social media in perpetrating false information; in particular, the celebrity death hoax is one that you have probably witnessed. Flegenheimer pointed out in 2012: 'Just about every day, and often more frequently, Twitter kills a public figure'. Celebrities whose deaths have been prematurely reported on Twitter include Miley Cyrus, Axl Rose, Macaulay Culkin, Betty White and Bill Cosby. In October 2014 the agent of American actor Judd Nelson was forced to circulate a photo of the actor holding up the day's newspaper with the date clearly visible to prove that he was still alive after the rumour that he had passed away spread on Twitter (Colker & Raab, 2014).

The serious issues raised by the risk of false information circulating on social media were underscored in 2014 by the publication of the online 'Verification Handbook', developed by the European Journalism Centre to provide journalists with 'step-by-step guidelines for using user-generated content during emergencies' (Silverman, 2014). While the aim of the handbook is to assist journalists in ensuring that accurate information is reported in what could be life-or-death scenarios, the developers also emphasize that the principles and strategies discussed can—and should—be used by any person, including the 'citizen reporter, relief responder, volunteer, journalism school student, emergency communication specialist, or […] academic researching social media' (Silverman, 2014). Nowadays, newsworthy events can be recorded in real time by anyone who is standing by with a digital camera or smartphone. Frequently, these eyewitness videos are uploaded directly to YouTube, or circulated on Twitter or other social media sites, without any context or any editorial control, as would be the case with a trusted news network. Separating that which is important and genuine from that which is trivial or fabricated is increasingly difficult because amateur videos and images often display a professional gloss or slickness, thanks to the media and filtering tools available to all. The need for intelligent evaluation is greater than ever so that we can untangle fact from fiction.

The digital detective never takes information at face value—especially information that reaches him or her through social media or is generated by 'the crowd'. In Chapter 5 we discussed the importance of carefully evaluating digital information and seeking out the clues that tell you whether information can be trusted. However, greater challenges arise when there has been a calculated effort to deliberately mislead, influence or, more seriously, defraud Internet users through the spread of false information, or when scams are implemented that have been designed to trick users into performing an action that will lead to some sort of negative consequence, frequently financial in nature. This chapter considers how you can recognize—and, more importantly, protect yourself against— fraudulent Internet activity.

10.3 REFLECTION: HOW SAFE DO YOU FEEL?

Take a few minutes to reflect on your own perceptions of online security. How would you react to the following statements?

- There are no issues with posting personal information online, as long as the security settings on the site have been set to the highest level of protection.
- Internet scams are very easy to spot because they are usually based on ridiculous or outrageous stories.
- There are very strict laws in place that prevent my personal online information from being shared with other people and companies.
- The government is concerned with protecting the personal data of all citizens and takes measures to enforce this protection.
- If you get caught in an Internet scam, there are always ways to get your money back, under data protection laws.
- It's fine to input a little personal information if it means getting free access to something.

In general, some evidence suggests that there is a growing lack of trust in the security of online information among Internet users in the past few years. In 2014, a Pew Research Center report on public perceptions of privacy and security in the United States found that, 'across the board, there is a universal lack of confidence among adults in the security of everyday communications channels—particularly when it comes to the use of online tools' (Madden, 2014). Participants in that study indicated that they felt insecure in a variety of situations, including using social media sites to share private information with another trusted person or organization, using chat or instant messages to share private information, sending private information via text messages and email and using their mobile phone when they want to share private information. Furthermore, in the wake of the explosive information leaked by whistle-blower Edward Snowden in 2013 about the activities of the National Security Administration in accessing the phone records and Internet search logs of US citizens, a very high percentage of participants expressed concern about the government's monitoring of phone calls and Internet communications. Most of the people surveyed felt that they should be doing more than they already were to protect their privacy online. However, it was also clear from the study that people frequently view the posting of personal information online as a kind of trade-off between their security concerns about what might happen to that information and the benefits they perceive will accrue from it, such as improved online services, personalized content or gaining free access to other services.

10.4 ONLINE IDENTITY RISK CALCULATOR

In 2012, the commercial vendor EMC launched a collaboration with the National Cyber Security Alliance to develop the Online Identity Risk Calculator, which is a 'free interactive assessment tool designed to help educate consumers about their personal exposure to online threats'. It can be accessed by navigating to this URL: http://www.emc.com/microsites/fraudgame/flash.htm.

Once you download the version of the tool that you require, you are invited to answer a series of questions about the nature and frequency of your online interactions. Your answers to these questions are used to calculate your online identity risk. Each individual answer generates 'identity risk scores', which are compiled to indicate an overall risk level. Questions include the following:
- How often do you access your online banking account?
- How often do you make purchases online?
- How many email accounts do you have and access on a regular basis?
- How many social networking sites do you use on a regular basis?

Your overall risk is calculated as low, medium or high, depending on your interactions. Although far from scientific, it is interesting to complete this exercise to reflect on your digital online behaviour and how open to cybercrime it might leave you. So, how safe **do** you feel? How much information are you willing to share online? The following sections consider the different scams that are perpetrated on the Internet and the measures you can put in place to protect yourself in online spaces.

10.5 A DIGITAL DETECTIVE'S GUIDE TO CYBERCRIME

One of the ways in which the Internet poses a threat to users is through *cybercrime*, defined in *Encyclopaedia Britannica* as 'the use of a computer as an instrument to further illegal ends'. Rather than a physical attack, cybercrime is described as 'an attack on information about individuals, corporations, or governments' (Encyclopedia Britannica, 2014); it concerns the digital identities or footprints we leave behind when we interact in online spaces. Cybercrime spans a wide range of different activities, including identity theft, copyright and intellectual property violations, malware, spam, hacking, trafficking of illegal images and documents, cyberterrorism, as well as the ubiquitous financial scams.

In Europe, the European Cybercrime Centre (EC3) at Europol was launched in January 2013 to 'build operational and analytical capacity for investigations and cooperation with international partners in the pursuit of an EU free from cybercrime' (European Cybercrime Centre, 2015). Its first report, the *Internet Organized Crime Threat Assessment (IOCTA)*, was published in 2014 to raise awareness among 'decision-makers at strategic, policy and tactical levels' of the different types of cybercrimes that are typically perpetrated online, and to advise on the measures that should be taken to protect citizens, businesses, and so on (European Cybercrime Centre, 2014). The US version, the Internet Crime Complaint Center (IC3; originally the Internet Fraud Complaint Center), was established in 2000 as a partnership between the National White Collar Crime Centre, the FBI and the Bureau of Justice Assistance to provide a means for members of the public to report online crime. Since then, its annual reports on Internet crime provide a revealing insight into the different types of fraudulent online activity that affect US citizens. However, although the IC3 reports are thorough, because of the difficulty in monitoring online crimes, the report's authors note that 'the true volume and scope of cybercrime is unknown' (Internet Crime Complaint Center, 2014, p. 8). Furthermore, the 'borderless' nature of cybercrime makes it difficult to implement cohesive or collaborative frameworks for handling investigative procedures and sanctions to deal with the ramifications of these activities.

The EC3 report broadly classifies cybercrimes into a number of different categories:

- Malware
- Child sexual exploitation online
- Payment fraud
- Criminal finances online
- Crimes relating to social engineering
- Data breaches and network intrusions
- Vulnerabilities of critical infrastructures

Here we focus on three of these categories: malware, payment fraud and crimes related to social engineering. How are they defined?

10.5.1 Malware

Malware is a portmanteau, which stands for malicious software, and is defined as 'software which is specifically designed to disrupt or damage a computer system' (Oxford Dictionaries, 2015). While malware can often arrive in the guise of non-malicious, seemingly benign software, it can cause extensive damage to a host device. Malware includes software such as computer viruses, worms, Trojan horses, ransomware, spyware, adware and scareware, some of which we explore below.

The EC3 report (2014) notes that malware covers a variety of hostile activities, ranging from 'logging keystrokes to steal sensitive user data, to sophisticated and professional malware which can intercept and alter data or hijack the victim's user session'. Devices on which malware has been downloaded are said to be 'infected'. Ransomware is a particular type of malware in which the victim's device is completely disabled by the software until a 'fee' is paid to release it. Another form, spyware, is malicious software that can gather personal information about you from your device, such as your Internet searches or banking details, which can then be sold to other organizations without your consent.

Malware can potentially be downloaded to your device in a number of ways:

- When you accept a prompt on your device without reading the 'small print'; for example, when installing software from a website, a pop-up might appear, suggesting that you need to download additional software or plugins, and you automatically click on the link provided. Or perhaps you receive a prompt informing you that your device is not adequately protected and that you need to download a particular security update.

- When you open an email attachment from an unknown or unfamiliar address—this is a very common way of infecting a device with malicious code; emails can seem to be legitimate, even using email addresses that look absolutely genuine. *Trojan horse* emails are explored in more detail below.
- When you download software (e.g., games) from any source that you have not verified as legitimate.
- When you have no antivirus software installed on your device or have not kept up with updates for the software you do have or for your operating system in general. Legitimate updates often contain the fixes for security vulnerabilities and so should always be installed as soon as possible.

10.5.2 Trojan Horse Emails

One very common means of installing malware on a victim's device is via a 'Trojan horse' email, named after the legendary story from the Trojan war, in which the Greeks used a giant wooden horse to enter and destroy the city of Troy by hiding their army inside. Trojan horse emails, which usually contain attachments, may seem genuine and look official, often seeming to come from legitimate email addresses. If, however, the attachment is opened by the recipient, it may cause damage in a number of ways:

- It can create a security vulnerability, or open a secret 'backdoor' on your device, leaving it exposed to future cyber attacks.
- It can install software that logs your keystrokes, thus allowing criminals to discover your login details and passwords for sites that you may use, as well as payment information.
- It can turn your device into a 'bot' that can be used by criminals to send spam, launch denial-of-service attacks or spread the virus to other computers (US-CERT, 2008).

How do you recognize a Trojan horse email? Some clues that you can look for include the following:

- The attachments in the email may contain unfamiliar extensions such as .msi, .bat, .com, .cmd, .hta, .scr, .pif, .reg, .js, .vbs, .wsf and .cpl, or they may have multiple extensions. .exe Files in particular are well known for spreading malware.
- The email is unsolicited and may appear to come from a person whom you don't know, or from a company or organization to which you have no personal links.
- There is some kind of positive or negative inducement in the subject line to encourage you to open the attachment—for example, notification of

a special offer or a warning that your account has been compromised. A very famous example was the 'ILOVEYOU' virus that circulated via email in the early 2000s; the inducement in this case was an invitation to the recipient to read the 'love letter' that was attached.

- The content of the email seems unusual, even if it appears to come from someone you know. This is where you need to use your instincts to detect whether something is amiss or out of the ordinary. Would your friend or colleague typically send an email like this?

10.5.3 Payment Fraud

Payment fraud covers a range of illegal activities, but by and large it refers to 'fraud that occurs when someone gains financial or material advantage by using a payment instrument or information from a payment instrument to complete a transaction that is not authorized by the legitimate account holder' (Sullivan, 2009). Payment card fraud is probably the most well-known example of this type of fraudulent activity, and it can take place in both the online and offline environments, as well as when the card is both present and not present during a transaction. For instance, you are now probably familiar with the small discreet notices posted on ATMs that remind you to cover the keypad when keying in your personal identification number (PIN) to obtain cash or carry out transactions, as well as the warnings to notify the bank if anything 'suspicious' about the machine is noticed. Although the widespread use of the 'chip and pin' card payment method has made card transactions much safer than before, a significant amount of card fraud in fact takes place *online*, where the card PIN is not needed.

Payment card fraud can occur via a number of criminal activities, including by obtaining lost or stolen payment cards and using them to make purchases; through card skimming, which is the extraction of card data from the magnetic strip of a payment card as the card is processed at various locations, using a special data collection or storage device; through 'shoulder surfing' at an ATM or at point-of-sale terminals in shops; through obtaining payment details via malware, as described above; through phishing, which is explained in the next section; or through 'access abuse', where 'persons (either in companies or privately) who are not entitled to know the bank details of another person or the company get access and use them in fraudulent ways' (PPRO, 2014). Online identity theft refers to the use of a stolen or false identity to obtain goods or services by deception and frequently results in financial loss. Identity fraud 'can be facilitated by the use of stolen or forged identity documents such as a passport or driving licence' (CIFAS, 2015). Account takeover has a similar effect but does not involve masquerading as an individual; rather, the cybercriminals simply hijack an existing bank account and steal from it.

The digital detective should be aware that payment fraud and identity theft may not just occur through criminals gaining access to private information; rather, it can sometimes involve information that we voluntarily make available online by filling out forms, registering for websites and so on. For example, we routinely send the following information into cyberspace:

- Internet protocol address
- Home/workplace address
- Usernames
- Passwords
- PINs
- National identification numbers (e.g., Social Security).
- Birth date
- Account numbers
- Answers to security questions (e.g., mother's maiden name, first pet's name).

While we might believe that websites are secure, this may not always be the case. You should always think twice about the information you are willing to give up, and guard your information online. For example, do not enable the 'autofill' function on websites where there is potentially sensitive personal information so that your login details will not be remembered on the browser. Changing your passwords regularly is also a recommended strategy, as is paying for online purchases with a credit card, rather than a debit card, because there tends to be more protection under law for credit card fraud, although this depends on the country you live in.

10.5.4 Crimes Related to Social Engineering

Social engineering criminal activity refers to 'a set of offline and online methods and techniques that aim to manipulate a victim into voluntarily releasing sensitive information or into transferring money' (IOCTA, 2014), and typically works on the fears, emotions, greed, carelessness and naivety of victims. Examples of this type of criminal activity that you might have heard of are *spam* and *phishing*, which is a particular form of spam. Spam is described as 'Irrelevant or unsolicited messages sent over the Internet, typically to large numbers of users, for the purposes of advertising, phishing, spreading malware, etc.' (Oxford Dictionaries, 2015). Although your primary experience of spam may be via email (or 'junk mail'), other channels also are susceptible, including social networks such as Facebook, blogs, Internet discussion boards, and short message service (text) messages, to name a few. Spam is a 'social engineering' crime because it depends on the curiosity, altruism or even vanity of the recipient to open the message, and perhaps to carry out the instructions within; the Trojan horse email described above is an example of this.

One of the most common social engineering crimes is the advance fee scam, most famously exemplified in the 'Nigerian Letter' or '419' scam. The modus operandi of this scam almost always follows the same pattern:

- You receive an unsolicited email from an apparently high-ranking official or member of a royal family who urgently needs to wire money out of their country and is imploring you to consider their plight.
- Their situation is inevitably complicated by political strife, persecution and bureaucracy.
- They therefore need someone from abroad who can receive the funds and who will then be rewarded with a small percentage (which is actually quite a lot of money).
- If you agree to 'help', however, problems keep arising that result in you revealing personal and financial details, and maybe even depositing some money in a bogus account (the 'advance fee', which is required to expedite the process).

The 'friend in need' scam works on a similar premise. This occurs when you receive a message, apparently from one of your friends, who is in some kind of trouble abroad; for example, they have been mugged and have lost their money and credit cards and have no way of getting home. You are asked to urgently forward some funds to allow them to travel back; details of where to send the money are provided. They do, of course, offer to pay you back afterwards.

10.5.5 Phishing

Phishing is a means of identity theft that 'uses email and fraudulent websites that are designed to steal your personal data or information such as credit card numbers, passwords, account data, or other information' (Microsoft, 2014). The strategies that cybercriminals use to 'phish' for personal information cover a number of different technologies. For example, victims may be targeted through 'automated redirects to a bogus website (pharming), SMS (smishing) or phone or VoIP (vishing)' (European Cybercrime Centre, 2014).

Clues to watch out for—which might help you avoid being a victim of phishing—include the following:

- Fake communications from online payment and auction sites such as eBay or PayPal, suggesting that your account security has been compromised, or that 'changes to the service agreement' have been implemented for your account, and that you need to log in to verify your account or risk the account being deleted.
- Fake emails from banks asking to you verify your account details by clicking on a link (real banks will **never** do this).
- Fake communications from Internet service providers suggesting that there is a problem with your account and you need to log in to check your details; this can take place over the phone or via email.
- Fake accusations of violating certain laws or committing undefined crimes.
- Fake communications from an information technology department, for example, an email from your university's IT Support Services 'notifying' you that you have exceeded your allocated space and asking you to log in to rectify this.
- A fake email informing you that you have won the lottery in a country you do not reside in and that you need to forward a small administration fee to facilitate the transfer of your winnings.
- Fake communications from your country's revenue service informing you that you are eligible for a tax rebate and that you need to verify your details to claim it.

'Smishing' attempts can include a text informing you that you have won a prize and only have to click on the link provided or call or text a number to claim this prize. In both cases you will be asked for personal information to 'process' your claim. Telephone or 'vishing' scams include the software company scam described in the next section.

10.6 SPOTLIGHT ON SPECIFIC SCAMS

The most recently available IC3 report (Internet Crime Complaint Centre, 2014) includes a more specific list of common scams, virtually all of which are perpetrated with financial gain in mind. It is likely that you have heard of some of them, or perhaps you even know someone who has been a victim of one or more scams. They include:

Auto-auction fraud	Software company telephone scams
Romance scams	Loan modification scams
FBI scams	Sextortion scams
Hit man scams	Gun sale scams
Ransomware/scareware scams	Fraudulent tech support call scams
Real estate rental scams	Photo and mugshot scams
Grandparent telephone scams	College and university scams
Timeshare marketing scams	Sim card swap scams
Work-at-home employment scams	Payday loan scams

Exploring how some of these scams work will offer us insight into the factors that trick or frighten people into complying with the instructions that appear on their screen or over their phone—even if they seem to be outrageous or far-fetched.

10.6.1 Romance Scams

This type of scam targets people who are seeking relationships online through dating websites such as match.com, eHarmony and PlentyofFish. The scammer reaches out to the victim, establishing a bond of trust through shared intimacies and sending poetry and other hooks, and seems to be very convincing and genuine. This then leads to fabricated stories of family tragedies, personal injuries or other hardships, usually culminating in a request for money to help them through the 'bad patch'. The unsuspecting victim may then forward the funds as requested, only for the 'friend' to disappear and become uncontactable as soon as the money is received.

10.6.2 FBI Scams

FBI scams work through intimidation and paranoia, and they prey on people's fear of 'being watched' by the government or law-enforcement agencies. Here, the victim receives an email or a pop-up message on their computer from what seems to be a high-ranking government official from the FBI (real names are often used) who suggests that they have been 'caught' engaged in an illegal computer activity that constitutes a violation of federal laws. They are warned that their computer will be 'locked' unless they pay a fine to avoid further criminal charges. Versions of this scam tailored to the laws and institutions of different countries also are common. Ransomware/scareware scams work on a similar premise, frightening people into believing they have been somehow caught in a crime, and using this fear to extort money. These scams work because there is still a great degree of uncertainty around the monitoring of Internet activity; often, people genuinely do not know if such targeted observation is possible or permitted by their governments.

10.6.3 Software Company Telephone Scams

Usually carried out over the telephone, these scams involve unsolicited calls from a scammer who claims to be an employee of a trusted software company. The victim is informed that some kind of virus or malware has been detected on their computer and that they are at risk of losing all of their data. The scammer asks the victim to log onto their computer and carry out a few simple instructions so that they can see how their computer became 'infected'. They then offer what seems to be competitively priced antivirus software to solve the problem, directing the victim to a website where a specific code must be entered, along with personal and payment information, to download the software.

10.6.4 Work-at-Home Scams

These scams offer what seems to be a unique and very attractive opportunity to earn significant amounts of money without having to leave your house. The 'jobs' that are advertised often involve very easy tasks, such as stuffing envelopes, processing medical claims, assembling craft items or selling products. Work-at-home schemes are often advertised in a slick way, using professional-looking websites and pop-ups with apparently genuine testimonials in order to recruit newcomers. Victims find themselves defrauded when they are asked to pay a fee for joining the scheme, to purchase materials that they are to use to carry out the job or to invest in stock for resale, which in reality is worth much less than claimed by the scammers.

10.7 SPOTTING A SCAM

The digital detective knows what to look for when something is not what it seems at first. Here are some of the factors to consider when spotting a scam:

- **If it seems too good to be true, it usually is**; for example, work-at-home schemes often offer a salary that is far above the marketplace rate for the type of work in question, and they seem to require no professional qualifications or experience from the applicant. Any message that apparently offers a reward for very little effort is almost always a scam.

- **There is urgency in the message** or a warning of unfortunate consequences if you don't act immediately, for example, If you don't act now, you will miss out on this amazing opportunity! If you don't pay this fine straight away, you will be arrested or have your computer seized! If you don't download the software now, you will lose all of the data on your computer!

- **A poorly written email with many spelling, grammar or punctuation errors** from an apparently 'official' source is a sign that it is not legitimate.

- **An email address that seems suspicious**, for example, an email that appears to come from your bank but uses a Yahoo! email address. Email software does not verify incoming email addresses—in other words, there is no way for your email software to tell whether an email is actually coming from the person it appears to be from. A quick way to check an email address is to hover your mouse cursor over the name in the 'From' line. From that you can tell whether the email is from a recognizable domain that is linked to the actual sender name. Alternatively, you can use a free online verifier, such as http://www.email-validator.net, which allows you to enter an email address to check its legitimacy.

- **The 'To:' field contains a name different from yours**, which indicates that this is a mass mailing where the 'To' field is not real or is selected randomly. Some of the words in the email might be CAPITALIZED, which is a tactic used to attract the attention of recipients. Some of the words may be distorted ('Lloan' instead of 'loan') in order to get around spam filters, or the link provided is not the URL of the company's official website.

- **A notification containing a company logo or graphic that doesn't seem right**; many phishing emails or fake websites include graphics that appear to be the official logo of an established company. If you take a closer look, however, you may realize that it is a mock-up or badly altered version of the original graphic.

- The communication may use **phrases** like 'Verify your account', **'Update your account'**, 'During regular account maintenance', 'Failure to update your records will result in account suspension' and similar instructions.

- **The emails may not address you personally**, as an official company or someone you know would, but include general greetings such as 'Dear (Bank/Company) Customer' or 'Dear friend'.

To ensure that visitors arrive at their official website, large established companies such as Amazon, Google and Apple, as well as banks and other businesses, use the **SSL (Secure Sockets Layer) protocol**. That means that you will see https in the URL address bar, rather than http://, and there may be some other differences in the address bar, such as a locked padlock icon at the start of the URL.

10.8 GENERAL STRATEGIES FOR OUTWITTING CYBERCRIMINALS

As you can see, the range and creativity of cyber scams is infinite, and new ways of manipulating the public are emerging constantly. As true digital detectives, however, you can adopt a variety of approaches to preempt any cyber attacks and protect yourself from scams. The key ingredient is vigilance, and you must develop sensible habits when interacting in the online environment.

- Ensure that you have fully up-to-date antivirus software installed on your devices.
- Activate a *firewall*, which is software that 'allows or blocks traffic into and out of a private network or the user's computer' (PCMag Encyclopedia, 2015). For example, in Windows, a firewall can be activated by going to the Control Panel, and turning on the *Windows Firewall* for each network location that you wish to protect.
- Do not open email attachments from people whom you don't know or that you were not expecting to receive.
- Download software only from sites that you trust or can verify.
- Regularly check your bank and credit card statements to ensure that no unauthorized activity has taken place.
- If you are invited to click on a URL in a communication, always check whether it is legitimate; in Chapter 5, we discussed how to analyze a URL when evaluating information resources. The same principles apply in this case. You can also use a lookup site such as http://www.whos. com/whois to identify the organizations and individuals behind domain names and Internet protocol addresses.
- When using ATMs, always take a close look at the machine before inserting your card; for example, does it have an extra mirror on the face, or any sticky residue that could indicate that a skimming device has been attached? Or is there anything stuck in the card slot or on the keypad? If anything seems amiss, do not use it.
- When making **online** purchases with a credit card, never input your card PIN—it is not required for these types of purchases.

- When using a payment card in person, always insist on being present when the actual transaction is carried out. Do not let anyone take the terminal device out of sight. This will help to prevent card cloning.
- If purchasing on an auction site such as eBay, always study the seller feedback, and confirm the full cost, including shipping, before completing a transaction. If selling on auction sites, never accept an offer from a buyer who wants to pay more than the requested amount for an item (allegedly to speed up the transaction). In all likelihood, the payment will fail after the item has been dispatched.
- When dealing with any company online, always check whether they have a physical address, rather than just a phone number or a post office box.
- Take extra care with any download of music or software that is free of charge; it may result in malware being installed on your computer.
- Disable the autofill function for forms on your browser, and do not permit your browser to 'remember' your password for sites that require personal information.
- Don't use public computers for online banking or any transactions that involve personal or financial information.

10.9 MANAGING YOUR PASSWORDS

One of the consequences of the way we use the Web today is that we must set up multiple accounts and enter registration information for the many sites and services that we want to use. Most of these sites request that you create a unique password, which should ideally be as difficult to guess as possible—sites refer to 'strong' passwords, which are more secure. The typical advice is to make sure that your passwords are atleast eight characters long and that they contain a mixture of upper- and lowercase letters, in addition to at least one number and possibly a symbol as well. This is good advice: It lowers the risk that someone will be able to figure out your password and access your account. It is also recommended that you change your passwords frequently, and that you avoid including information in the password that might identify you, like your date of birth or a complete word that is related to you in some way.

However, while this is a sensible approach to take, it does mean that we can end up juggling numerous different passwords, and eventually it may seem impossible to manage them all. This is especially true for sites that you use only sporadically. How are you supposed to remember all of them? As a result of this, many people choose to use the same password repeatedly, for different sites. While this might help you, it also renders you more vulnerable in terms of online privacy. Reusing the same password exposes you to the possible consequences of a 'password leak', which can occur when sites are attacked by cybercriminals. According to Hoffman (2013), 'When your password leaks, malicious individuals have an email address, username, and password combination they can try on other websites. If you use the same login information everywhere, a leak at one website could give people access to all your accounts'. So, using the same password for every account is risky. Another option people sometimes take is to enable the 'autofill' function on their browsers, which means that login information is automatically entered when you load different sites; as we know, however, this is also not advisable, since anyone who uses the same browser will also have access to your accounts. How can you protect your security online and effectively manage the multiple passwords you require?

10.9.1 Password Management Software

One strategy is to use a password manager, which is 'a software application that helps a user store and organize passwords' (Wikipedia, 2015). A password manager stores all of your passwords in encrypted form and requires you to create only a single master password to log into the service. So, the application does the job of remembering for you. When your passwords for the different sites and accounts are stored in the password manager, logging into a site simply requires you to enter the master password into the password manager, which then automatically enters the appropriate login information into the website; for even greater convenience, if you're already logged into your password manager, it automatically fills in the data for you, without you having to go to a login page at all. Some password managers also offer the option of generating a secure password when you are creating a new account, so you don't even have to think of one yourself.

While some password managers have a cost attached, there are also many free applications to choose from. Some of the most popular password managers available include the following:
- LastPass (https://lastpass.com)
- Dashlane (https://www.dashlane.com/tpc)
- KeePass (http://keepass.info)
- Roboform (http://www.roboform.com/)
- PasswordBox (https://www.passwordbox.com/)
- Password Boss (https://www.passwordboss.com/)

10.10 CHALLENGES

1. Individually or in a group, develop a *Concise Guide to Internet Safety* for the following groups: (a) school-age children between 8 and 12 years old; (b) teenagers aged between 14 and 17 years; (c) older adults, aged 65 years and older. What specific kind of information about protecting oneself online does each of these groups require? What is the best way to present this information for each group? When developing your guide, think about the following:

   a. The type of online activities the individuals in these groups are likely to engage in on a regular basis. For example, are schoolchildren likely to be doing online shopping? You should research the groups carefully before beginning the guide.

   b. The likely level of *existing* knowledge and understanding about the Internet within each group.

   c. The most effective way of delivering the message to each group. For example, is it better to have a handout, a website or a booklet? Are text, images or even videos likely to have the desired impact?

2. To create an accurate profile of the cyber threats you might be exposed to in your daily life, maintain a month-long personal log of your Internet activities that may carry potential security issues using, for example, Microsoft Excel). At the end of the month, review your activities and decide whether you need to take more steps to protect yourself online. Are you habitually taking risks online? Some of the items to record might include:

   a. any **e-commerce** sites that you used during this period. How did you pay for the goods or services that you purchased? Did the site require you to set up an account? Were you given the option to store your payment details for the next time? Were you asked to verify your payment card? Did you receive a confirmation email? Did you have any concerns about the security of your payment through the site? What information about the security of your transaction did the site provide?

   b. The status of the **antivirus software** on your computer. Is it up to date? Did you receive any warnings about potential security breaches? Did you run any security scans on your computer during this time?

   c. Any **emails** that you received that you were concerned about. Did any of them come from addresses that seemed suspicious? Were there strange links or attachments with any emails? What action did you take if this happened? Did any of them seem to come from institutions such as banks where you currently have an account?

    d. Any **downloads** to your devices. Were they free of charge? Did you check the trustworthiness of the sites you downloaded from? What information did you have to give in order to obtain the download?

    e. Any **apps** that you downloaded to your mobile devices. Were they free of charge? Did they require a link to your account on social media sites such as Facebook? Were in-app purchases involved? Do these apps record your geographic location? What personal information did you have to provide to obtain and use the apps?

    f. Any other online interactions that involve payment, registration or the provision of personal information.

3. Locate the **data protection** website for the country or state in which you live; for example, in the Irish Republic, this website is http://www.dataprotection.ie/, and in the United Kingdom it's at https://ico.org.uk/. In the United States, different states may have different laws; for example, information for California can be found at https://oag.ca.gov/privacy. Answer the following questions using the information on the site:

    a. What rights do you currently have when a person or organization takes or records your personal details?

    b. When, or under what circumstances, do these rights apply?

    c. What information must data controllers give you about the personal information they hold about you?

    d. How do you go about gaining access to personal information that persons or organizations hold about you?

    e. Do you have the right to change information held about you, or prevent its use in any way?

    f. What action can you take if you are concerned about the data about you that are being held by a person or organization?

REFERENCES

CIFAS. (2015). *Identity Fraud*. Retrieved from https://www.cifas.org.uk/glossary_i.

Colker, D., & Raab, L. (2014, October 26). Judd Nelson's agent sends photo to dispel Twitter rumors of actor's death. *LA Times*. Retrieved from http://www.latimes.com/entertainment/gossip/la-et-mg-judd-nelson-not-dead-20141026-story.html.

Encyclopaedia Britannica. (2014). *Cybercrime*. Retrieved from http://www.britannica.com/EBchecked/topic/130595/cybercrime.

European Cybercrime Centre. (2014). *Internet organized crime threat assessment (IOCTA)*. Retrieved from https://www.europol.europa.eu/iocta/2014/toc.html.

European Cybercrime Centre. (2014). *Crimes related to social engineering*. In Internet Organised Crime Threat Assessment (IOCTA). Retrieved from https://www.europol.europa. eu/iocta/2014/chap-3-6-view1.html.

European Cybercrime Centre. (2015). A collective EU response to cybercrime. *Europol*. Retrieved from https://www.europol.europa.eu/ec3.

Hoffman, C. (2013, March 22). *Why you should use a password manager and how to get started* (Blog post). How-to Geek. Retrieved from http://www.howtogeek.com/141500/ why-you-should-use-a-password-manager-and-how-to-get-started.

Internet Crime Complaint Centre. (2014). *2013 internet crime report*. Retrieved from http:// www.ic3.gov/media/annualreport/2013_ic3report.pdf.

Jeffries, S. (2011, September 29). Sock puppets, twitterjacking and the art of digital fakery. *The Guardian*. Retrieved from http://www.theguardian.com/technology/2011/ sep/29/sock-puppets-twitterjacking-digital-fakery.

Lee, D. (2014).The top memes and viral videos of 2014. *BBC News*. Retrieved from http:// www.bbc.com/news/technology-30625633.

Madden, M. (2014, November). *Public perceptions of privacy and security in the post-Snowden era*. Pew Research Center. Retrieved from http://www.pewinternet.org/2014/11/12/ public-privacy-perceptions.

Microsoft. (2014). *Phishing – frequently asked questions*. Retrieved from https://www.microsoft. com/security/online-privacy/phishing-faq.aspx.

Oxford Dictionaries. (2015). Retrieved from *http://www.oxforddictionaries.com*.

PC Mag Encyclopedia. (2015). *Definition of firewall*. Retrieved from http://www.pcmag. com/encyclopedia/term/43218/firewall.

PPRO. (2014). *Payment fraud types and how to prevent them*. Retrieved from https://www.ppro. com/blog/payment-fraud-types-and-how-to-prevent-them/.

Silverman, C. (Ed.). (2014). *Verification handbook: A definitive guide to verifying digital content for emergency coverage*. Netherlands: European Journalism Centre (EJC). Retrieved from http://verificationhandbook.com.

Sullivan, R. J. (2009, October). *The benefits of collecting and reporting payment fraud statistics in the United States. Federal Reserve Bank of Kansas City*. Retrieved from https://www.kansascityfed. org/PUBLICAT/PSR/Briefings/PSR-BriefingOct09.pdf.

US-Cert. (2008). *Recognizing and avoiding email scams*. Retrieved from https://www.us-cert. gov/sites/default/files/publications/emailscams_0905.pdf.

Wikipedia. (2015). *Password manager*. Retrieved from https://en.wikipedia.org/wiki/Password_ manager.

CHAPTER 11

A Hidden Agenda

11.1 THE DILEMMA: "PEOPLE CAN SEE ONLY WHAT I WANT THEM TO SEE ON THE WEB. I CONTROL THE IMAGE THAT I PROJECT, DON'T I?"

In this chapter we reflect on the *digital footprint* that you intentionally and unintentionally leave behind in the online environment and consider how this trail of *digital crumbs* can affect the different parts of your life in both a positive and negative way. We explore the different channels and media by which information about you can be circulated online, and the possible consequences that this can have for your personal online reputation and for other aspects of your life in the *nondigital world*. The chapter examines different strategies for guarding your privacy and controlling the image that you project in a world where it has become commonplace to share publicly the minutiae of daily life and sometimes even the very thoughts that are in your head. A particular focus is social media sites, where a personal profile does not just contain basic demographic information, but is often expanded to include *likes* and *dislikes*, location tracking through status updates and *check-ins*, as well as the networks of relationships and social connections we develop with other online users.

In this chapter, you will:

- understand why your personal online reputation should matter to you in the twenty-first century.
- learn about digital footprints and how they are created.
- discover how data about you are collected online and what they are used for.
- develop strategies for discovering your personal online profile.
- learn how to protect your online reputation and create a positive personal online presence.

11.2 THE POWER OF AN ONLINE PRESENCE

[B]ecause of the "sharability" of online content, it is more difficult for people to maintain control over what they post and what might happen to it in the future. The Internet is full of anecdotes of people who have lost their jobs, ruined their

Digital Detectives
ISBN 978-0-08-100124-0

reputations or wrecked their marriages because of something they posted on an online social networking site.

Jones and Hafner (2012, p. 152)

In March 2015, Steve Blakeman, the Managing Director of Global Accounts at OMD Worldwide, published an article with an eye-catching title on the business networking site LinkedIn. He exhorted readers to "Burn your Résumé" because "LinkedIn has made it obsolete." Although the headline was designed to be dramatic, Blakeman's reasoning in the article demonstrates just how powerful social media sites and the self-image we project through them have become in the various aspects of our lives. Blakeman suggests that paper résumés are too *two-dimensional* to capture the personality and social fit of a prospective employee. A website, such as LinkedIn, "has the capacity to show high quality photographs/videos, can be more easily updated so is more likely to be real time and it shows who you know (and how you are connected) for easy cross reference" (Blakeman, 2015). He also emphasizes that the professional image that you project through interacting with and publishing on social media sites is essential for advancing in the job you are doing at the moment and for making yourself stand out to current and future employers.

The increasing use of social media sites by recruiters is a hot topic. A recent survey of more than 1800 recruiting and human resources professionals by online recruiting platform Jobvite (2014) found that "93% of recruiters use or plan to use social [media] to support their recruiting efforts," and that "55% of recruiters have *reconsidered* a candidate based on their social profile." A similar survey by CareerBuilder (2013) of more than 2000 human resources professionals in the United States also found that 43% of hiring managers who currently use social media to evaluate clients claimed that they had uncovered information that resulted in them choosing *not* to hire a person. The kind of information that caused them to reject prospective clients included inappropriate photographs; claims of drinking or drug use; bad-mouthing previous employers; racist, sexist, or otherwise derogatory comments; lying about previous employment; and poor communication skills in general. While these are all understandably off-putting factors, it was perhaps easier to conceal them before the age of social media. Now, with the tendency of social media users to post large amounts of personal information online, private and intimate thoughts are making their way to the public eye, frequently assisted by individuals themselves.

The list of anecdotes describing how employees have lost their jobs as a result of comments, images, or videos posted casually on social media sites is growing all the time. One of the most recent high-profile cases concerned a public relations executive for a US-based company, who was fired in 2013 after posting an offensive tweet on her Twitter account as she was about to board a flight to South Africa, "Going to Africa. Hope I don't get AIDS. Just kidding. I'm white!" The tweet immediately *went viral*. This lack of judgment resulted in her immediate dismissal after her flight landed and widespread condemnation of what was universally perceived as a racially insensitive comment (Pilkington, 2013). Another similar case in 2011 concerned an employee of a media strategy company working on behalf of Chrysler in the United States, who posted an objectionable tweet about motorists in Detroit: "I find it ironic that Detroit is known as the #motorcity and yet no one here knows how to [expletive] drive" (Nudd, 2011). Although the tweet was later deleted, Chrysler was forced to post an apology on its blog, and the employee was fired. In addition, the contract with the media company was not renewed by Chrysler in the wake of the controversy. These are just two examples of the long reach of social media and how difficult it is to control content once it has been released into the online world.

11.3 WHY DOES ONLINE REPUTATION MANAGEMENT MATTER?

Anyone who uses social networking sites is inescapably a participant in the "attention economy," with successful participation dependent on being able to manage information about oneself, to effectively engage in self-promotion, and to figure out how to protect one's privacy when necessary.

Jones and Hafner (2012, p. 153)

As the above examples show, the management of your online image has possible consequences far beyond the impact it has on your social life alone. The importance of online reputation management has grown to such an extent in recent years that a dedicated industry has been established, consisting of companies that "can be hired to help individuals locate and remove problematic content from the Internet" (Magnuson, 2011), as well as to build effective social media strategies from scratch to promote and market products and services. Companies with names such as reputation.com, Webimax, Reputation Management Consultants, Brand Resurrection, and Reputation Rhino all compete to deliver services including brand management and *reputation repair*. During the past decade, the job of *social media consultant* also has emerged; this is defined as "someone who works with businesses of all sizes creating and managing social media marketing campaigns [and] stays up on all of the latest news and changes as it applies to the industry" (Edwards, 2014).

Research also has shown that people's information behavior is affected by their perceptions of how they appear or wish to appear on social media. A recent study by the Pew Research Center supports the theory that people tend "not to speak up about policy issues in public—or among their family, friends, and work colleagues—when they believe their own point of view is not widely shared" (Hampton *et al.*, 2014). The survey of more than 1800 adults sought opinions on Edward Snowden's revelations in 2013 about National Security Agency surveillance in the United States. The survey found that, "in both personal settings and online settings, people were more willing to share their views if they thought their audience agreed with them" and that "if people thought their friends and followers in social media disagreed with them, they were less likely to say they would state their views on the Snowden-NSA story online and in other contexts, such as gatherings of friends, neighbors, or co-workers." The researchers termed this phenomenon a *spiral of silence*, which illustrates people's reluctance to stand out from the crowd, especially when it comes to disagreeing with the perceived majority viewpoint.

Kaplan and Haenlein (2010, pp. 62–64) identified six different types of social media that support greater or lesser levels of self-disclosure and self-presentation by participants, combined with social presence and media richness. Communication and the forging and maintaining of online relationships are determined by the combination of these factors:

- Collaborative projects, such as wikis and social bookmarking sites.
- Blogs.
- Content communities, such as Flickr and YouTube, that facilitate the sharing of media content between users.
- Social networking sites, such as Facebook and MySpace.
- Virtual game worlds, which are "platforms that replicate a three-dimensional environment in which users can appear in the form of personalized avatars and interact with each other as they would in real life" (p. 64). World of Warcraft is a popular example of a virtual game world.
- Virtual social worlds, such as Linden Lab's Second Life.

Some of these media provide extensive opportunities for creative self-presentation and disclosure online; for example, virtual social worlds enable users literally to inhabit a virtual world that mimics the real world. With a few restrictions, the virtual world also allows them to create and customize a persona and an environment that are unique. Social networking sites also enable the projection of an individually crafted image, from the careful selection of images to display through the various *likes*, *shares*, and searches that characterize your interaction with content, to the status updates and *check-ins* that map your daily activities. Other media, such as content communities, offer more limited scope for self-expression since they often require just a basic profile from users. All of them, however, have a role to play in the creation, development, maintenance, and protection of your online reputation:

> *Reputation management has now become a defining feature of online life for many Internet users, especially the young ... Search engines and social media play a central role in building one's reputation online, and many users are learning and refining their approach as they go.*
>
> **Madden and Smith (2010)**

Take a moment to reflect on your online behavior. Have you ever done any of the following?

- Uploaded a video of yourself to a public website?
- *Tagged* your friends in photographs from a night out?
- Become involved in a heated discussion with someone on a message board?
- Registered for a website account without reading the site's privacy policy?
- Accepted a friend request on Facebook or a connection on LinkedIn from someone you have never met in person?
- Uploaded your résumé to a public website?
- Started and maintained a personal blog?
- Shared personal photographs on a public site, including the geographic location of the pictures?
- Entered a competition on Facebook?
- Posted online a critical review of a restaurant, hotel, or other service?
- Cleared your search history on a Web browser?
- Clicked on an advertisement that popped up on a website you were browsing?
- Clicked the box stating "I agree to the Terms and Conditions" on a website, without actually reading them?

All of these actions carry consequences for your online image and contribute to how you are perceived in the online world. Almost anything you do online leaves a *trace* of your presence that may become a permanent record, even if you believe you have deleted this information. In truth, there is nothing on the Web that is completely private. Even simply visiting a Web site once begins the process of information collection. Let us explore the concept of a *digital footprint* and see how information about you is collected online.

11.4 WHAT IS A DIGITAL FOOTPRINT?

Just as a *carbon footprint* describes the total greenhouse gas emissions (carbon dioxide and methane) caused by a person, organization, or event, your digital footprint refers to the *digital emissions* you leave behind in the online world through the activities that you undertake there. In the same way taking many long-haul flights can result in a higher carbon footprint, extensive interactions on the Internet can increase your own digital footprint. A digital footprint is defined as follows:

> A trail left by an entity's interactions in a digital environment; including their usage of TV, mobile phone, internet and world wide web, mobile web and other devices and sensors. Digital footprints provide data on what an entity has performed in the digital environment and are valuable in assisting behavioral targeting, personalization, targeted marketing, digital reputation, and other social media or social graphing services.
>
> **Thakur (2011)**

Your digital footprint is the sum total of your online activity, whether intentional or unintentional. How is it generated?

11.5 HOW ARE DATA ABOUT YOU COLLECTED ONLINE?

Data about you can be collected *passively* or *actively*. When you browse the Web, your interactions cast a *digital shadow* consisting of the sites that you access, the cookies that are placed on your device (these are explained below), your Internet protocol (IP) address and geographic location, the time you access certain sites, and other traces. In certain cases it is possible that a *key logger*, which is a type of surveillance software or spyware, is keeping track of every keystroke you make on your device and transmitting this information to a third party without your knowledge.

In Chapter 3 we discussed how *filter bubbles* and the introduction of personalized searching on Internet search engines such as Google are ensuring an increasingly customized search experience for users. The results you retrieve in your searches often are tailored to your preferences, which are deduced from previous searches you have carried out (your search history), your geographic location, and links that you have clicked on. Search preferences are recorded through *cookies* that are placed on your device; a cookie is defined as "a small file of letters and numbers that is downloaded on to your computer when you visit a website [which] can do a number of things, e.g., remembering your preferences, recording what you have put in your shopping basket, and counting the number of people looking at a website" (Information Commissioner's Office, 2015). From a positive perspective, cookies have *enhanced* the usability of the Web and have helped to make interactions more secure. They provide a useful way of "tying multiple actions by a single user into one connected stream," which is necessary for complex interactions such as online shopping and payment (Internet Society, 2015). websites usually set a cookie in your browser when you first visit the site. Cookies can be useful in that they can prevent you from having to enter your login details into a website each time you visit it, or they can record the preferences you have set for a particular website to save you from having to reset them each time you log in.

However, cookies can also be used to record your activities on the Web and to distribute or even sell this information to companies without your knowledge or consent. They can "create detailed profiles about where you browse, as well as other information about you. These profiles can be used to make certain advertisements show up on your screen when you browse the Web. This is called Behavioural Advertising or targeted advertising" (Office of the Privacy Commissioner of Canada, 2011). When you visit websites with advertisements on them, you should also be aware of the potential presence of third-party cookies; in this case, the cookies are sent from external companies (the third parties) to your device in order to record information about your activities. This information is then analyzed to target you for customized advertisements. This process is known as *Web leakage*. Enabling advertising is an important source of revenue for many websites; however, in many cases, no restrictions are placed on the amount of information that may be disclosed, thus leading to a significant amount of Web leakage of user information.

Your own voluntary actions can lead to information about you being collected in a number of different ways. Think about the different online interactions you might engage in every day:

- Filling out surveys so that you will be placed in a drawing for a prize.
- Taking online quizzes or tests for fun (What type of car are you? What country should you live in?). There are many examples of these types of quizzes on Facebook.

- Completing online registration forms to gain access to sites, online shops, and so on.
- Using a GPS app to find the best route to a location.
- Subscribing to newsletters or mailing lists so you can avail yourself of special offers.
- Indicating your preferences and creating playlists on music streaming services.
- Adding items to your *wish lists* on commercial sites.
- *Liking* posts, pages, videos, and images on social networking sites.
- Bookmarking and tagging online documents.
- *Following* people on Twitter, and sharing and re-tweeting links.
- *Checking in* with your location on social media sites.
- Commenting on blogs or social media posts.
- Searching for, and then booking, flights and accommodation for your next trip abroad.

With each interaction, you inadvertently (or knowingly) share information about yourself: what you like and dislike, what your interests are, what you purchase, what you listen to, what you read, what you eat, where you like to go—and who you *are*—in terms of your location, name or screen name, age, gender, family, friends, and numerous other variables.

11.6 WHO WANTS DIGITAL DATA ABOUT YOU?

You might wonder who, outside of your immediate circle, would be interested in what you do online. After all, a lot of our activity might seem boring or banal to others! If we examine the issue from a commercial perspective, it becomes more obvious. Most of us now enjoy availing ourselves of content and applications on our computers or mobile devices that are apparently free; for instance, music or video streaming apps, games, public transportation apps, score trackers for sporting events, and many more. The idea of legally downloading something free is appealing, and again, many of us accept that, in return for these services, we will be asked to provide some personal identifying details or to create an account. Online information behavior suggests that we consider this to be a fair trade-off and that we are generally happy to click on the *I agree to the Terms and Conditions* box without giving them much thought—and usually without reading them. However, it's also likely that you have heard the following phrase at some point in the past few years, particularly in relation to this use of free apps and online services:

If you're not paying for it, you're not the customer—you're the product!

But what does this expression mean? The key issue here is the potential *monetary value* of the data about individuals that commercial firms can obtain from analyzing online information behavior by, for example, looking at your clickstream and placing cookies to record what you look at and listen to, what you purchase, and where you go. In terms of targeted third-party advertising, from which most Internet sites make their profits, the *likes* and preferences that characterize your online interactions can be a gold mine for companies that want to sell to you. As we discussed in Chapter 3, your Web browsing has probably been interrupted at some point by a pop-up ad that appears to be *directly* related to something you had recently been searching for, watching, or reading. The apps and services you download are not as free as they seem. An exchange is taking place, even though you might not be aware of it. "Instead of cash, people pay Google *in kind*: with their identity, their behaviour, their habits and their preferences" (Scally, 2015; emphasis added). As Bartlett (2013) points out, "What may seem innocuous, even worthless information—shopping, musical preferences, holiday destinations—is seized on by the digital scavengers who sift through cyberspace looking for information they can sell: a mobile phone number, a private email address." Monetizing personal digital data is the name of the game for businesses today.

The sheer amount of data about individuals that is collected, especially by Internet giants such as Google, Facebook, and online retailers such as Amazon, has meant that *Big Data* itself has become big business. Although there is no universal definition, the following is a useful conceptualization of Big Data:

Big data refers to things one can do at a large scale that cannot be done at a smaller one, to extract new insights or create new forms of value, in ways that change markets, organizations, the relationship between citizens and governments, and more.
Mayer-Schönberger and Cukier (2013)

The work of Cambridge University's Psychometrics Centre is further testament to the growing interest in the data that can be harvested from social media sites. As far back as 2007, a researcher there launched the myPersonality app, which encouraged Facebook users to complete a range of psychometric tests, get feedback on their scores, and share their scores with friends. By 2012, over 6 million Facebook users had completed the test, creating an enormous data bank of psychological scores and social media information, which researchers were permitted to access. Many researchers from all over the world took advantage of this incredible resource, and more than 30 scholarly papers based on the data have been published. The center now works with many commercial companies that wish to use the techniques and methods pioneered by the center in their market research (Lewsey, 2015).

For the most part, there are no—or at least very few—legal restrictions on selling these data on to interested parties, and the lucrative nature of this market has led to the establishment of giant *data brokers* or clearinghouses, such as Acxiom and Epsilon, which collect, analyze, package, and sell on personal data as a valuable commodity. Lists of individuals, categorized by attributes such as gender, sexual orientation, medical conditions, location, and any number of different variables, are now available for commercial companies to buy in order to target the most profitable niche markets. In the past this information was typically gathered through labor-intensive and costly market research, by, for example, asking customers to complete survey questionnaires or interviews about their habits and preferences. Online browsing and interaction have opened a whole new, relatively low-cost world of market research and advertizing; much of this data collection is carried out without users' knowledge. It is estimated that each of us gives away "up to £5000 worth of data every year" (Bartlett, 2013). The reality is, however, that there is no clear picture of how much and what type of data are collected about individuals, as well as, importantly, how this information is used.

In 2013, the *Financial Times* (http://on.ft.com/14yjj65) created an interactive calculator on its website to enable you to calculate how much your personal data might be worth, if sold. You are asked to check a variety of boxes under the headings of Demographics, Family & Health, Property, Activities, and Consumer. The site then calculates approximately what marketers would pay for your individual data and estimates what a *package* of data similar to yours would cost. Interestingly, data about individuals are generally not valued at an especially high rate. According to the *Financial Times*, "General information about a person, such as their age, gender and location, is worth a mere $0.0005 per person, or $0.50 per 1000 people" (Steel, Locke, Cadman, & Freese, 2013), although data about consumers, who are undergoing major life changes, such as becoming a parent, moving house, or getting married, are considered to be worth more. Very sensitive personal information, such as medical conditions that individuals are suffering from, is worth more again. The most valuable data of all are information about an individual's social influences; people who seem to display a high degree of influence online are a valuable target for companies wishing to create a *buzz* about their products. As digital detectives, it is important to be aware of the existence of this *digital dossier*—the detailed profile about you that can be created—based on your online information behavior; this will enable you to make informed choices about how much information to give away and how much to hold back.

11.7 HOW DO I APPEAR ON THE INTERNET?

There are a number of ways for you to monitor your online presence in order to evaluate the type of image you are projecting. First, create a *Digital Footprint* folder on your computer, where you can store all of the content about you that you find on the Web.

11.7.1 *Ego Surfing*: The First Step

Ego surfing is a self-explanatory term defined as "the act of using search engines to seek references to one's own website or to view webpages that mention your own name (or company name)" (Webopedia, n.d.). This is a strategy that can be used to locate *data spills* about yourself, that is, information that you do not want to appear publicly. *Self-googling* is usually the first step in this process. What comes up in the search results when you enter your own name?

Take a short break from reading this chapter and type your own name into Google. Answer the following questions:

- What are the first five results that appear? Are they all about you or about other people with the same name?
- What images of you appear under the *Image* search?
- Do you think the first five results that are about you give a positive or negative impression?
- If a stranger googled your name, what could they deduce about your character?
- Would you be happy if a potential employer saw the first five results?
- Do the first five results give any indication of your academic, sporting, professional, or other achievements?
- Are there any sites or pages about you that are missing from the first five results?
- Is there anything you wish you could erase?

Remember, as we discussed in Chapter 3, research has shown that users often do not go beyond the first page of search results after typing in a query, and they may not even click on more than the first one or two links. As the saying goes: first impressions count. Carefully search for yourself, not just on Google, but on a variety of different search engines, including Yahoo!, Bing, and DuckDuckGo, to name but three. Expand your search to include other information related to yourself, as follows:

"Your Name" AND university

"Your Name" AND workplace

"Your Name" AND sports club

"Your Name" AND "City you live in"

Take a screenshot of anything interesting that you find, and save it in your Digital Footprint folder.

11.7.2 Google Alerts

You can also set up a Google Alert for your own name, which will let you know at intervals when your name is mentioned on the Web. Navigate to https://www.google.com/alerts; in the search box *Create an alert about…*, enter your own name, using quotation marks to make sure that your full name is treated as a phrase search. Beside the *Create alert* button, click on *Show options* to specify the alert settings, such as how often you wish to be alerted, what kinds of sources you wish to be searched, the language and/or region of the search results, and the email address to which you wish the alerts to be delivered. However, you should also be aware that you might receive alerts about other people who have the same name. To be more specific, you can add details or create new alerts that are unique to you, for example, your email address or your name plus the institution where you study or work. Think of the information people might enter if they were searching for you specifically; for example, they might search for your name, plus the city where you live or a sports club where you are a member. These are all alerts you can set up for yourself.

11.7.3 People-Search and Visualization Websites

While search engines like Google are a useful place to start, there are also a number of search engines that are designed specifically to facilitate searches for people-related information. While the commercial side of online people-finding has been exploited by companies—there are many services that you must pay for—there are also several excellent free resources that enable you to broaden the search for your digital footprint. Some of these are outlined below.

11.7.3.1 Pipl

The first of these search engines is Pipl (https://pipl.com). What is special about Pipl is that it searches the Deep Web to find people-related information, which gives you results beyond what you might find through the standard search engines. Pipl searches across social media sites and blogs, such as Facebook, Flickr, and LinkedIn, and also finds any mentions of your name in public records, such as birth and property databases. Another useful feature of Pipl is that it allows you to search by email address, online username, and reverse phone number lookup. Unlike many of the existing people search engines, Pipl has an international scope and searches beyond the United States. When you search Pipl, it produces a single-page *report* on the person you are looking for, which includes links to their personal social media pages, Amazon wish lists, bookmarking sites where they have an account, as well as basic career, education, and location information. Pipl is useful because it can retrieve accounts on sites that you may have forgotten about and now wish to delete or use again.

11.7.3.2 PeekYou

PeekYou (http://www.peekyou.com) is another example of a people search engine that has an international scope. In a similar way to Pipl, PeekYou "collects and combines scattered content from social sites, news sources, homepages, and blog platforms to present comprehensive online identities" (PeekYou, 2015). Searching for a real name or username, PeekYou allows you to search by either *World* or specific American states. Potential *matches* are displayed on the results page, and you have the option to focus the results by social media, public records, phone, email, Web search, or images. Scrolling down the results page provides a huge amount of information. Of particular interest is the *Documents* category, which includes PDFs that may be related to the name you searched for.

11.7.3.3 Life Online Mirror

The Life Online Mirror (http://mirror.nationalmediamuseum.org.uk) is a fascinating online installation project that was created by the National Media Museum in the United Kingdom, in collaboration with Cambridge University researchers in psychology. The aim of the project is to show you a *digital reflection* of yourself, extrapolated from your online activity. To achieve this, the creators use a personality analysis system (the *Big 5*) and compare your personality traits with a vast database of people to try and predict your personality to a high degree of accuracy. The Life Online

Mirror does this by requesting access to your Facebook profile or by asking you to answer a number of questions. The questionnaire asks you about the online news sources you regularly check, the celebrities you follow on Twitter, the music you are likely to stream or download, the social networks you use, and the technology brands you favor. Based on these answers, you receive an estimated personality profile, with descriptions under five specific personality traits. Some of the profile attributes require you to link to specific social media accounts for further information. This can be a fun activity, even if it is not completely accurate, and an interesting way of considering what your online activity might say about your personality.

11.7.3.4 University of Cambridge Psychometrics Centre

Following the conclusion of the *myPersonality* app, which ran from 2007 to 2012, there are currently two tests that you can take via the myPersonality project website:

- **Apply Magic Sauce** (http://applymagicsauce.com/test.html): This requires you to log into your Facebook account. The test endeavors to predict your personality based on your Facebook *likes*. You receive a profile snapshot that attempts to guess your age, psychological gender, sexual preference, relationship status, and political orientation, among other attributes.
- **Traditional personality testing** (http://tests.e-psychometrics.com) includes *Predictive Big Data*, an audit of public attitudes toward big data and predictive technologies, *Diener's Satisfaction with Life Scale*, and *My Personality*, which measures five fundamental dimensions of personality.

11.8 PROTECTING YOUR PRIVACY: CONTROLLING YOUR ONLINE REPUTATION

In general, what do people do to protect their online reputations or, more proactively, to ensure that their digital footprint is a positive one? A Pew Internet study of privacy management found that "social network users are becoming more active in pruning and managing their accounts" (Madden, 2012) through engaging in activities, such as *unfriending* or restricting friends on social media sites, *untagging* themselves from photographs that have been posted online, restricting public access to their profiles, and deleting unwanted comments. All of this is collectively known as *profile pruning* and represents a key strand of your personal online reputation management strategy. You can select one of two strategies in controlling your online reputation. First, you can choose to *minimize* your digital footprint by reducing your public online interactions and placing strict privacy controls on the browsers, sites, and apps that you use. Second, you can create, publish, and promote *positive* content about yourself that conveys an image you proactively choose and wish to portray to the world. The best strategy is, of course, a blend of both approaches.

11.8.1 Crumble the Cookies

All digital detectives should know that you can control cookies through the privacy settings on the Internet browser that you use; this reduces the information that can be gathered about your online activities. For instance, you can set your browser to:

- delete all or selected cookies.
- block all cookies.
- allow all cookies.
- block third-party cookies only.
- clear all cookies when you quit the browser.
- block cookies from certain sites and allow them from others.

In Google Chrome, cookies, images, JavaScript, and plug-ins are all allowed by default. However, the procedure to adjust your privacy settings is straightforward. First, click on the Chrome menu on the browser toolbar; this is located at the top right-hand corner and is an icon depicting three horizontal parallel lines. Select *Settings*, and then scroll down to click on *Show advanced settings*. On this screen, you should once again scroll down until you come to the *Privacy* section. You will see a button called *Content settings*. This is where the cookie controls are found. Here you will see a number of options:

- **Allow local data to be set**: This setting allows both first-party and third-party cookies by default.
- **Keep local data only until you quit your browser**: This setting allows sites to keep local data, including first-party and third-party cookies, and then erases this information when you exit the browser.
- **Block sites from setting any data**: This setting blocks all cookies from your browser. Using this setting means that you will have to sign in to certain sites every time you wish to access them.
- **Block third-party cookies and site data**: If you select this option, only cookies from third parties on sites that you access will not be accepted in your browser. First-party cookies on sites will still be permitted.

Even when you opt to block cookies, you can choose to make exceptions for certain sites. In Chrome, by clicking on *Manage exceptions*, you can include sites or domains for which you wish to have a different cookie setting. Also, by clicking on the button *All cookies and site data*, you can choose to remove all or selected cookies from your browser. Chrome's privacy settings also give you the option to *Send a "Do Not Track" request with your browsing traffic*. However, this does not guarantee that sites will adhere to this request; they may track you nonetheless.

The pathway on Internet Explorer is slightly different. Here, click on the *gears* symbol in the top right-hand corner, then *Internet Options*. Choose the *Privacy* tab; you will see a vertical slider scale, which allows you to set the privacy level of your browser from *Accept All Cookies*, which is the lowest level, to *Block All Cookies*, which is the highest level. There are various settings in between, such as *Medium*, which blocks or restricts first- and third-party cookies under certain conditions. You should choose the level of protection with which you are most comfortable.

11.8.2 Mobile Browsing

The same rules apply whether you browse the Web on your desktop or mobile devices. Be aware of your privacy settings. For mobile apps, individual app settings can be adjusted by first accessing general settings and then selecting the relevant app. For example, the settings for the Safari browser on Apple iOS devices allow you to block pop-ups, set a *Do not Track* option, choose a fraudulent website warning alert, and control cookies by giving you the option to *Always block, Allow from websites I visit, Allow from current website only*, or *Always allow*. You can also choose to enable passwords and autofill for online forms, which can include credit card information, if you wish.

11.8.3 Install a Tracker Blocker

Cookies can also be managed by tracker blockers. For instance, Ghostery (https://www.ghostery.com/en) is a good example of a free tracker blocker that can be installed on your browser. Once installed, Ghostery scans any webpages that you navigate to and identifies the ad networks, behavioral data providers, Web publishers, and anyone else who is interested in what you do online. Then it presents you with a list in the *findings panel*, which you can access by clicking on the *ghost* icon beside the address bar in your browser. You then have a choice to block the trackers manually, to prevent them following your activity, or to ignore them.

11.8.4 Blitz Your Browser

When you browse normally, all of the information about the sites you visit is stored in *Web browser history files*, which means that anyone who has access to these files can see what you have been viewing online. One way of protecting your privacy is to delete your browsing history every time you finish a session. In Google Chrome, you will find the History option under the general settings menu, or press Ctrl-H for a shortcut. Here, you are able to view your browsing history for the day. You can click on the *Clear browsing data* button to remove all items or select individual items for deletion. In Internet Explorer, the *Delete History* option is found in the *General* tab in the *Internet options* menu.

Another way of avoiding being tracked while you browse is to browse anonymously or *incognito*, which means that the sites you visit will not be stored in the browser history. In Chrome, you can do this by clicking *New incognito window* under *Settings*, or press Ctrl-Shift-N for a shortcut. For the same effect in Internet Explorer, select *Safety* in the *Settings* menu, then *InPrivate Browsing*. You can also browse privately on your mobile devices; for Safari users on iOS devices, in-private browsing can be set by tapping the *Pages* icon (shaped as two squares) in the lower right-hand corner, then tapping *Private*. When private browsing has been activated, Safari appears black or dark, instead of white or gray.

11.8.5 Browse the Alternatives

In the past few years, a number of alternative search engines have appeared that claim not to track your search behavior, in effect allowing you to search anonymously. Three of the best known are the following:

- **DuckDuckGo** (www.duckduckgo.com): The creators of Duck-DuckGo state clearly in their privacy policy that they "do not collect or share personal information" about those who use their search engine. In effect, this means that searches you carry out on DuckDuckGo cannot be linked to you or your device because they do not store information, such as the IP address of your computer, as other search engines do. In addition, DuckDuckGo uses no browser cookies *by default*, which means that your activities cannot be tracked.
- **Ixquick** (www.ixquick.com): Ixquick is a powerful search engine that also operates under a privacy policy stating that they do not collect or share any personal information about their users. Specifically, they note that they "do not record your IP address, we do not record which browser you are using (Internet Explorer, Safari, Firefox, Chrome etc.),

we do not record your computer platform (Windows, Mac, Linux, etc.), and we do not record your search words or phrases."

- **Disconnect Search** (https://disconnect.me/): This is an extension for Chrome and Firefox browsers that enables you to use search engines such as Google privately. Disconnect Search protects your privacy in a number of ways, including routing your search queries through their own servers, which makes it appear that your searches are coming from Disconnect Search, instead of your device.

11.8.6 Be Social Media Savvy

A growing number of social networking services, such as Snapchat, support a greater degree of privacy than we have become used to over the past decade, whereby photos, messages, and *shares* expire quickly, ostensibly wiping away the record of your communication from public view. You should be aware, however, that no application is totally secure, even apps such as Snapchat: "all digital communications leave a forensic trail, and cyber risk experts have shown that it is possible to recover a wide range of 'artifacts' from these messages before, after and during transmission" (Curtis, 2014). No matter what service you are using, awareness remains the key to maintaining your privacy and ensuring that you minimize the digital trail you leave in your wake. Most social media sites have a range of privacy settings that enable you to restrict the access other people have to your content. Since the default setting is often *public*, as a digital detective you need to spend some time figuring out who you wish to include or exclude from your online social world.

For social media sites, ask yourself a few key questions that can help to guide you in selecting the appropriate privacy settings. You should consider this checklist of questions in relation to each social media site that you use.

- How can your profile be found online?
- Who can request a connection with you?
- Who can send you private messages?
- Who can see what you post, upload, favorite, or link to?
- Who can comment on, *like*, *thank*, or add tags to your profile or the items that you post or upload?
- Who can view personal photographs or videos that you may have posted online?
- Who can see your location?
- Who can see what other people post or upload about you?
- Who can *share* what you post or upload with other people?

- How can you *prevent* people viewing your posts and photographs, or commenting about you, if you need to?
- How can you delete your profile, if you choose to?

For each question and each social media site or app, think about what your preferences might be; for example, do you want anyone in the world to be able to request a connection with you or just people who are specifically directed to your profile (e.g., *friend* you on Facebook, *follow* you on Twitter)? Do you want your friends to be able to *tag* photographs of you and post them without checking with you first? Do you want to be able to block content from certain people and share it with others? On social media sites, all of these variables can be controlled and filtered to a greater or lesser extent by managing your privacy settings.

11.8.7 Example: Facebook

Facebook, one of the most widely used social networking sites in the world, offers you some means of controlling access to your profile and content. Clicking on either the *padlock* or *arrow* icon at the top right-hand corner of your main Facebook page allows you to access the settings that you require to set up the appropriate controls. On the left-hand side of the *General Account Settings* page are links for *Privacy*, *Timeline and Tagging*, and *Blocking*. These links are the gateway to control of your profile. The available settings under each link are listed in Table 11.1.

You have various control options for each setting, such as limiting access to *Public, Friends, Only me*, or a customizable option that allows you to select specific users to include and exclude. Being able to manage tags means, for example, that you can prevent *friends of friends* from viewing items that are tagged by your friends, or you can review and approve tags before they are posted, rather than having to request that they be removed after the items appear on the site. You should take time to go through each of these settings and make a clear decision about how public or private you wish your profile and activities to be.

There are, of course, some things that you should *never* share on social media sites:

- Your address and phone number (mobile and landline).
- Personal conversations or exchanges.
- Your social or vacation plans.
- If your social media profiles are linked (e.g., Facebook and LinkedIn), avoid posting information on one site that you would not want to appear on the other (or unlink your profiles). Be aware that this could happen.

Table 11.1 Facebook Privacy Settings

Privacy	Who can see my stuff?	Who can see your future posts?
		Review all your posts and things you're tagged in?
		Limit the audience for posts you've shared with friends of friends or Public?
	Who can contact me?	Who can send you friend requests?
		Whose messages do I want filtered into my inbox?
	Who can look me up?	Who can look you up using the email address you provided?
		Who can look you up using the phone number you provided?
		Do you want other search engines to link to your timeline?
Timeline and Tagging	Who can add things to my timeline?	Who can post on your timeline?
		Review posts friends tag you in before they appear on your timeline?
	Who can see things on my timeline?	Who can see posts you've been tagged in on your timeline?
		Who can see what others post on your timeline?
	How can I manage tags people add and tagging suggestions?	Review tags people add to your own posts before the tags appear on Facebook?
		When you are tagged in a post, who do you want to add to the audience if they aren't already in it?
		Who sees tag suggestions when photos that look like you are uploaded?
Blocking	Restricted List Block users Block app invites Block event invites Block apps Block Pages	N/A

- Sensitive information about your workplace that could be used by competitors.
- Photographs of your children, if you have any, or of other people's children (e.g., relatives, friends, neighbors).
- Any information about your personal finances.

- Any of your passwords, with anyone, even close friends. Recall the section on password management from Chapter 10.
- Any password *hints* or security questions.
- Any negative comments about your place of education, workplace, and so on.
- Anything that you are even slightly uncertain about.

11.8.8 Flood the Web with Positivity

While you can take various measures to protect your privacy and restrict what people can see about you online, the best way to take advantage of the power of online reputation is to ensure that what people *do* see places you in the best possible light. You should adopt a proactive approach to your online profile and develop your own personal reputation strategy. This strategy should consist of the following building blocks:

- **Professional networking**: Even though you might be at the very beginning of your time in higher education, it is *never* too soon to develop a professional online presence. An important step is to set up a high-quality LinkedIn profile and keep it up to date with information about your achievements, education, work experience, awards, volunteer activities, publications, and so on. Your profile picture on LinkedIn should be friendly and approachable, but semiformal and professional; for instance, in the photo, you should wear the kind of clothes you might wear in the workplace. You should then make connections with classmates, colleagues, and anyone within your networks with whom you can engage in a supportive way. You can request recommendations from people you have worked with and those who can positively endorse you. Join groups that are relevant to your professional and personal interests, and participate in online discussions. Share content that you think your connections might find useful. You should include links to other sites about you that you may like people to view, for example, your blog or personal website.
- **Blogging**: A recent survey by Fractl and Buzzstream (Morrison, 2015) of more than 1200 participants found that *blog articles* are the most consumed type of online content across all generations—Millennials, Generation X, and Baby Boomers—ranking higher than images, e-books, comments, memes, and quizzes. A well-curated blog is the perfect way to create a fresh online presence with the potential to strengthen your reputation. As part of your strategy, think about starting a blog on a topic that you are interested in or very knowledgeable about. Frequently use words

that you would like to be associated with if someone performs a search for you; for instance, if you are interested in a career in communications, blog about media-related topics and use as many key terms as you can, including the tags you attach to your posts. This will help to move your link up the list of search results when someone searches for those key terms. Platforms such as WordPress, Tumblr, and Blogger have made it easy to create and maintain personal blogs.

- **Personal website**: If you do not wish or do not have the time to maintain a blog, consider setting up a personal website using a service such as WordPress or Tumblr. (You can always do both, of course!) You can keep all of your content in one place and create a strong personal brand, almost like a one-stop shop for you!

- **Personal versus professional**: Think about whether you need to maintain separate personal and professional online profiles. Which sites fall into each category? For example, you might choose to use Facebook and Instagram for personal content only and completely restrict the privacy settings on these sites, whereas you use your public Twitter and LinkedIn accounts for work or education-related postings that everyone can see.

- **Social bookmarking and content curation sites**: Use social bookmarking and content curation sites to bolster your association with topics relating to your educational or professional interests.

11.9 THE RIGHT TO BE FORGOTTEN

In May 2014, the perceived power and influence of an online reputation was cemented further by an extremely significant legal development in Europe: The European Commission ruled that search engines, including Google, must offer individuals the *right to be forgotten*, that is, the right to request that information about them be removed from a search engine's database under particular conditions (Travis & Arthur, 2014). According to the Commission, "This applies where the information is inaccurate, inadequate, irrelevant or excessive for the purposes of the data processing" (European Commission, 2014). As a result, search engines have received various requests for information to be removed from the Internet, sometimes resulting in the deletion of content we would not have expected to have been removed (e.g., newspaper articles).

As a result, the impact of the *right to be forgotten* condition has been mixed. While the ruling has proven helpful to people who have been trolled or otherwise unfairly treated online, the ruling also has allowed some people to airbrush unsavory aspects of their lives (e.g., a criminal past) from the

Internet. The call to have mentions of some people's names deleted also has raised questions about freedom of speech, such as the call for deletion that has led to removal of entire news articles. The ruling has left search engines in a situation where they are, in effect, the unintended censors of information and the Internet (see e.g., Goldman, 2015).

If information can be deleted from the Internet, there should be no problem with dealing with unfortunate posts, erroneous information, and trolls, right? Not quite. Although the *right to be forgotten* offers some leeway in reprinting your digital footprint, you must file a request to have information removed. It is unfeasible to anticipate that ongoing or frequent requests would be approved without questions being raised and debates occurring about your own responsibility in posting information and whether information you post yourself can or should be removed under the *right to be forgotten* ruling. Remember that, regardless of the origin of information on the Internet, it takes time to process a removal request, and this means that the undesired information will remain in the public domain at least temporarily—and potentially long enough to cause damage to your digital image. The obvious choice here is to manage content as much as possible, taking care with what information you ultimately decide to share and with whom you elect to share that information.

It is important to note, however, that the *right to be forgotten* currently applies only to search engine subdomains within the European Union, such as google.ie and google.co.uk. The legislation specifically states that, "Even if the physical server of a company processing data is located outside Europe, EU rules apply to search engine operators if they have a branch or a subsidiary in a Member State which promotes the selling of advertising space offered by the search engine" (European Commission, 2014).

11.10 CHALLENGES

1. Carry out a full online audit of your digital footprint using the approaches suggested in this chapter. What do you think is the impression given by your online presence? Does it reflect your true personality? What actions could you take to change or improve your online reputation?
2. For this exercise, team up with another student (preferably someone you don't know well). You both must have a device connected to the Internet, with access to a browser. For 15 min, each of you must try to find out as much as possible about the other person by searching the Web. Now, share what you found with your partner. What does this exercise tell you about online reputation and privacy? Were you surprised by

what your partner was able to discover about you? Do you think you need to take any actions to alter your digital footprint as a result?

3. Create a personal website using a free platform such as WordPress.com, wix.com or weebly.com. The aim of this website should be to showcase your achievements, abilities, skills, and professional attributes to potential future employers. How can you create a professional image that will serve as an online résumé?

4. Individually or in a group, develop a social media strategy for an institution, commercial company, or voluntary organization of your choice. What approach would you advise this organization to take to create a positive online presence and to help them to achieve their aims? You should think about the following:

   a. What should the organization's website look like? What features and content should they include to attract their target audience?

   b. What social media sites should they use to engage with their target audience/clients (e.g., Facebook, LinkedIn, Twitter, Google+)? What kind of content would be appropriate to include in their online profile(s)? What should they *avoid* doing?

   c. What different media could they use to create a positive image (e.g., videos, images, a blog)?

   d. What interactive tools could they use to engage fully with their target audience (e.g., quizzes, online reviews, QR codes)?

   e. Would it be useful for this organization to develop a mobile app? If so, what would the purpose of the app be?

REFERENCES

Bartlett, J. (2013, December 7). *iSPY: How the internet buys and sells your secrets*. The Spectator. Retrieved from http://www.spectator.co.uk/features/9093961/little-brothers-are-watching-you.

Blakeman, S. (2015, March 11). *Burn your résumé – LinkedIn has made it obsolete*. LinkedIn Pulse. Retrieved from https://www.linkedin.com/pulse/burn-your-r%C3%A9sum%C3%A9-linkedin-has-made-obsolete-steve-blakeman.

CareerBuilder. (2013). *More employers finding reasons not to hire candidates on social media, finds CareerBuilder survey*. Retrieved from http://www.careerbuilder.com/share/aboutus/pressreleasesdetail.aspx?sd=6/26/2013&id=pr766&ed=12/31/2013.

Curtis, E. (2014, March 12). *Is Snapchat as private as it seems?* The Telegraph. Retrieved from http://www.telegraph.co.uk/technology/internet-security/10692856/Is-Snapchat-as-private-as-it-seems.html.

Edwards, M. (2014, April 3). *Why you should hire a social media consultant*. LinkedIn. Retrieved from https://www.linkedin.com/pulse/20140403135916-133448973-why-you-should-hire-a-social-media-consultant.

European Commission. (2014). *Factsheet on the right to be forgotten ruling*. Retrieved from http://ec.europa.eu/justice/dataprotection/files/factsheets/factsheet_data_protection_en.pdf.

Goldman, D. (2015, January 4). *Google: The reluctant censor of the Internet*. CNN Money. Retrieved from http://money.cnn.com/2015/01/04/technology/google-censorship.

Hampton, K. N., Rainie, L., Weixu, L., Dwyer, M., Inyoung, S., & Purcell, K. (2014). *Social media and the spiral of silence*. Pew Research Center. Retrieved from http://www.pewinternet. org/files/2014/08/PI_Social-networks-and-debate_082614.pdf.

Information Commissioner's Office. (2015). *What are cookies?*. Retrieved from https://ico. org.uk/for-the-public/online/cookies.aspx.

Internet Society. (2015). *Why did we start leaving such big footprints?*. [Online tutorial] Retrieved from http://www.internetsociety.org/your-digital-footprint/why-start.

Jobvite. (2014). *Social recruiting survey*. Retrieved from https://www.jobvite.com/wp-content/uploads/2014/10/Jobvite_SocialRecruiting_Survey2014.pdf.

Jones, R. H., & Hafner, C. A. (2012). *Understanding digital literacies: A practical introduction*. New York: Routledge.

Kaplan, A. M., & Haenlein, M. (2010). Users of the world, unite! The challenges and opportunities of social media. *Business Horizons, 53*, 59–68.

Lewsey, F. (2015). *How to read a digital footprint*. University of Cambridge. Research Features. Retrieved from http://www.cam.ac.uk/research/features/how-to-read-a-digital-footprint.

Madden, M. (2012). *Privacy management on social media sites*. Pew Research Center's Internet & American Life Project. Retrieved from http://www.pewinternet.org/files/old-media//Files/Reports/2012/PIP_Privacy_management_on_social_media_sites_022412.pdf.

Madden, M., & Smith, A. (2010). *Reputation management and social media: How people monitor their identity and search for others online*. Pew Research Center's Internet & American Life Project. Retrieved from http://www.pewinternet.org/files/old-media//Files/Reports/2010/PIP_Reputation_Management_with_topline.pdf.

Magnuson, L. (2011). Promoting privacy: Online and reputation management as an information literacy skill. *College & Research Libraries News, 72* (3), 137–140.

Mayer-Schönberger, V., & Cukier, K. (2013). *Big data: A revolution that will transform how we live, work and think*. London: John Murray.

Morrison, K. (2015, May 7). *How different generations consume content online [Infographic]*. Social Times, Adweek Blog Network. Retrieved from http://www.adweek.com/socialtimes/how-different-generations-consume-content-online-infographic/619882.

Nudd, T. (2011, March 9). *Chrysler throws down an F-bomb on Twitter*. Adweek. Retrieved from http://www.adweek.com/adfreak/chrysler-throws-down-f-bomb-twitter-126967.

Office of the Privacy Commissioner of Canada. (2011). *Cookies – following the crumbs [Fact sheet]*. Retrieved from https://www.priv.gc.ca/resource/fs-fi/02_05_d_49_e.asp.

PeekYou. (2015). *How it works*. Retrieved from http://www.peekyou.com.

Pilkington, E. (2013, December 22). *Justine Sacco, PR executive fired over racist tweet, 'ashamed'*. The Guardian. Retrieved from http://www.theguardian.com/world/2013/dec/22/pr-exec-fired-racist-tweet-aids-africa-apology.

Scally, D. (2015, May 14). *De-Google your life: It's worth the hassle if you value your privacy*. Irish Times. Retrieved from http://www.irishtimes.com/business/technology/de-google-your-life-it-s-worth-the-hassle-if-you-value-your-privacy-1.2211355.

Steel, E., Locke, C., Cadman, E., & Freese, B. (2013, June 12). *How much is your personal data worth?* Financial Times. Retrieved from http://www.ft.com/cms/s/2/927ca86e-d29b-11e2-88ed-00144feab7de.html#axzz3e3uym5NJ.

Thakur, B. (2011, November 25). *What does your digital footprint reveal? [Blog post]*. Retrieved from http://bhaskarthakur.com/blog/your-digital-footprint.

Travis, A., & Arthur, C. (2014, May 13). *EU court backs 'right to be forgotten': Google must amend results on request*. The Guardian. Retrieved from http://www.theguardian.com/technology/2014/may/13/right-to-be-forgotten-eu-court-google-search-results.

Webopedia. (n.d.). *Ego surfing*. Retrieved August 25, 2015, from http://www.webopedia.com/TERM/E/ego_surfing.html.

CHAPTER 12

Fact or Fiction? Negotiating New Learning Spaces

12.1 THE DILEMMA: 'REAL LEARNING HAS TO TAKE PLACE IN A CLASSROOM, RIGHT?'

Online learning has increasingly become a feature of learning opportunities, whether in a formal university setting or in informal venues, such as social media and corporate websites. While learning informally online may or may not already be part of your learning tool kit, the transition to online opportunities in the academic setting may be quite new and different. A successful transition to a learning experience that may be highly mediated by technology—using learning management systems (LMSs), e-tutorials, collaborative authoring tools, podcasts, and many more resources—often requires some additional attention. Many institutions have adopted mobile applications as one-stop shopping for communication and learning tools (Green, 2011). This chapter introduces you to the benefits of synchronous, as well as self-managed remote and asynchronous learning activities, which may be complementary to, rather than in competition with, traditional face-to-face classroom activities. New resources that may be unfamiliar, such as an LMS, are described in terms of their structure, function, and privacy properties. Becoming a savvy user of web-based tools, such as blogging platforms, online survey software, document sharing resources, and other creative tools will expand your formal educational experience.

In this chapter, you will:
- learn about the range of online learning opportunities.
- consider ways to excel in an online learning environment.
- identify ways in which to utilize different learning modes in a virtual setting.
- explore essential e-resources to facilitate learning.
- adopt a systematic personal information management approach that takes advantage of a range of digital tools to facilitate learning online.

Digital Detectives
ISBN 978-0-08-100124-0

12.2 MAKING THE TRANSITION TO THE VIRTUAL CLASSROOM

The trend in university education is to tailor teaching to facilitate personal learning (McLoughlin & Lee, 2010). As universities shift the focus of learning from delivery of content to a more personalized, student-centred approach, students may find that they have a greater role in shaping their educational experience. In this educational environment, students must manage their individual learning to ensure that they acquire the necessary skills to move forward after their university degrees, with digital competencies assisting them in this process.

Where do you feel you learn best? Formal and/or informal learning contexts may be attractive to students. From the time we are young, the formal classroom setting plays a formative role in our learning. More and more, the digital environment also is playing a strong role in our learning. However, receiving instruction from a person in a physical classroom environment may still be the obvious mode of learning that we associate with institutional learning. There are many ways that we might learn; the classroom context is only one. Our challenge is to take advantage of both traditional and new online modes of learning as appropriate to our learning needs.

The traditional learning context in universities has long been the classroom. Formal learning opportunities in the university environment are dominated largely by lectures delivered by subject experts and infused with activities, such as labs and small-group tutorials, as appropriate for a given discipline. Depending on the courses taken, one or more of these learning opportunities may be integrated into a learning schedule for a given course.

The online learning environment offers alternative means of learning, importantly facilitating the achievement of learning goals via remote and varied locations. While possibly simply offering a different location for learning this environment may also provide new means of learning. For instance, lectures are still possible as synchronous events online, as well as podcasts or vodcasts that can be reviewed multiple times.

Online learning in a formal education setting may be new to you. While this contextual change for learning may seem like an easy transition, students need to beware of the many challenges associated with this form of learning, just as challenges exist for learning in a traditional lecture theatre. It is essential to consider the online environment as a tool for learning and how best to utilize this environment for formal, as well as informal learning.

12.3 FORMAL ONLINE LEARNING SPACES

Universities and colleges today most frequently use some sort of software for online teaching and learning, often an LMS. Examples of LMSs used in higher education include Blackboard, Desire2Learn, and Moodle. Various names and meanings are associated with this sort of educational system, for example, learning content management system and virtual learning environment. This sort of system is likely to play a significant role in the organization and delivery of your learning at university.

LMSs offer a range of modes of learning online, supporting fully online learning and blended online and offline learning environments. For example, your instructor may post important learning documents, such as your syllabus, assessment instructions, and weekly learning activities, for you to view or download. Content may provide a basis for online activities, such as exercises and quizzes, and shared learning spaces for collaborative input. The online space for a given course is organized and managed by the course instructor to facilitate your learning.

Importantly, the online course space provides to the student a measurable opportunity to demonstrate engagement with the course content in this environment. The LMS tracks your views of documents, participation in online journals, completion of e-tutorials and quizzes, and so on. This form of digital footprint can help you demonstrate a record of achievement, as well as alert the instructor to areas that may have been difficult for you.

12.4 PREPARING FOR SUCCESSFUL LEARNING ONLINE

Successful online learning critically requires your presence, that is, your full attention. Students often have the misperception that learning organized around an online space requires no preparation or participation. They may treat university timetable slots for online learning as optional or unnecessary. This misunderstanding of learning can lead to missed opportunities to acquire essential learning for progression in a course. All learning requires your active involvement. Be sure to give online learning your undivided attention, just as you should learning in a physical classroom.

Several key points can help you achieve learning success online:

1. **Explore the online learning environment as soon as you have registered for a course delivered in part or wholly online.**
   Your instructor will add documents and activities to the online learning space for a given course for you. This is not a random act. Instructors

have a plan to help you acquire learning around a given topic, so pay close attention to the online learning space. Before engaging with course materials, ensure you familiarize yourself with wayfinding in this particular online space. The university may have an institutional template for all courses that provides standardized information points and organization (e.g., course description, course contacts, learning materials). An institutional template facilitates similar wayfinding across courses for you. In addition, there may be course-specific points of information that instructors may provide for particular courses. Again, becoming familiar with these unique course attributes will help you to navigate the course effectively in the online environment.

If the LMS or an individual course features an online tour, be sure to take the tour before you embark on learning about course content. Knowing the layout of the course early can help you finesse navigation easily and quickly. When you are in a hurry at some point to access or upload content, you will be glad you know your way around!

2. **Download and review course materials immediately.**
   Download and carefully review the course syllabus. Remember that the syllabus is the instructor's blueprint for the course. Essential information, such as class times, instructions to access information, the instructor's contact details and office hours, a weekly schedule of topics, learning objectives and activities, is generally found in the course syllabus.

   In addition, take time at the beginning of the course to download and ensure you understand assessment requirements, including assessment instructions and feedback forms that form the basis of grading. Make a plan now for timely completion of this work.

3. **Learn how to submit assessment online well in advance of deadlines.**
   In the online environment, assessment is submitted online. Ensure that you understand how to upload and submit your work via your course LMS space well in advance of the assessment deadline. A university's late penalties apply to assessments submitted online, and it is essential to understand the online submission process to deliver assessments on time. The good news here is that students view LMSs, specifically Blackboard, as being easier to use than Facebook for posting files and homework (Milburn, Braham, & McClinton, 2014). However, the panic of a deadline can make any process fraught. You can ensure greater ease of submitting assessments online by taking note of the pathway to submission well before your assessment is due. Remember that systems, such as LMSs are

frequently updated; as a result, it is important to double-check the online submission process periodically, particularly at the beginning of each academic year.

4. **Use a digital diary on the go.**

   If you are still using a paper-based diary or no diary at all, now is the time to consider a digital alternative that you can access anytime and anywhere. Email providers, such as Google and Yahoo!, as well as LMSs, offer free calendar facilities. Use your mobile phone to consult your diary on the go. Take note of class meeting times, weekly topics, reading in preparation for class, and so on, and add each key date to your calendar. Use sharing functions to plan and share meeting times and tasks with teams.

5. **Ensure you complete all assigned activities each week.**

   Refer to and review your diary on a daily basis, as well as on a weekly rotation, to ensure that all tasks have been completed. Your instructor has provided learning activities timed to help you achieve the learning objectives for the course. Keeping on top of small, weekly tasks will help you progress your learning continuously, and this gradual learning approach will help you retain what you have learned.

6. **Set aside time to study in preparation for online quizzes and tests.**

   Online quizzes and tests may be presented in different question formats (e.g., multiple choice, true/false) as selected by your instructor. As you plan for ongoing activities, also consider the timing of quizzes and tests online. Give yourself the same preparation time as you would need in an offline learning environment. Familiarize yourself with the structure of the quiz or test. What are the test parameters: length of the test, number of questions, question format, open book? Importantly, leave yourself plenty of time to ensure that you are on top of the content to be covered in an online quiz or test.

7. **Prepare for e-guest visits.**

   Plan ahead for online activities, such as visitors. Being prepared signals your interest and engagement with the topic at hand, and you never know when a classroom guest from outside the university might lead to an important connection or even a job after graduation. Read assigned materials and check company websites in preparation, just as you would in the offline environment. Think of at least two questions to ask the e-guest, based on your prepared reading. You may be required to post questions in an asynchronous discussion space, or you may need to ask questions in a synchronous online discussion.

8. **Enhance your learning experience with materials outside the course.**
   Remember that you should apply the same principles for online activities to your preparation for learning beyond a virtual setting. For instance, explore online tours provided by your university library to explore new tools and learn new skills you can apply in the online classroom environment.

12.5 EXCELLING IN THE VIRTUAL CLASSROOM

Online interaction can be both rewarding and challenging. Students often have preferences for online or offline learning interactions, and they may select one learning environment over the other for varying reasons. Interestingly, the online environment can increase interactions for quieter students, who may not feel comfortable speaking up in the traditional classroom in the midst of other learners. A group of learners may be present together with that same student online, but the familiar feeling of perceived anonymity online creates a nonthreatening environment where participation can flow. Engagement is central to learning in the online environment. It is essential to become comfortable in the virtual environment to learn effectively there. Certain approaches can facilitate your online class interactions and communication.

The synchronous and asynchronous online environments pose different challenges. The asynchronous environment—that is, an online space in which interaction can occur at different times and often when others may not be online—enables the individual student to post, reflect, and digest content at their own pace and in their own time. The synchronous environment—that is, an online space in which participants meet together simultaneously—requires students to interact with others in that moment. The time in which an individual can type or voice a comment is immediate, as it would be in a traditional classroom.

Excelling in either the synchronous or asynchronous learning environment requires attention to some particular aspects of this environment. For instance, studying in a digital space is predicated on a basic understanding of the technology you are using to access this space. Before beginning to contribute to a course online, check your personal technology for a working connection to the online learning environment; this includes general connections to the Internet and your university's LMS. Within the LMS, a virtual space for specific class sessions is likely available. The technology around this classroom space should be explored before class begins. Students normally are expected to negotiate this access in advance and on their own. If you experience difficulty, consult with the information technology help desk on campus.

Once you have entered an online classroom space, familiarize yourself with the technical features available. For example, there is usually a means for raising your hand to ask a question during class. A whiteboard is often available, which can be used to add content freehand or to show slides. Communication with others is possible synchronously through a chat box conversation or as voice input. Instructors may provide a sample classroom space, in which you can practice navigating and using classroom tools ahead of time, so that you can focus on content when in class.

The same attention to technological functionality is required in the asynchronous environment. It is essential to try out procedures for posting content before deadlines. Post a test message to the discussion board. Set up a wiki space within the LMS and customize it. Check for system idiosyncrasies and note particular pathways to complete tasks. Remember that there is normally a *Help* option offered in a given LMS, which provides step-by-step assistance.

12.6 COLLABORATIVE OR USER-GENERATED CONTENT AND LEARNING IN THE DIGITAL WORLD

Collaborating with others to enhance learning is as important online as it is in the traditional classroom. Peer learning, a form of self-constructed learning, harnesses collaboratively created information and spaces to help explore subjects and embed learning. Peer learning has gained in popularity as a tool to help engage students.

A peer learning space may be formally or informally constructed. For instance, an instructor may ask students to share work via an online discussion space and to comment on each other's postings or submitted work to help everyone reflect more deeply on learning around concepts and information. For example, Purdue University offers an LMS called *Mixable*, an in house developed LMS. Mixable provides peer learning spaces online, where students can connect with classes, discuss ideas with each other, and review their peers' assessments.

Alternatively, students sometimes construct their own digital peer learning spaces. Various software tools can support peer learning, including file sharing and content construction via tools, such as Google *Drive*. Tools, such as Dropbox (www.dropbox.com) offer free file storage space and file sharing; Dropbox can also be integrated with other platforms for file access and file sharing.

Because university students often prefer software solutions that do not involve cost (e.g., Fulton & Gleave, 2013), mobile device applications, such as WhatsApp, are popular for contacting colleagues for study, organizing team meetings, and generally communicating. While Facebook's popularity has shifted among various demographics, the tool is still used by university students for teamwork, offering an easily accessed and used space for communication and collaboration through Facebook's Groups option. According to Milburn *et al.* (2014), students perceive Facebook as more easily used than Blackboard for communication tasks, such as discussions and sending notifications.

12.7 MANAGING MY PERSONAL TECHNOLOGY AND INFORMATION TO UTILIZE ONLINE LEARNING ENVIRONMENTS

Success with academic work depends, in part, on developing an appropriate work approach to facilitate efficient and effective completion of assigned learning tasks. The online environment can prove useful, but it is essential to bear in mind that academic achievement in the digital world is about more than selecting mobile applications and tools. Importantly, creating an overall system for productivity, utilizing the tools you choose, shapes your academic success.

The term *personal information manager*, or *PIM*, is important here. The acronym PIM is currently more commonly used to mean personal information management, a process of asserting personal control over information around us. Jones (2008) explores this concept of how we go about organizing information in his text, *Keeping Found Things Found*. In the digital world, a PIM is a form of software that provides personal organization functions, including tracking information and managing information. A PIM tool is much like the previously popular personal digital assistant (PDA), an electronic device that performed similar organizational functions. Interestingly, you are unlikely to have heard the term *personal information manager*; instead, we refer to *productivity tools* to help us manage some aspect of information in our daily lives. For some people, no term is used, whereas others simply refer to a particular tool itself, for example, their Google Calendar.

A PIM or productivity tool often is associated with maintaining multiple forms of information, for example, address books, to-do lists, calendar dates, reminders, communication, project management, and RSS feeds. A single tool may perform one or many functions, synchronizing information across multiple devices or with the Cloud, a web-based means of storing and accessing digital information. Productivity software is highly useful for educational purposes, facilitating planning, information acquisition, and project execution and management. Consider using a productivity tool to track your digital world at university. Start with your learning objectives, year-by-year educational planning, and module scheduling. All of this can be done via your smartphone. The smartphone is your new PDA.

12.8 POSITIVE LEARNING OUTCOMES VIA ESSENTIAL e-LEARNING RESOURCES

Instructors may provide a variety of e-resources in a given LMS course area for student consumption. Remember that your instructor has embedded digital tools and sources of information that correspond with specific aspects of learning for the particular course; you must take advantage of this material. To personalize your learning, consider additional digital tools and resources you can add to the mix to enhance your learning. All of the digital tools listed below fall under the heading of productivity tools. Adapt as appropriate for your learning and add to this list.

1. **Personal organization**

    As discussed above, a range of calendars, such as Google Calendar, are available and accessible via the Internet and/or mobile devices. Many of these tools have integrated task lists and other functions to provide the overall organization of previously used PDAs and the current PIM or productivity management approach.

    Task list applications also are common. For example, *Remember the Milk* (www.rememberthemilk.com) tracks and reminds the user of to-do items, and it automatically synchronizes information across multiple devices. *Bla Bla List* (http://blablalist.com) enables list creation and sharing with others. Various e-calendars (e.g., Google or Yahoo! calendars) have embedded task list functions. Integrate your use of the to-do list function with your daily and weekly calendar review schedule.

2. **Time management**

    Students must juggle multiple tasks at once. By tracking your time, you can ensure you are completing tasks as efficiently as possible. For instance, try

SlimTimer (http://slimtimer.com) to create a task, and then set a timer to gauge how long it takes you to complete that task. Review your progress and consider how you might improve your personal time management.

3. **Learning goal management**

    As discussed in Chapter 2, creating learning goals and reflecting on our achievement of those goals on an ongoing basis are both important factors in our learning. A simple journal application downloaded to a mobile device can facilitate continuous recording of information. Options for diary or journal applications are endless, for example, *Private Journal*, *My Secret Diary*, and *Day One*. Find a journal with a layout you like and start writing. Students also use blogs to document their lives. Try *WordPress* (www.WordPress.com) or Google's *Blogger* (www.blogger.com); both are available as mobile applications.

4. **Project management**

    Teamwork can prove difficult for students for a variety of reasons. Differing schedules and availability to meet, as well as ownership of tasks and management of task completion, are all challenges that teams must overcome. Successful teamwork involves ensuring that all team members have responsibility for a role or section of the task and tracking the work completed and yet to be completed. *Freedcamp* (https://freedcamp.com) is a web-based tool that supports team projects, task assignment, and so on, allowing multiple projects to be tracked at once.

5. **Collaboration**

    Effective team communication is another challenge for students working together on a task. Software tools, such as *Zoho* (www.zoho.com) offer integrated communication and collaboration solutions via a smartphone or the Web. Zoho brings together Google Mail, presentations, document and report organization, and online communication.

6. **Brainstorming**

    Whether working alone or with a team, at some point you will need to think creatively about task. Brainstorming is a common approach to thinking about problem solving. A productivity application called *bubbl.us* (https://bubbl.us) provides a digital means of capturing mind maps, which can then be exported in different formats.

7. **Webpage tracking**

    Since the late 1990s, several social bookmarking sites have been developed and become popular as a means of bookmarking Web content for future reference. Social bookmarking allows digital bookmarks to be organized and managed. Some tools have extended the simple noting of content; for example, *MyStickies* (www.mystickies.com) enables the user to highlight text within an item and then bookmark the page. With more content tagged than by the traditional digital bookmark, MyStickies is intended to expand the retrievability of an item.

8. **Finding scholarly sources of information**

   While your institution may subscribe to a variety of databases that can facilitate your ability to locate scholarly materials for use in assessment, there are sources of scholarly materials available on the Internet (see also Chapter 8). For example, *Google Scholar* is a well-known database of citations and often the full text of scholarly published documents. However, open-access repositories may also be useful to you. For example, *Scientific Research* (http://www.scirp.org) is an open-access academic publisher that provides access to a range of academic publications, including articles, books, and conference papers; the service features a mobile application that can be used on both Android and Apple devices.

9. **Presenting information**

   Presentations are a common feature of students' academic lives. Multiple tools can assist you with the development of presentations. The usual presentation software tool used in universities is Microsoft's PowerPoint; explore this tool for advanced features to add colour and movement to your slides. Many other presentation software tools, such as *Prezi* (www.prezi.com) and *SlideRocket* (http://www.sliderocket.com), offer multiple features to enhance audience engagement.

   Use specialized software to add unique features to a particular slide. For example, a drawing tool called *Gliffy* (www.gliffy.com) can be used to take some of your ideas and create a flowchart of them for presentations and reports. Word cloud applications, such as *Wordle* (www.wordle.net) and *WordItOut* (http://www.worditout.com), can help add interest to slides by presenting words in picture format.

10. **Generating reference lists for assessment**

    Students often struggle with preparing a list of references for assessment. The work is detail-intensive, and mistakes are often made because of the tendency to leave this task until the end of the assessment process. Your university may subscribe to tools, such as *Endnote* or *Flow*, for the management and preparation of references that follow specific citation style guides. You may also wish to experiment with simplified web-based tools, such as *WritingHouse* (http://writinghouse.org), which facilitate the creation of reference lists in American Psychological Association, Chicago, Harvard, and Modern Language Association citation styles.

12.9 HOW WILL e-SKILLS HELP ME AFTER UNIVERSITY?

The digital skills you develop during your university education can have a positive impact on your work and daily lives beyond the university environment. Adoption of a digital environment touches every part of our lives. Learning to communicate and take part in meetings online will facilitate your participation in the workplace, particularly with organizations that have colocated employees. Understanding how to manage your time will help you to process information efficiently in your work and daily lives. Use your developing digital skills and supporting productivity tools to help you become a more effective learner and digital citizen.

12.10 CHALLENGES

1. Explore the LMS used by your university.
   a. Identify the courses for which you are registered.
   b. Check for system messages and announcements to students from the overall LMS administrator or university, and act on these messages immediately where your input is required.
   c. Examine how information has been organized in the LMS. Make a list of key features that support your use of the LMS for your learning.
   d. Locate the online help manual for this LMS. Keep track of this information for future reference.
2. Using the Google or Yahoo! calendar function, set up a time management calendar.
   Note: If you have a calendar with one of these services already, then add your time management calendar to your general, personal calendar. If this is your first time using Google or Yahoo! services, remember that you need to set up an account with them before proceeding.
   a. Theme your calendar with a colour of your choice.
   b. Add all dates and deadlines relevant to your learning for the coming year (e.g., assessment deadlines, team meetings).
   c. Share team meeting entries with the members of the relevant project team(s).
   d. Add a task list to your calendar and rank priority items.
3. Create a personal productivity system. Select and set up three productivity tools that will enhance your education. How does each tool manage multiple information tasks? How do these tools back up your information?

REFERENCES

Fulton, C., & Gleave, H. (2013). Students and mobile phone apps: everyday uses for problem-solving. Panel: use of mobile apps in information seeking: an international viewpoint. In *Beyond the Cloud: Rethinking information Boundaries, Association for information Science & technology (ASIS&T) annual meeting, November 1–5, 2013, Montreal, Canada.*

Green, K. C. (2011). *Campus computing: Big gains in going mobile.* Retrieved from http://www.campuscomputing.net/item/campus-computing-2011-big-gains-going-mobile.

Jones, W. (2008). *Keeping found things found: The study and practice of personal information management.* London: Elsevier Inc.

McLoughlin, C., & Lee, M. J. W. (2010). Personalized and self-regulated learning in the Web 2.0 era: international exemplars of innovative pedagogy using social software. *Australasian Journal of Education Technology, 26*(1), 28–43. Retrieved from http://ascilite.org.au/ajet/ajet26/mcloughlin.html.

Milburn, A. B., Braham, A., & McClinton, J. (2014). Integrating qualitative components in quantitative courses using Facebook. *Interdisciplinary Journal of E-Learning and Learning Objects, 10,* 229–246. Retrieved from http://www.ijello.org/Volume10/IJELLOv10p229-246Milburn0872.pdf.

REFERENCES

ALA Digital Literacy Task Force. (2011). *What is digital literacy?* ALA, Office for Information Technology Policy. Retrieved from http://connect.ala.org/node/181197#sthash .LtRAktge.dpuf.

American Psychological Association. (n.d.). APA Style. Quick answers – References. Retrieved from http://www.apastyle.org/learn/quick-guide-on-references.aspx.

Badke, W. B. (2004). *Research strategies: Finding your way through the information fog.* New York: iUniverse, Inc.

Barry, C., & Lardner, M. (2010). A study of first click behavior and user interaction on the Google SERP. In *19th international conference on information systems development (ISD 2010). Prague, Czech Republic, August 25–27, 2010.* Retrieved from http://hdl.handle.net/10379/1492.

Bartlett, J. (December 7, 2013). *iSPY: How the internet buys and sells your secrets.* The Spectator. Retrieved from http://www.spectator.co.uk/features/9093961/little-brothers-are-watching-you.

Benson, V., & Filippaios, F. (2010). Effects of digital footprint on career management: evidence from social media in business education. Knowledge management, information systems, e-learning, and sustainability research. *Communications in Computer and Information Science, 111,* 480–486. Retrieved from https://kar.kent.ac.uk/28769/1/TECHEDU.pdf.

Bergman, M. K. (2001). White paper: the deep web: surfacing hidden value. *Journal of Electronic Publishing, 7*(1). Retrieved from http://quod.lib.umich.edu/cgi/t/text/idx/j/jep/3336451.0007.104/–white-paper-the-deep-web-surfacing-hidden-value?rgn=main;view=fulltext.

Brown, D. (2007). *Scientific communication and the dematerialization of scholarship; glossary.* Proquest-CSA Discovery Guides. Retrieved from http://archive-com.com/page/1795906/2013-04-02/http://www.csa.com/discoveryguides/scholarship/gloss_f.phph.

Budapest Open Access Initiative. (2002). *Read the Budapest Open Access Initiative.* Retrieved from http://www.budapestopenaccessinitiative.org/read.

Careerbuilder. (2013). *More employers finding reasons not to hire candidates on social media, finds Careerbuilder survey.* Retrieved from http://www.careerbuilder.com/share/aboutus/pressreleasesdetail.aspx?sd=6/26/2013&id=pr766&ed=12/31/2013.

CIFAS. (2015). *Identity Fraud.* Retrieved from https://www.cifas.org.uk/glossary_i.

Clark, W., Logan, K., Luckin, R., Mee, A., & Oliver, M. (2009). Beyond web 2.0: mapping the technology landscapes of young learners. *Journal of Computer Assisted Learning, 25*(1), 56–69.

Colker, D., & Raab, L. (October 26, 2014). *Judd Nelson's agent sends photo to dispel twitter rumors of actor's death.* LA Times. Retrieved from http://www.latimes.com/entertainment/gossip/la-et-mg-judd-nelson-not-dead-20141026-story.html.

Creative Commons. (n.d.). About the licenses. Retrieved from https://creativecommons.org/licenses.

Curtis, E. (March 12, 2014). *Is Snapchat as private as it seems?* The Telegraph. Retrieved from http://www.telegraph.co.uk/technology/internet-security/10692856/Is-Snapchat-as-private-as-it-seems.html.

Deep Web Technologies. (n.d.). What is the deep web? Retrieved from http://www.deepwebtech.com/company/resource-center/faqs/#deepweb.

Edwards, M. (April 3, 2014). *Why you should hire a social media consultant.* LinkedIn. Retrieved from https://www.linkedin.com/pulse/20140403135916-133448973-why-you-should-hire-a-social-media-consultant.

Eells, L., Vondracek, R., & Vondracek, B. (2012). Fishing the deep web: the search for information. In C. A. Jennings, T. E. Lauer, & B. Vondracek (Eds.), *Scientific communication for natural resource professionals*. Bethesda, Maryland: American Fisheries Society. Retrieved from http://www.fisheriessociety.org/proofs/sci/eells.pdf.

Ego surfing. (n.d.). Webopedia. Retrieved from http://www.webopedia.com/TERM/E/ego_surfing.html, 25.08.15.

Eijkman, H. (2010). Academics and wikipedia: reframing web 2.0+ as a disruptor of traditional academic power-knowledge arrangements. *Campus-Wide Information Systems*, 27(3), 173–185.

Encyclopedia Britannica. (2014). *Cybercrime*. Retrieved from http://www.britannica.com/EBchecked/topic/130595/cybercrime.

English Wikipedia. (n.d.). In Wikipedia. Retrieved from http://en.wikipedia.org/wiki/English_Wikipedia, 06.08.15.

European Commission. (2014). *Factsheet on the right to be forgotten ruling*. Retrieved from http://ec.europa.eu/justice/data-protection/files/factsheets/factsheet_data_protection_en.pdf.

European Cybercrime Centre. (2014). *Internet organized crime threat assessment (iOCTA)*. Retrieved from https://www.europol.europa.eu/iocta/2014/toc.html.

European Cybercrime Centre. (2015). *A collective EU response to cybercrime*. Europol. Retrieved from https://www.europol.europa.eu/ec3.

Ferrari, A. (2013). *DIGCOMP: A framework for developing and understanding digital competence in Europe*. Joint Research Centre (JRC): Scientific and Policy Reports. Report EUR 26035. Seville, Spain: JRC, European Union. Retrieved from https://ec.europa.eu/jrc/sites/default/files/lb-na-26035-enn.pdf.

Focus Ireland. (2013). *Roisin's story: The new face of homelessness*. Retrieved from https://www.focusireland.ie/about-homelessness/customer-and-staff-stories/roisin-s-story, 19.08.15.

Fulton, C. (2010). *Information pathways: A problem-solving approach to information literacy*. Lanham: Scarecrow Press.

Giles, J. (2005). Special report: internet encyclopedias go head to head. *Nature, 438*, 900–901.

Gilster, P. (1997). *Digital literacy*. New York: Wiley Computer Publications.

Goldman, D. (2015). *Google: The reluctant censor of the internet*. CNN Money. Retrieved from http://money.cnn.com/2015/01/04/technology/google-censorship, 04.01.15.

Google. (2014). *About google search history*. Retrieved from https://support.google.com/accounts/answer/54068?hl=en.

Google Scholar. (n.d.). About Google Scholar. Retrieved from https://scholar.google.com/intl/en/scholar/about.html.

Green, K. C. (2011). *Campus computing: Big gains in going mobile*. Retrieved from http://www.campuscomputing.net/item/campus-computing-2011-big-gains-going-mobile.

Hampton, K. N., Rainie, L., Weixu, L., Dwyer, M., Inyoung, S., & Purcell, K. (2014). *Social media and the spiral of silence*. Pew Research Center. Retrieved from http://www.pewinternet.org/files/2014/08/PI_Social-networks-and-debate_082614.pdf.

Harpring, P. (2010). *Introduction to controlled vocabularies: terminology for art, architecture, and other cultural works*. J. Paul Getty Trust. Retrieved from http://www.getty.edu/research/publications/electronic_publications/intro_controlled_vocab/index.html.

Head, A. J. (2013). *Learning the ropes: How freshmen conduct course research once they enter college, project information literacy research report*. Retrieved from http://projectinfolit.org/images/pdfs/pil_2013_freshmenstudy_fullreport.pdf.

Head, A. J., & Eisenberg, M. B. (2009). *Lessons learned: How college students seek information in the digital age. Project information literacy first year report with student survey findings*. University of Washington's Information School. Retrieved from http://projectinfolit.org/images/pdfs/pil_fall2009_finalv_yr1_12_2009v2.pdf.

Head, A. J., & Eisenberg, M. B. (2010). How today's college students use Wikipedia for course-related research. *First Monday, 15*(3). Retrieved from http://firstmonday.org/article/view/2830/2476.

Head, A. J., & Eisenberg, M. B. (2010). *Truth be told: How college students evaluate and use information in the digital age.* Project information literacy progress report. Retrieved from http://projectinfolit.org/images/pdfs/pil_fall2010_survey_fullreport1.pdf.

HLWiki International. (2015). *Snowballing.* Retrieved from http://hlwiki.slais.ubc.ca/index.php/Snowballing.

Hochstotter, N., & Lewandowski, D. (2009). What users see – structures in search engine results pages. *Information Sciences, 179*(12), 1796–1812.

Hoffman, C. (March 22, 2013). *Why you should use a password manager and how to get started [blog post]. How-to Geek.* Retrieved from http://www.howtogeek.com/141500/why-you-should-use-a-password-manager-and-how-to-get-started.

IAB Ireland. (2015). *Digital glossary – IP address.* Retrieved from http://iabireland.ie/research-case-studies/glossary/digital-glossary.

Information Commissioner's Office. (2015). *What are cookies?* Retrieved from https://ico.org.uk/for-the-public/online/cookies.aspx.

Institute of Electrical and Electronics Engineers (IEEE). (n.d.). Discovery services. Retrieved from http://ieeexplore.ieee.org/Xplorehelp/#/tools/toolsForAdministratorsAndLibrarians/discoveryServices.

Internet Crime Complaint Center. (2014). *2013 internet crime report.* Retrieved from http://www.ic3.gov/media/annualreport/2013_ic3report.pdf.

Internet Society. (2015). *Why did we start leaving such big footprints?* [Online tutorial]. Retrieved from http://www.internetsociety.org/your-digital-footprint/why-start.

ISBN.org. (2014). *FAQs: General questions.* Retrieved from http://www.isbn.org/faqs_general_questions.

Jeffries, S. (September 29, 2011). *Sock puppets, twitterjacking and the art of digital fakery.* The Guardian. Retrieved from http://www.theguardian.com/technology/2011/sep/29/sock-puppets-twitterjacking-digital-fakery.

Jobvite. (2014). *Social recruiting survey.* Retrieved from https://www.jobvite.com/wp-content/uploads/2014/10/Jobvite_SocialRecruiting_Survey2014.pdf.

Jones, R. H., & Hafner, C. A. (2012). *Understanding digital literacies: A practical introduction.* New York: Routledge.

Jones, W. (2008). *Keeping found things found: The study and practice of personal information management.* London: Elsevier Inc.

Kaplan, A. M., & Haenlein, M. (2010). Users of the world, unite! the challenges and opportunities of social, media. *Business Horizons, 53*, 59–68.

Kumar, M. (2012). *What is the deep web? A first trip into the Abyss.* The Hacker News. Retrieved from http://thehackernews.com/2012/05/what-is-deep-web-first-trip-into-abyss.html.

Laniado, D., & Tasso, R. (2011). Co-authorship 2.0: patterns of collaboration in Wikipedia. In *Presented at ACM hypertext 2011, 22nd ACM conference on hypertext and hypermedia, June 6–11, 2011.* Retrieved from http://airwiki.ws.dei.polimi.it/images/2/23/Coauthorship2.pdf.

Lee, C. (2010, November 18). *How to cite something you found on a website in APA style [Blog post].* Retrieved from http://blog.apastyle.org/apastyle/2010/11/how-to-cite-something-you-found-on-a-website-in-apa-style.html.

Lee, C. (2013, October 18). *How to cite social media in APA style (Twitter, Facebook, and Google+) [Blog post].* Retrieved from http://blog.apastyle.org/apastyle/2013/10/how-to-cite-social-media-in-apa-style.html.

Lee, D. (2014). *The top memes and viral videos of 2014.* BBC News. Retrieved from http://www.bbc.com/news/technology-30625633.

Lewsey, F. (2015). *How to read a digital footprint*. University of Cambridge. Research Features. Retrieved from http://www.cam.ac.uk/research/features/how-to-read-a-digital-footprint.

Lim, S. (2009). How and why do college students use Wikipedia? *Journal of the American Society for Information Science and Technology, 60*(11), 2189–2202.

Madden, M. (2012). *Privacy management on social media sites*. Pew Research Center's Internet & American Life Project. Retrieved from http://www.pewinternet.org/files/old-media//F iles/Reports/2012/PIP_Privacy_management_on_social_media_sites_022412.pdf.

Madden, M. (November 2014). *Public perceptions of privacy and security in the post-Snowden era*. Pew Research Center. Retrieved from http://www.pewinternet.org/2014/11/12/public-privacy-perceptions.

Madden, M., & Smith, A. (2010). *Reputation management and social media: How people monitor their identity and search for others online*. Pew Research Center's Internet & American Life Project. Retrieved from http://www.pewinternet.org/files/old-media//Files/Reports/2010/PIP_Reputation_Management_with_topline.pdf.

Magnuson, L. (2011). Promoting privacy: Online and reputation management as an information literacy skill. *College & Research Libraries News, 72* (3), 137–140.

Mayer-Schönberger, V., & Cukier, K. (2013). *Big data: A revolution that will transform how we live, work and think*. London: John Murray.

McLoughlin, C., & Lee, M. J. W. (2010). Personalized and self-regulated learning in the web 2.0 era: international exemplars of innovative pedagogy using social software. *Australasian Journal of Education Technology, 26*(1), 28–43. Retrieved from http://ascilite.org.au/ajet/a jet26/mcloughlin.html.

Microsoft. (2014). *Phishing – frequently asked questions*. Retrieved from https://www.microsoft. com/security/online-privacy/phishing-faq.aspx.

Microsoft Academic Search. (2013). *About Microsoft academic search*. Retrieved from http://ac ademic.research.microsoft.com/About/Help.htm.

Microsoft Safety & Security Center. (2014). *What is a cookie?* Retrieved from http://www. microsoft.com/security/resources/cookie-whatis.aspx.

Milburn, A. B., Braham, A., & McClinton, J. (2014). Integrating qualitative components in quantitative courses using Facebook. *Interdisciplinary Journal of E-Learning and Learning Objects, 10*, 229–246. Retrieved from http://www.ijello.org/Volume10/IJELLOv10p229-246Milburn0872.pdf.

Ministry of Justice. (October 12, 2015). *New law to tackle revenge porn*. Retrieved from https://www.gov.uk/government/news/new-law-to-tackle-revenge-porn.

Morrison, K. (May 7, 2015). *How different generations consume content online [Infographic]*. Social Times, Adweek Blog Network. Retrieved from http://www.adweek.com/socialtimes/how-different-generations-consume-content-online-infographic/619882.

NASA. (July 27, 2015). *Media usage guidelines*. NASA. Retrieved from http://www.nasa.gov /audience/formedia/features/MP_Photo_Guidelines.html.

Naughton, J. (March 9, 2014). *25 things you might not know about the web on its 25th birthday*. The Guardian. Retrieved from http://www.theguardian.com/technology/2014/mar/0 9/25-years-web-tim-berners-lee.

Nudd, T. (March 9, 2011). Chrysler throws down an F-bomb on Twitter. *AdWeek*. Retrieved from http://www.adweek.com/adfreak/chrysler-throws-down-f-bomb-twitter-126967.

OECD. (2013). *Glossary of statistical terms*. Retrieved from http://stats.oecd.org/glossary/detail .asp?ID=198.

Office of the Privacy Commissioner of Canada. (2011). *Cookies – Following the crumbs [fact sheet]*. Retrieved from https://www.priv.gc.ca/resource/fs-fi/02_05_d_49_e.asp.

Oxford Dictionaries. (2015). Retrieved from http://www.oxforddictionaries.com.

Pangrazio, L. (2014). Reconceptualising critical digital literacy. *Discourse: Studies in the Cultural Politics of Education*, 1–12. http://dx.doi.org/10.1080/01596306.2014.942836.

Pariser, E. (2011). *The filter bubble: What the internet is hiding from you*. London: Penguin Viking.

Parr, C. (2015, April 23). MOOCs: Fluctuating rates in online investment. *Times Higher Education*. Retrieved from https://www.timeshighereducation.com/news/moocs-fluctuating-rates-in-online-investment/2019816.article.

Password Manager. (2015). In *Wikipedia* Retrieved from https://en.wikipedia.org/wiki/Password_manager, 14.08.15.

PC Mag Encyclopedia. (2015). *Definition of firewall*. Retrieved from http://www.pcmag.com/encyclopedia/term/43218/firewall.

PeekYou. (2015). *How it works*. Retrieved from http://www.peekyou.com.

Pilkington, E. (December 22, 2013). *Justine Sacco, PR executive fired over racist tweet, 'ashamed.'*. The Guardian. Retrieved from http://www.theguardian.com/world/2013/dec/22/pr-exec-fired-racist-tweet-aids-africa-apology.

PPRO. (2014). *Payment fraud types and how to prevent them*. Retrieved from https://www.ppro.com/blog/payment-fraud-types-and-how-to-prevent-them/.

Prescott, J., Wilson, S., & Becket, G. (2012). Students want more guidelines on Facebook and online professionalism. *The Pharmaceutical Journal, 289*(August), 1–3.

Purcell, K., etal. (2012). *How teens do research in the digital world*. Pew Internet & American Life Project. Retrieved from http://www.pewinternet.org/2012/11/01/how-teens-do-research-in-the-digital-world.

Rheinhold, H. (September/October 2010). Attention and other 21st-century social media literacies. *Educause Review*, pp. 14–24. Retrieved from https://net.educause.edu/ir/library/pdf/ERM1050.pdf.

Rouse, M. (2011). *DarkNet definition*. TechTarget Network. Retrieved from http://searchnetworking.techtarget.com/definition/darknet.

Rowley, J. E., & Hartley, R. J. (2008). *Organizing knowledge: An introduction to managing access to information*. Hampshire: Ashgate.

Sandeen, C. (2013). Assessment's place in the new MOOC world. *Research & Practice in Assessment* 8: 5–12.

Scally, D. (May 14, 2015). *De-google your life: It's worth the hassle if you value your privacy*. Irish Times. Retrieved from http://www.irishtimes.com/business/technology/de-google-your-life-it-s-worth-the-hassle-if-you-value-your-privacy-1.2211355.

Silverman, C. (Ed.). (2014). *Verification handbook: A definitive guide to verifying digital content for emergency coverage*. Netherlands: European Journalism Centre (EJC). Retrieved from http://verificationhandbook.com.

Smith, C. (2015). *By the numbers: 25 amazing vine statistics*. Retrieved from http://expandedramblings.com/index.php/vine-statistics.

Soanes, C., Waite, M., & Hawker, S. (2001). *The Oxford dictionary, thesaurus, and wordpower guide*. Oxford: Oxford University Press.

SPARC Europe. (2015). *Institutional repositories*. Retrieved from http://sparceurope.org/repositories.

StatCounter GlobalStats. (2015). *Search engine (desktop, mobile, tablet, console)*. Retrieved from http://gs.statcounter.com/#all-search_engine-ww-monthly-201408-201507-b.

Steel, E., Locke, C., Cadman, E., & Freese, B. (June 12, 2013). *How much is your personal data worth?* Financial Times. Retrieved from http://www.ft.com/cms/s/2/927ca86e-d29b-11e2-88ed-00144feab7de.html#axzz3e3uym5NJ.

Stein, K. (2013, December 5). PENN GSE study shows MOOCs have relatively few active users, with only a few persisting to course end. *PENN GSE Graduate School of Education Press Room*. Retrieved from https://www.gse.upenn.edu/pressroom/press-releases/2013/12/penn-gse-study-shows-moocs-have-relatively-few-active-users-only-few-persisti.

Stokes, P., & Martin, L. (2008). Reading lists: a study of tutor and student perceptions, expectations and realities. *Studies in Higher Education, 33*(2), 113–125. http://dx.doi.org/10.1080/03075070801915874.

Suber, P. (2015). *Open access overview*. Retrieved from http://legacy.earlham.edu/~peters/fos/overview.htm.

Sullivan, R. J. (2009, October). *The benefits of collecting and reporting payment fraud statistics in the United States. Federal Reserve Bank of Kansas City.* Retrieved from https://www.kansascityfed. org/PUBLICAT/PSR/Briefings/PSR-BriefingOct09.pdf.

Tardy, C. M. (2010). Writing for the world: Wikipedia as an introduction to academic writing. *English Teaching Forum, 48*(1), 12–19 27.

Thakur, B. (November 25, 2011). *What does your digital footprint reveal? [blog post].* Retrieved from http://bhaskarthakur.com/blog/your-digital-footprint.

Travis, A., & Arthur, C. (May 13, 2014). *EU court backs 'right to be forgotten': Google must amend results on request.* The Guardian. Retrieved from http://www.theguardian.com/technology/-2014/may/13/right-to-be-forgotten-eu-court-google-search-results.

United Nations Educational Scientific and Cultural Organization (UNESCO). (2013). *Global media and information literacy assessment framework: Country readiness and competencies.* Paris, France: UNESCO.

University of British Columbia Library. (n.d.). Scholarly vs. popular sources. Retrieved from http://help.library.ubc.ca/evaluating-and-citing-sources/scholarly-versus-popular-sources.

US-Cert. (2008). *Recognizing and avoiding email scams.* Retrieved from https://www.us-cert. gov/sites/default/files/publications/emailscams_0905.pdf.

Vasager, J., & Fontanella-Khan, J. (September 15, 2014). *Berlin pushes google to reveal search engine formula.* Financial Times. Retrieved from http://www.ft.com/cms/s/0/9615661c-3ce1-11e4-9733-00144feabdc0.html#axzz3K4nl0o7P.

Wikipedia. (n.d.). In Wikipedia. Retrieved from http://en.wikipedia.org/wiki/Wikipedia, 06.08.15.

Wikipedia: Education Program/Ambassadors. (n.d.). Wikipedia. Retrieved from https://en. wikipedia.org/wiki/Wikipedia:Education_program/Ambassadors.

Wikipedia: Systemic Bias. (n.d.). In Wikipedia. Retrieved from http://en.m.wikipedia.org/wiki/Wikipedia:Systemic_bias, 06.08.15.

Wurman, R. S. (1989). *Information anxiety.* New York: Doubleday.

YouTube. (2015). *Statistics.* Retrieved from https://www.YouTube.com/yt/press/statistics.html.

INDEX

Printed in Great Britain
by Amazon

41290174R00146